1832 1417

The Dynamics of Strategic Change

Corporate Strategy, Organization, and Change

Series General Editor
Andrew Pettigrew, University of Warwick
Associate Editors
Henry Mintzberg, McGill University; Peter Lorange, The
Wharton School, University of Pennsylvania

Also in this series:

The Dynamics of Strategic Change

C. R. HININGS and
ROYSTON GREENWOOD

with the assistance of
Stewart Ranson and Kieron Walsh

Basil Blackwell

Copyright © C. R. Hinings and Royston Greenwood 1988

First published 1988

First published in USA 1989

Basil Blackwell Ltd
108 Cowley Road, Oxford, OX4 1JF, UK

Basil Blackwell Inc.
432 Park Avenue South, Suite 1503
New York, NY 10016, USA

British Library Cataloguing in Publication Data
Hinings, C. R. (Christopher Robin), 1937–
    The dynamics of strategic change.
    1. Companies. Organisational change.
    Management
    I. Title. II. Greenwood, Royston, 1944–
    III. Series
    658.4'06

ISBN 0—631-15989-4

Library of Congress Cataloging in Publication Data
Hinings, C. R. (Christopher Robin)
    The dynamics of strategic change/Christopher Hinings and Royston
    Greenwood : with the assistance of Stewart Ranson and Kieron Walsh.
        p.   cm. — (Corporate strategy, organization, and change)
    Bibliography: p.
    Includes index.
    ISBN 0-631-15989-4
    1. Organizational change. I. Greenwood, Royston. II. Title.
    III. Series.
    HD58.8.H56 1988
    658.4'06—dc19   88-23337
                                                                          CIP

Typeset in 10 on 12pt Times
by Photo-Graphics Ltd, Honiton, Devon
Printed in Great Britain by T. J. Press (Padstow) Ltd., Padstow, Cornwall

Contents

Preface

This book has been 'in the making' for a considerable period of time. It has been a longitudinal effort. The first recognizable draft was produced in 1979–80 when Bob Hinings had a Social Science Research Council Personal Fellowship and spent some time as a Visiting Professor at the Institute of Organizational and Industrial Sociology in Copenhagen. The current book has evolved from that never-completed manuscript. After 1979 the various members of the original research team moved on to a variety of different projects within the Institute of Local Government Studies. Then, in July 1982, Royston Greenwood moved to the Department of Organizational Analysis in the Faculty of Business, University of Alberta. He was followed by Bob Hinings in January, 1983. Since that time, we have developed many of the original ideas in a somewhat different direction than was initially envisaged.

This has happened because, as we all know, time does not stand still. Since the general development of an economic recession in the Western world during the late 1970s and early 1980s, organizational theorists have become more interested in the subject of strategic organizational change. Writers publishing over the past four or five years have had a major impact on our thinking. So, we attempted to incorporate a whole series of new developments into the book, which resulted in a total rewriting of the manuscript that was in place. The particular innovations are in the concepts of archetypes and tracks which position the whole thrust of the book. Similarly, there has been an attempt to deal with some of the more recent literature on leadership and the sequencing of evolution and revolution in organizational change. In effect, our ideas underwent a transformation.

However, the book could not have been written without the contributions of Stewart Ranson and Kieron Walsh, for two reasons. The first reason was their intellectual contribution from 1973 until 1980. The research group that was assembled at the Institute of Local Government Studies, University of Birmingham, developed the essential framework for understanding the dynamics of organizational change through the concepts of prescribed and emergent structure, interpretive schemes, interests and power. The second contribution was that of data collection and analysis. Each member of the team had a caseload of organizations from 1973 to 1978 and the initial attempts at analysis were done by the four members. Thus, the contribution of Stewart and Kieron to the book was important in establishing some of the basic ideas and modes of analysis.

Other organizations and individuals have also been important during the fifteen year life of this undertaking. The Institute of Local Government Studies was an exciting, innovative place to work during our tenure there. It provided an environment that encouraged the development of new ideas and long-term research engagement within a particular institutional sphere. That intellectual excitement was embodied in the then Director, John Stewart. He was instrumental in getting the initial project going, in encouraging its continued development, in giving a whole range of advice and in bringing his vast knowledge and insight about local government to bear on our work.

The University of Alberta has proved to be a very supportive environment for continued work on the ideas and the data. Particular support was given during 1986–7 when Bob Hinings held a McCalla Research Professorship, enabling the completion of the manuscript. Our colleagues in the Department of Organizational Analysis have commented on our work at a variety of seminars, and Richard Field read and commented on parts of the manuscript.

A number of colleagues and friends at other universities have made helpful comments on the ideas and the manuscript, particularly Danny Miller and Lynne Zucker, and also David Hickson, John Kimberly and Andrew Pettigrew.

Finally, we would like to thank Merle Lobo and Karen Macdonald who carried out the sometimes arduous task of typing the manuscript and having to cope with one author's constant alterations which were always the highest priority!

Bob Hinings
Royston Greenwood
Edmonton, Alberta

Introduction

Throughout the Western industrial world there has been a state of organizational turmoil for at least the past decade. In the USA, for example, the auto industry has faced a number of major challenges, not least of which has been the situation facing the Chrysler Corporation. In his book, Lee Iacocca (1984) describes the successful attempt to transform Chrysler, although he starts the story by saying that

> If I'd had the slightest idea of what lay ahead for me when I joined up with Chrysler, I wouldn't have gone over there for all the money in the world. (p. 141)

As the story unfolds it becomes obvious why that statement was made. Turning Chrysler around involved every aspect of the business, including its relations with government, suppliers, dealers and customers, its product line and methods of production, its control and incentive systems, its ways of planning, the relations between staff work and operational managers and the ways in which the company dealt with its employees. And not only were all aspects of the business affected: their interdependence was also a continuing source of difficulty.

A further problem that faced Iacocca, as he and his team of senior managers struggled with the situation facing Chrysler in 1979, was that the circumstances producing that situation did not stand still. The transformation of Chrysler had to be accomplished against a moving background. Again, to quote Iacocca,

> Once I had my team in place, I was confident that Chrysler's recovery would only be a matter of time. But then I hadn't counted on the economy to fall apart. And I certainly hadn't counted on Iran. (p. 182)

Similarly, in Canada over the past five years, its 'senior' company, the Hudson's Bay Company originally founded in 1642, has been facing very difficult times. The general downturn in the economy that occurred in the early 1980s faced all retail organizations with problems of maintaining earnings and market share. But The Bay suffered more than most and chalked up major losses which were seen by Canadians, generally, as all the worse because of the 'blue-chip' status of the company and its place as a Canadian institution. As Peter Newman (1985) has suggested, the Hudson's Bay Company is part of Canadian history.

Because of The Bay's special position, facing up to the implications of its declining situation was traumatic for management and workers alike. Attempting to bring The Bay back into profit required examination and transformation of long-held beliefs, styles and methods of management. The whole image of the retail operation throughout every province came under scrutiny. Many stores were removed from The Bay chain of stores and renamed as part of the downmarket but successful Zeller's empire (with its slogan of 'only you'll know how little you paid'). Product lines were altered, new forms of merchandising were introduced, many staff were laid off, union contracts were renegotiated and many senior managers, including the chief executive, were fired.

Of course, other retail organizations – including Sears, Woolco, and Eatons – did not stand idly by and watch The Bay (directly or through its 'Zellers' subsidiary) reclaim its market share. They were, and are, similarly reacting to changes in the nature of the retail business. So The Bay found itself trying to implement a traumatic reorganization within a continuously moving market context.

A further example of such organizational turmoil comes from the case of ICI as documented by Pettigrew (1985; 1988). ICI was Britain's largest industrial company but, in spite of its scale and the scope of its products, found itself in increasing competition with its European rivals, especially the major West German companies Hoechst, Bayer and BASF. As Pettigrew describes the situation,

> . . . the arrival of the Thatcher government in 1979, pursuing strict monetarist economic policies, meant high interest rates, a recession in industrial production, and mounting unemployment. The further fall in ICI's United Kingdom customer base and, worse still, the sharply rising value of sterling in 1980 and 1981 in relation to the US dollar and

deutsche mark meant cheaper chemical imports from Europe and North America. . . (p. 24)

The result was a dramatic worsening of ICI's profitability from 1980 to 1983, something which came as a great shock to such a blue-chip company. In response ICI attempted to focus its marketing strategy more clearly; the chief executive, Sir John Harvey-Jones, and his fellow board members attempted to change their mode of operation. They attempted to move towards more decentralization so that more entrepreneurial values would be adopted. There were attempts to lessen the amount of bureaucracy. All the divisions of the company lost assets and manpower and two divisions, Petrochemicals and Plastics, which made the largest losses were merged into one division after many plants were closed. Changes continued between 1983 and 1986 with the eventual merger of all the United Kingdom heavy chemicals divisions into one group.

Similarly at Cadbury-Schweppes a marked deterioration in market share and profitability sparked a process of repositioning and reorganization. In the mid-1970s there was a dramatic fall in market share, in particular from the impact of Mars (Child and Smith, 1987). The response was to examine products, manufacturing and marketing. Historically Cadbury's had maintained a large number and broad range of branded products. With a deteriorating market situation Cadbury's reduced its product range and began to examine the possibility of more mass manufacture and to rethink its marketing strategy. For a company such as Cadbury's, so much part of the British industrial structure and proud of its distinctive traditions, the idea that radical change was necessary was difficult to swallow. Indeed, at one point in the change process the unthinkable was suggested, namely that the Bournville production facility should be shut down!

In order to cope with the consequences of its changing competitive position Cadbury's had to launch a whole series of initiatives including concentrating on core businesses, emphasizing performance through an industrial engineering approach, reducing capital investment, introducing job flexibility, subcontracting, decentralizing functions and a four-shift system. This is only a partial list of all the changes (for more detail see Smith et al., 1988). By 1982 all this culminated in 'Operation Fundamental Change'. Over a period of ten years every aspect of the business has been subject to examination.

Strategic Organizational Design Change

The above vignettes could be repeated. They represent not the unusual case but the contemporary norm. And, if Zane Barnes of Southwestern Bell is correct, the ability to manage change will be of increasing, rather than decreasing, importance:

> It is crystal clear that our economy is undergoing a fundamental shift. It is changing rapidly and basically from a production base to an information base. It is equally clear that our economy is no longer national but global in scope. . . . My point is simply this – managing organizational change is a topic American business needs to examine and understand, because fundamental change will be the order of the day for the foreseeable future. And, obviously the company that can adapt its culture to change, quickly and successfully, will have a powerful competitive advantage. (Barnes, 1987, p. 43)

Despite the importance of the need to understand how to manage change the actual magnitude of the changes required, and the associated tendency by managers to underestimate that magnitude, often results in those changes being undermanaged. Undermanagement is also caused by the lack of systematic frameworks available to managers for understanding and analysing situations of major organizational transformation.

The general issue of understanding such transformations – or strategic organizational design change – is examined in this book. The central focus is upon radical strategic changes in organizational design (i.e. patterns of structural arrangements and management systems) which signal a fundamental shift in the basic orientation of the organization. Such changes are analysed conceptually and empirically in settings where attempts have been made to redesign organizational arrangements. The theory developed allows for the possibility of both successful and unsuccessful redesign attempts. The empirical material illustrates the conditions that facilitate organizational transformation and the conditions that hinder its achievement. The material also illustrates the nature of the transformational process.

The basic components of the theory are established in chapters 1–3. Chapter 1 sets out the idea of organizational *archetypes*. Archetypes are defined as compositions of structures and systems given coherence or orientation by an underlying set of ideas, values and beliefs. We argue that organizations tend to operate and remain within the parameters and assumptions of any given archetype and find it difficult to move between archetypes. Such movements where they do occur represent a reorientation or transformation for the organization, i.e. a strategic design change.

Chapter 2 introduces the language of organizational *tracks*. For, although the archetype thesis suggests that most changes within an organization are consistent with the assumptions and limitations of the prevailing archetype, changes that move an organization away from coherence do occur. The idea of tracks is an attempt to map or capture the movement of organizations over time within or between alternative archetypes. The chapter is especially central to the theoretical framework because the subsequent chapters seek to explain why and how organizations move along a particular track and not along others. We ask, in other words, why some organizations remain locked within a particular archetype whereas others achieve transformational change. Similarly, we ask why some organizations begin to move from one archetype to another but fail to arrive, becoming marooned or locked between archetypes.

Chapter 3 deals with the dynamics of change, setting out a framework for understanding why organizations move away from their current design, why they follow particular tracks and how some organizations are able to complete such changes while others are less successful or fail. The concepts of situational constraints, values, interests, power and organizational capacity are introduced. The chapter outlines three primary *dynamics of change*. The thrust of the argument is that changes of the kind examined here involve the complex interaction of organizational context and internal organizational processes. Moreover, change has to be conceptualized as an 'unfolding' series of circumstances and actions. Change is not a static subject. The situation and the issues of change continually re-form, partly because of the unanticipated consequences of actions taken and partly because of the moving context. The quotes from Iacocca catch this theme nicely.

The purpose of these early chapters, in other words, is to give a framework for understanding why organizations move away from, or retain, their current design, why they follow particular tracks, and why some organizations are able to complete such transformations while others with similar intent are less successful or fail. Throughout these early chapters, empirical material is used continuously to illustrate the ideas being developed; chapters 5 onwards, however, apply the developed framework more systematically to a series of major attempts to alter the structure, processes, cultures and methods of operation of a particular set of organizations. These later chapters, in other words, afford a more systematic appraisal elaboration of the ideas introduced in chapters 1–3. (Chapter 4 gives details of the research design underlying these empirical chapters.)

1 Understanding Organizational Design: Archetypes

Introduction

The vignettes of change sketched in the Introduction contain very little explicit articulated discussion of organization design *per se*. In Lee Iacocca's autobiography there is minimal discussion of the appropriate organizational design for Chrysler. In all the articles in newspapers and business periodicals on the Hudson's Bay Company there is, similarly, very little concern with matters of organizational structure and process. ICI did make statements about decentralization and reducing bureaucracy. For all four organizations the emphasis is on repositioning and revitalizing the company, i.e. on searching for new markets and products and redefining old goals and purposes. Yet, as Kimberly and Quinn (1984) point out, repositioning and revitalizing, *of necessity*, involve the reorganization of structures of authority and responsibilities and the redesign of management systems. Chrysler, The Bay, ICI and Cadbury's have all been involved in redesigning their internal structures and processes.

Our interest is with reorganizations of such a scale that they involve and reflect the transformation of structures and systems, brought about by the displacement of central ideas, values and beliefs. In a nutshell, the analysis is concerned with reorganizations that involve movement *between* archetypes. Therefore, an essential initial step is to define what is to be understood by a design archetype.

A design archetype may be summarized in terms of two general statements. First, organizational structures and management systems are best understood in terms of overall patterns rather than by analysis of narrowly drawn sets of organizational properties. This is the '*holistic*' perspective asserted by Miller and Friesen (1984). Second, organizational patterns are provided by the ideas, values and beliefs – i.e. the 'interpretive schemes' (Ranson et al., 1980) – embodied within structures and systems. Recognition of a design pattern is thus a function of uncovering and isolating the interpretive schemes underpinning structures and systems. A design archetype, in short, may be formally defined as *a particular composition of ideas, beliefs and values connected to structures and systems*.

The 'Holistic' Approach

1   *Prescribed Framework*

The idea of organizational design has traditionally focused on the concept of structure, i.e. the patterning of relationships, differentiation of tasks and positions, formulation of rules and procedures and prescriptions of authority. Much work has concentrated on establishing both the considerable variation that occurs in organizational structures and the patternings that occur between structural elements. From this work taxonomies and typologies of organizations have been produced (cf. Pugh et al., 1969; Mintzberg, 1979; McKelvey, 1982).

This traditional approach is important because of its emphasis on structural forms as instruments for achieving calculable and predictable control of organizational performance. It is because of this instrumentality that reorganization almost inevitably follows organizational repositioning and revitalization, much in the manner pioneered by Chandler (1962). Chandler noted that the structure of an organization followed from the strategies that owners and managers adopted in the face of changes in markets and technologies, suggesting that the active interventions of management have replaced market forces.

The traditional approach, illustrated by Chandler, focuses upon the authoritative or, as we would prefer to describe it, *prescribed framework* laid down to secure coherent organized effort. The process of managing is aimed at ensuring an adequate level of performance. This is achieved, in part, by means of an officially intended structure of roles and responsibilities and a pattern of vertical and horizontal integration. Thus, tasks are allocated – or differentiated – between divisions, departments, branches, sections and roles. An authority system is set up as one means of integrating this organizational differentiation. Lateral devices such as committees, teams and task forces are used to complement the hierarchy. Integration is further prescribed by means of policies, plans, schedules, budgeting systems, human resource systems and so on. These structures and systems of differentiation and integration constitute a prescribed framework for action.

Prima facie the prescribed framework is an important level of analysis. Many reorganizations are centrally concerned with it. They centre around amalgamating or splitting departments, redefining responsibilities, taking out or putting in levels in hierarchies, introducing new reporting and control systems and developing new patterns of recruitment or systems of appraisal and reward. In fact, any attempted organizational transformation will include all, or a significant proportion of, these elements even when the transformation is more centrally concerned with moving into new markets or introducing new products. For example, when an organization moves from a functional to a divisionalized structure – the path identified by Chandler for firms pursuing diversification of products and/or markets – there has to be a rethinking of the distribution of tasks between departments, the introduction of new strategic planning systems, the working out of new performance evaluation systems and a redefining of relationships between the centre and the relatively autonomous units.

It is important not to lose this idea of the elements of the prescribed framework as being interdependent and interactive. Central to the idea of design archetypes, as we indicated earlier, is that a better understanding of organizations is obtained by identifying and interpreting overall patterns or orientations amongst key design variables and the avoidance of what Miller (1981) rebukes as the 'partist approach'. The partist approach selects limited numbers of organizational variables which are analysed in an essentially discrete fashion. For example, the extent of centralization may be correlated with the extent of standardization. The holistic approach, on the other hand, as developed by Miller and Friesen (1984), would embrace the study of multiple variables (environment, strategy and structure) examined in terms of 'common configurations of mutually reinforcing elements of strategy, structure and environment' (Miller and Friesen, 1980, p. 593). That is, according to the holistic perspective organizations should be conceived not as loosely coupled clusterings of structural properties but as overall gestalts

> composed of tightly interdependent and mutually supportive elements such that the importance of each element can best be understood by

making reference to the whole configuration. (Miller and Friesen, 1984, p. 1)

Avoidance of the 'partist approach' does not necessarily involve the inclusion of environmental *and* strategic *and* structural variables within the definition of gestalt/archetype. On the contrary, it has been persuasively argued that to do so may conceal important theoretical linkages between these variables (Hambrick, 1983). What *is* important, however, is that the study of organizational designs should be approached in a manner consistent with the logic of the gestalt/archetype perspective. That is, the focus should be (i) upon a wide and *inclusive* rather than narrow and exclusive conception of design in order (ii) to isolate *patterns* or configurations of design.

More specifically, we believe that in much contemporary work the study of organizational design has been overly narrow and too focused upon structures to the neglect of organizational systems. Elements of bureaucracy – the division of labour, standardization of work practices, formalization of rules and written documentation and the centralization of hierarchically located authority – have been taken as definitive of organizational design. Emphasis in such work is placed upon the configurations of differentiation and integration involved in the pattern of vertical and horizontal allocations of authorities and responsibilities. Essentially missing from such definitions are the processes and systems that connect and activate structural frameworks. Systems of resource allocation, appraisal and compensation systems, information and control processes – each of which is an integral aspect of organizational design – have been largely ignored. Pursuance of a more holistic approach, in contrast, would involve coverage of organizational structures *and* systems (Daft and Macintosh, 1984).

It would be misleading, however, to consider the idea of a design archetype as though it were a matter of a broader coverage of structures and systems established in the prescribed framework. As both academic analysis has pointed out and managerial experience has confirmed, the prescribed framework often has a problematic relationship to the day-to-day work of an organization. Therefore a fuller understanding of organizational arrangements has to embrace the *emergent pattern of interactions*.

2 Emergent Interactions

Any attempt to make the prescribed framework of activity into a total prescription of organizational activity is not possible even in the most policy-specific and manual-oriented organization. The early critics of Weberian bureaucracy as a rational calculative control system demonstrated the possibility of organizational members displacing goals, subverting roles and amplifying rules (Selznick, 1949; Gouldner, 1955; Merton, 1968). To survive and continue every organization has its emergent interactions, i.e. activities, norms of behaviour and ways of operating, that are *not* formally prescribed.

Members of organizations have actually to transact their work, formulate policy and allocate resources. No ledger of rules can envisage every possibility even in the most bureaucratic system. Attempts to do so can become dysfunctional. Some rule systems are so cumbersome in their attempt at comprehensiveness that to operate them would produce organizational inefficiency. Organizational members do and must 'fill in' the rules, or ignore them, to *aid* performance. Similarly, no authority system can predefine all situations. As a result, authority is defined in general terms which require operationalization and application to particular situations. The point is that interpretation and operationalization of rules and systems of authority are necessary on a day-to-day basis, producing a pattern of emergent interactions.

A conceptualization of organizational design, therefore, should accommodate not only the prescribed framework but also the emergent and realized patterns of interaction within organizations, describing how actors actually accomplish their work, develop policy and allocate resources.

The distinction between *prescribed framework* and *emergent interactions* is important because it catches the two elements contained in the term social structure, i.e. the patterning of relationships and the continuity of interaction in time (Giddens, 1976). In a reorganization an organization defines a set of relationships in terms of responsibilities for different but interrelated tasks, and the set of systems and procedures through which they will work. An important part of Iacocca's reorganization at Chrysler, for example, was to redefine the responsbilities of, and the systems linking, dealers, sales and production.

But organizations do not redesign their structures and systems which then remain static until the next environmental jolt which leads to a further redesign. Day-to-day work in organizations is made up of activities and interactions. Structures and systems operate over time and have a continuity. For example, the Alberta Department of Energy and Natural Resources introduced an integrated resource management planning system in 1976 (Langhorn and Hinings, 1988). At the prescribed level this system redefined relationships between units such as the Alberta Forest Service, Public Lands Division, Fish and Wildlife Division etc., and introduced new procedures to direct work. However, at the emergent level, it was a matter of working out, *over time*, what set of activities and pattern of interaction was necessary to support the new system. The very newness of the system, with its implications for altering existing interactions, meant that the degree of specification would be limited. In addition the lack of experience with such systems in the department meant a great deal of exploratory behaviour had to be employed. Indeed, it took up to seven years for the system to be operating at what its designers regarded as optimum efficiency, and over this time there was an interdependence and interaction between emergent interactions and prescribed frameworks as reciprocal changes occurred in each.

In trying to understand organizational design, therefore, the analyst and the manager have to take account of this interdependent nature of framework and interaction. Organizationally prescribed frameworks are means for shaping interaction and as such are continually produced in interaction. Yet there is also a transformative capacity to interaction, arising from the impossibility of complete specification of behaviour and the development of new situations. Through the necessary process of continual interaction required to produce work, prescribed frameworks are subject to modification and replacement. Structures are not static but dynamic through the reciprocal nature of framework and interaction.

The Basis of Classification: Interpretive Schemes

The thrust of the analysis thus far is that the various elements of organizational design should be conceived as a whole, embracing both prescribed and emergent structures and systems. Following Miller and Friesen (1984) and Ranson et al. (1980) we have proposed that the study of organizational design arrangements look at a broad rather than narrow range of design variables at the level of both prescribed

Table 1.1 The elements of organizational design

---

1 *Prescribed framework*
   structure of roles and authorities, vertically and horizontally

   decision systems (e.g. policy and resource allocation mechanisms)

   human resource systems (e.g. recruitment, appraisal, compensation systems)

2 *Emergent interactions*
   structure of roles and authorities

   decision systems

   human resource system

---

framework and emergent interactions. This line of reasoning is summarized in table 1.1.

The idea of a design archetype, however, involves much more than the coverage of the design elements portrayed in table 1.1. A more pressing and definitive issue is the basis upon which patterns in structures and systems are to be discerned and understood. What is it, in other words, which gives meaning to the pattern?

The crucial ingredient of the archetype argument is that structures and systems 'hang together' to form a coherent design. Therefore, the critical research problem is how to uncover – i.e. recognize and interpret – such coherent patterns. Exactly how *is* the researcher to know when a pattern of relatively enduring significance has been found? What is the process by which an underlying orientation, that gives direction or coherence to an apparently patterned array of structures and systems, is to be observed?

Miller and Friesen (1984) are less than clear on this issue and largely rely upon the use of statistical manipulation of large samples of organizations, observed over periods of 20 years or more, to produce configurations or clusterings of relationships between variables. That is, statistical analysis identifies recurring patterns of design arrangements. Our position, following Ranson et al. (1980) and Greenwood and Hinings (1988), is different. The pattern or orientation of a composition of structures and systems is provided by the set of ideas and values – i.e. the 'interpretive scheme' (Ranson et al., 1980) –

embodied within them. Structures and systems, from this perspective, are not neutral instruments but embody intentions, aspirations and purposes. *Therefore*, the classification and recognition of a design pattern or gestalt is a function of isolating the sets of ideas, values and beliefs which underpin design characteristics. An 'orientation', to us, is the coherent structural expression of an interpretive scheme.

The interplay of structures and values can be illustrated through a number of existing studies. The first of these, based upon Cole's (1982) work, is at a somewhat general level. Cole analysed the dissemination and impact of ideas about worker participation in Sweden, Japan and the USA. Although ideas on participation had their origins in the USA, the values associated with them were not consistent with those traditionally held by senior management in the USA. The degree of hierarchical distance, emphasis upon respect for authority and the heavy reliance upon external management control systems, all of which were pervasive values within US organizations, prevented the widespread introduction of worker participative practices. Such practices are connected to egalitarian norms and values, and the denial of specialist expertise as a prerogative of management.

In Japan and Sweden, prevailing managerial ideologies were more able to embrace the new ideas about structural form because the constituent values were less alien. Again, though, it is not simply a matter of values *leading* structure but of interaction. It is not just that the managerial values in the USA emphasize expertise, authority systems and impersonal control systems but that such values are given meaning and substance in organizational practices, especially at the prescribed level. Emergent practices – e.g. a section manager using quality circles – have to be 'tested' against prevailing values. If new practices survive the test they can form a basis for the unfolding of new meanings which can eventually become institutionalized in new prescribed structures and systems.

Cole's work is at the societal level of analysis. Other studies, however, illustrate the connection of structures and values within particular organizations. One such study is Hackman's (1984) account of People Express Airline. It is an example of an organization that at the time of Hackman's account 'has not experienced the kinds of organizational transitions that usually are observed in the early years of an organization's life – and has enjoyed considerable success nonetheless' (p. 55). Essentially People Express avoided restructuring towards more specialized work activities, a greater use of formalized means of communication and closer specification of responsibilities and changes in decision-making practices than Greiner's (1972) work on phases of growth would suggest. An important part of the explanation for this was the 16 precepts for operation laid out by the 16 top managers at the start-up of People Express. They are 'now used throughout the firm as the primary guides for decision-making about organizational policies, structures, and practices' (Hackman, 1984, p. 30).

Over time, and in the face of external and internal pressures that suggested the need for a transition, Hackman found that senior managers developed greater understanding of these precepts and found them useful as guides for decision making. But a further important point that he makes is that 'lots of things *are* getting designed and structured throughout the organization, largely from the bottom up, and in ways that are consistent with the precepts' (Hackman, 1984, p. 58). This illustrates the importance of emergent patterns of interaction. We would argue that, while such interactions emerge in the light of existing values, there is always sufficient loose coupling for them also to serve as vehicles for the questioning of, and changes in, the values–structure relationship.

Again, this kind of interpretation is suggested by Hackman in his analysis of the role of the chairman of the company. The maintenance of central precepts and their organizational consequences is a vital leadership role (Tichy and Ulrich, 1984). But Hackman foresaw a gradual transfer of power to other senior managers. While such a transfer would occur in the light of the established ideas of how to operate, it would also contain the possibility of allowing People Express 'to become a qualitatively different kind of organizational entity' (Hackman, 1984, p. 59). Even with a strong culture, movements towards decentralization introduce the possibility of change through differing interpretations of the specific organizational meaning of the values.

A second example of how values give meaning to structural form is provided by Barrett and Cammann's (1984) analysis of the National Steel Corporation (NSC). They show both the difficulties and high levels of activity involved when an organization is faced with the requirement of change, precisely because of the values–structure relationship. The problem derives from the NSC's being a large, mature and stable organization that faced an increasingly turbulent economic environment. Barrett and Cammann suggest that the NSC was a typical mature organization with a stable culture which did not define change favourably. As they put it,

People in the organization understood its methods of working, its structure of authority, and its position in the marketplace. . . . Generally, each individual did his job, guarded his territory, expected to be rewarded when he did well, and otherwise minded his own business. (p. 219)

As a result it became necessary to set in train a series of changes that began from a redefining of the purposes of the organization and of the way that organizational members see their roles and relationships. From these redefinitions and new meanings can be derived the actual structures and systems necessary for accomplishing the new purposes. But the new structures did not follow automatically, because of the continuing power and legitimacy of existing ways of operating. So, while the new values being developed by top management emphasized autonomy, participation and the idea of a 'diversified operating company', local managers continued to operate as though most decisions were still being made at head office. The values embodied in the existing structure did not allow freedom of action, and the reward structure was competitive, not participative.

Reorganization at the NSC was required to embody the new business and organizational concepts. To achieve that, it was necessary, at the outset, to demonstrate the validity of those concepts through the reorganization of top management. Secondly, it was necessary to put a great deal of senior management effort into demonstrating the legitimacy of new ways of operating. The office of the chairman led the way. As Barrett and Cammann (1984) put it, this activity gave

a clear signal that the implementation of the mission was occurring in a visible and significant manner. It legitimized certain people and groups working together that had not cooperated well in the past. (p. 230)

In this case, we see difficulties that face managers in breaking the links between existing meanings and structures in order to reorient and transform an organization by introducing new values and ideas and their structural emanations. It also indicates the important strategic role of top management in shaping and implementing the process of transformation.

A third example of the values–structure relationship is to be found in the work of Tolbert and Zucker (1983) on municipal reform. Working with a population of cities that adopted civil service reform they suggest that the process of institutionalization is important in understanding why civil service reform structures became widespread. By institutionalization they mean 'the process through which components of formal structure become widely accepted, as both appropriate and necessary, and serve to legitimate organizations' (p. 25).

The elements of structure dealt with as reform were essentially aspects of a legal–rational bureaucracy. The three structural devices were, instituting a system of written examinations for municipal officials, giving administrative personnel tenure and setting up a central agency for personnel appointments. Such a set of structural arrangements reflect values about the appropriate ways of responding to particular issues. One of the reasons for adoption was

> in response to conflict generated by different conceptions of the appropriate role and function of municipal government held by older, established groups and/or community business leaders, and those held by lower status groups in the community, particularly the politically organized immigrants. (Tolbert and Zucker, 1983, p. 30)

Organizational arrangements, then, are a way of dealing with different values and conceptions. But, interestingly, Tolbert and Zucker go on to suggest that this particular way of organizing in cities became institutionalized within the governmental system. That is, the programmes for structural change came to be seen as a necessary component of a 'proper' organizational structure. For a period of time, the connection between values, legitimacy and organizational structure becomes tightly coupled. 'The rapid institutionalization of the reform rested on the assumed isomorphism between it and the ideal rational bureaucratic form' (Tolbert and Zucker, 1983, p. 25).

The above examples illustrate how organizational structures reflect and embody values and beliefs. They are less clear, however, on the extent to which structures and systems are consistently aligned to such underlying values and beliefs. Partly, of course, this is an empirical question but the idea of structures and systems developing a coherent orientation is defensible because of a limited amount of available empirical work (e.g. Miles and Snow, 1978; Mintzberg, 1979; Hood and Dunsire, 1982; Miller and Friesen, 1984).

Two interesting examples of how underpinning ideas and values provides a pervasive coherence or orientation to structures and systems are available from the private and public sectors. Heclo and Wildavsky's (1974) study of British central government noted the prevailing and fundamental importance attributed throughout the civil service to the ideas and values of trust and confidence. Arriving at optimal or 'correct' decisions appeared secondary to the goals of minimizing and containing disruptive behaviours. The Whitehall 'village community' worked to exclude civil servants who neglected such values or who sought a different priority. In effect, there were clearly understood ways of 'how things ought to be done'. Furthermore, organizational arrangements, such as systems of recruitment, appraisal and career advancement, reinforced the expression and practice of these values (Chapman, 1984). Resource allocation mechanisms were similarly designed to minimize potentially disruptive disagreements and laid down how disputes should be handled, how to consult, how to bargain, how to behave *without* rocking the boat. In effect, the basic structures and processes of the civil service organization were underpinned by and reflexive of a set of values of what ought to be.

The second example, this time from the private sector, is Worthy's (1985) study of Sears, Roebuck. Worthy has catalogued the principles which General Wood embodied within Sears, Roebuck from the early 1920s until the 1950s. Thus, according to Worthy, when General Wood assumed control of Sears he redefined the company's strategic purpose from that of buyer for the farmer to that of supplier to the American mass market. From this definition of purpose flowed a whole series of functional strategies and organizational implications. Buying strategies, for example, stressed that Sears's proper role was that of distributor, not producer. Retailing strategies involved supplementing the traditional mail-order catalogue business with the rapid expansion of stores in towns and cities (far distant from the original rural market of Sears before Wood). Recruitment policies for staffing of the stores were developed differently from those of the mail-order business and an ambitious executive development programme was launched to produce the reserves of talent needed to fuel the expansion of stores. The overall organization became more decentralized to reflect the complexity of the distribution system. In other words, having repositioned the organization in terms of strategic purpose, or domain, structures and systems had to follow suit in order to reinforce the basic values espoused in the strategic purpose.

In effect, the position put forward here is that patterns of organizational design, i.e. design archetypes, are to be identified by isolating the distinctive ideas, values and meanings that are pervasively reflected in and reproduced by clusters of structures and systems. An organizational archetype, in this sense, is a particular composition of ideas, beliefs and values connected with structural and system attributes. We would go on to suggest, drawing upon the examples cited above, that the ideas, beliefs and values, or interpretive schemes, may be considered in terms of their definition of three principal and constraining vectors of activity. That is, interpretive schemes set 'frames' for (a) the *appropriate domain of operations*, i.e. the broad nature of organizational purposes or mission, (b) the appropriate *principles of organizing*, and (c) the *criteria of evaluation* to be used *within* the organization for assessment of organizational performance.

The Characteristics of Archetypes

An important implication of defining archetypes in terms of underpinning interpretive schemes is that the transition from one archetype to another may not easily be achieved. Design archetypes may have the attribute of a paradigm with its connotation of world view and intractability. This is not to imply that change is denied by the concept of design archetypes. Miller and Friesen's (1984) research into archetypes observed considerable change, but in most instances change was the adjustment of structures and systems to secure consistency and coherence *within* an archetype. Their research showed that 'momentum' (i.e. the gravitation towards and consolidation within an archetype) was dominant whereas reversals in the direction of change were rare. Essentially, organizations operate within the contoured mould of existing design orientations.

Three reasons are put forward in the literature for the failure of organizations to appreciate and alter pervasive and prevailing assumptions. The first, identified with Hedberg (1981), Starbuck (1976; 1983), Meyer (1982) and Weick (1979), is that structures and processes are often designed to monitor selectively, thus missing critical information. Even where relevant information *is* detected, interpretation is in terms of prevailing references and orientations:

> Because the search for solutions to new problems does not extend much beyond already known solutions, the organization is motivated to transform ill-defined problems into a form that can be handled with existing routines. (Miles and Snow, 1978, p. 156)

Similarly,

> ... the filtered stimuli elicit responses that exploit caches of slack resources and are constrained by behavioral repertoires crystallized in structures. (Meyer, 1982, pp. 519–20)

Kimberly (1987) extends the idea of existing repertoires constraining the range of choices and, importantly for present purposes, puts it in a historical setting by emphasizing the idea of an organizational biography. He suggests that when an organization is set up four important decisions are made, to do with domain, governance, expertise and organizational design. That is, the founders of an organization decide what kinds of products will be produced for what kinds of markets, what the structure of accountability within the organization will be, what sorts of people will be recruited and how the organization will be internally designed. He then suggests that these four features become constraints as the organization develops.

For example, Iacocca's (1984) description of turning Chrysler around is a history of five years in that company from 1978 to 1983. Iacocca's pursuit of change was constrained, at the outset, by what he described as 'problems'. One constraint was the range of products offered by Chrysler and the social groups to which they appealed (blue-collar, older and less educated). Another was the existence of large numbers of plants distributed throughout the world. These constraints, which were the legacy of previous decisions on domain, restricted the options available.

But, as Kimberly (1987) makes clear, the impact of this history is not just a technical matter. Chrysler's situation resulted from particular sets of beliefs and values as well as the technical–rational pressures of its context. Iacocca suggests that a financially rather than engineering oriented top management had had an unfortunate impact on the company. Decisions about strategy and direction were circumscribed by the values of senior management as much as by issues of economic rationality. Past decisions about, for example, domain had become constraining values about the 'proper' business of a company.

In short, Kimberly is theorizing, and Iacocca illustrating, that at any point in time an organization is constrained by its existing organizational design and the kinds of people and expertise which it entails. Past decisions become current constraints and are themselves imbued with values. Thus, the *need* for changes in organizational design may not be recognized within the organization. The *existing* organizational design constrains future movement. The first explanation of design inertia, in short, assumes that organizations simply do not recognize the need for reorientation because they are caught within the meanings and structural form of the prevailing design archetype.

A second explanation (Miller and Friesen, 1980; 1984) assumes that though the need for change may be recognized it is subject to a calculus of costs and benefits:

> potentially disruptive changes must be delayed until the costs of not restructuring become high enough to justify the widespread structural modifications that may be required to re-establish harmony among structural elements. (Miller and Friesen, 1984, p. 208)

A third explanation stems from a view of an organization as a political system composed of constituencies of interests seeking to advance and sustain claims upon scarce and valued resources (Cyert and March, 1963; Greenwood et al., 1977; Pfeffer, 1981; Walsh et al., 1981). From this perspective organizations are not hierarchical ordered machines smoothly orchestrated to achieve task ends and purposes but shot through with Dalton's 'internal combustics' (1964) as a consequence of structural differentiation. Struggles for resources connect to structural arrangements by providing some actors preferential access to key decision processes and, thus, the opportunities to preserve and recreate a pattern of advantage and disadvantage (Ranson et al., 1980; Walsh et al., 1981; Clegg and Dunkerley, 1982).

Patterns of privilege and disadvantage are largely sustained by the institutionalization of the structures which support them. Organizational arrangements become regarded as the appropriate, perhaps even the only, way of doing things; 'alternatives may be literally unthinkable' (Zucker, 1984, p. 5). As a result, privileged dominant coalitions maintain their interests by denying structural reorientation. Attempts to reorient an organizational design have to overcome the sustaining forces of favoured interests and embedded privilege which is usually achieved only with considerable difficulty.

For these three reasons, *adjustments* to structures or processes to achieve archetype coherence, rather than structural and system transformation or *reorientation* (movement from one archetype to another), is the more usual progression. The prevailing hegemony of ideas and the logic of task accomplishment become part of accepted assumptions and rigidify organizational design.

Of course, as noted earlier, movements between design archetypes can and do occur. But the nature of these organizational movements, and the forces that can sustain inertia or promote change, have been fitfully and inadequately addressed in the literature. The majority of studies of organizational change have focused upon *intra*-archetypical change, or have failed to recognize the existence of constraining design types and ideological bases. Furthermore, there has been a focus on *change* rather than inertia, and on *successful* rather than abortive change efforts. A more appropriate approach, and one that is followed in this book, would concentrate on the movements (or tracks as we shall call them in chapter 2) of organizations through time, some of which may exhibit reorientations and some of which may exhibit *abortive* and *aborted* movements to and from design archetypes.

Summary

The argument presented in this chapter is that organizational design can be usefully approached through the notion of archetypes. Archetypes are defined as clusters of prescribed and emergent structures and systems given order or coherence by an underpinning set of ideas, values and beliefs, i.e. an interpretive scheme. This is portrayed in table 1.2. Essential to the idea of archetypes is that prescribed and emergent structures and systems, i.e. design arrangements, can be understood only in terms of the ideas, beliefs and values contained within them. We have argued, both theoretically and through empirical examples, that structures and systems are not purely instrumental, related only to task constraints. Any set of structures is an expression of a set of

Table 1.2 The elements of a design archetype

Interpretive schemes	Organization design
1 *Domain*	1 *Prescribed framework*
2 *Principles of organizing*	structure of roles and
3 *Evaluation criteria*	responsibilities
	decision systems
	human resources systems
	2 *Emergent interaction*
	structure of roles and
	responsibilities
	decision systems
	human resources systems

values and ideas about the organization and appropriate ways of organizing. It is a means of operationalizing purposes, goals and objectives. As such, structures are imbued with values and commitments and serve particular interests, which make the process of producing and managing transformations difficult.

It is very much the connection between ideas, beliefs and values on the one hand, and structures and systems on the other, which gives the concept of archetype. Equally essential to the idea of archetype is that structures and systems have to be examined as a whole because they can be expected to form patterns. Archetypes represent holistic relationships between different aspects of structure, systems and meaning. Understanding change requires examining how far any particular organization is moving from one design archetype to another and how far its current situation shows design coherence. It is the overall 'gestalt' or coherence of design characteristics that is crucial, not their individual occurrence. Given the argument of interdependence between structures, systems and interpretive schemes, the search for organizational patterns becomes central.

Pfeffer (1982) has reached a similar conclusion, stressing that 'one of the critical administrative tasks involves the articulation of the organization's paradigm' (p. 228). From our perspective a critical need is to identify what design archetypes are in operation within organizations. Having done that, it then becomes possible to trace the movements between them and to explain those movements. We are also saying that the concept of organizational design archetype must probe behind structures in both their prescribed and emergent form and uncover the ideas and values which act as premises and assumptions that shape and give logic to them.

At the outset of this chapter we stated that our interest is with reorganizations that involve movement between archetypes. Such movements represent *strategic* organizational design change because the panoply of structures and systems constituting the organization's design has been recast in the shape of a new set of ideas and values about the organization's purpose, ways of operating and relevant performance criteria. Our interest, however, is not simply with successful reorganizations. We are equally interested in why some attempted reorganizations of strategic dimensions are unsuccessful and in why some organizations determine along a course towards strategic change whereas others, apparently facing similar contextual opportunities and pressures, do not. These interests are elaborated in the next chapter where the focus is upon the notion of organizational 'tracks'.

2 Organizational Tracks

Introduction

The argument that organizations have to be understood holistically is not because our primary concern is with the articulation and elaboration of an exhaustive set of organizational archetypes. We agree with McKelvey (1982) that establishing a well-based taxonomy of organizations is important for the theoretical development of the subject. But such a task is beyond the scope of this book. The concern here is with strategic *change*, both its presence and absence, and with establishing the incidence, nature and causes of movements between design archetypes. In the context of our interests, the identification of design archetypes is an interesting and illuminating but essentially *preparatory* step for the explanation and mapping of change.

An essential point, already made, and one that has long been part of the change literature (cf. Bennis et al., 1984) is that movement in organizations does not occur easily. Not all organizations pass through transitions, nor do they depart from similar positions or have common destinations. Organizations that attempt to transform themselves do not always succeed. Similarly, organizations find themselves in transformational situations without having planned to be there. This means that the language of tracks has to provide for the study not only of organizations which attempt and wittingly manage major transformations but also of those involved in abortive shifts and that do not experience, wittingly or otherwise, strategic change.

If we go back to some of the illustrative material presented earlier we can see some of these tracks. Chrysler would seem to be a major success story. The radical transformation and turnaround of the company was achieved with a repositioning in the market, a revitalization of ideas and cultures and systematic organizational reorganization. Yet, as Iacocca makes clear, this both was a much more difficult process and required a much longer time period than anyone had anticipated. Chrysler is a 'new' organization. It has followed a track involving massive change which has brought success.

People Express, on the other hand, failed to transform itself in organizational terms, illustrating the necessity of congruence between values, structures and environment. Hackman's (1984) account of People Express is called 'The transition that hasn't happened', and it emphasizes the tightness between the founding ideas or culture and structures and modes of operation. During 1985–6, People Express faced major market difficulties and consequential losses. But the company did not alter its basic organizational design. Towards the end of his paper Hackman poses the question of whether People Express can operate indefinitely in its particular and distinctive way, 'or is a day of reckoning to come?' (p. 56). He put forward three possible answers to this question, the first of which is that People Express had merely put off the inevitable. Hackman goes on to say that such an answer would mean that

> A significant transition in how the firm does its business must occur, and when it does, the organization will probably pay a considerable price for having deferred so long doing what long-term viability requires. Every time it looked as if a major transition was about to occur at People Express, a crisis appeared or a spurt of growth was initiated, and attention turned to those pressing matters. One could argue that this pattern cannot continue indefinitely, and that one of these days the consequences will catch up with the organization. (p. 57)

Hackman's two other possible answers are that People Express had managed to avoid the need for a transition, or that it had managed to transcend the conventional notions about organizational life cycles. In our terms, at the time of Hackman's writing there had been an absence of strategic organizational design change. The track for People Express was one of momentum within a given organizational design type. (Subsequently, of course, People Express has been taken over by Texas Air which has resulted in considerable change.)

The Bay may or may not be successful in achieving a change from one design archetype to another. As yet the judgement of the market jury is not returned. The Bay is still struggling, in the sense of attempting both to redefine its markets and to achieve a redesigning of its organization. Whether it will be an aborted attempt at change is not clear. The Bay has a distinct culture based on its long history and past dominance of particular sectors of the retail market and it is proving difficult for the company to shift archetypes. At The Bay organizational structures and systems were highly consistent with the prevailing dominant set of values. Changing structures, therefore, involve changing values and underlying meanings, which, as already noted, is no easy task.

Organizations, then, can be 'sorted' in terms of whether and how they change. The notion of *tracks* is an attempt to provide a systematic basis for the process of sorting. It is important, therefore, to be clear as to what is meant by tracks. An archetype, it was stated in chapter 1, is a composition of structures and systems given coherence by an underpinning set of ideas, values and beliefs. Tracks are about the extent to which organizations remain over time within the assumptions and parameters of a given archetype or move between archetypes. A movement away from an archetype involves the decoupling of structures and systems (in total or in part) from a previously prevailing interpretive scheme. Movement into a new archetype involves the recoupling of structures and systems (in total) to a new set of ideas, beliefs and values. The key characteristic of a track, in short, is whether design arrangements become decoupled from a prevailing interpretive scheme and attached to suffusing ideas and values. Tracks, in other words, are about the *configuration of interpretive decoupling and recoupling*, of which, as we shall see in a moment, there are several variants. They are to do with whether there is any loss of design coherence and any displacement of underpinning interpretive schemes over time.

There is a subsidiary characteristic of tracks that is of concern later in this chapter, namely the *sequence of decoupling*. The purpose of looking at *configurations* of interpretive decoupling is to observe whether organizations do or do not move between archetypes and, as will be seen, the relative pace at which they do so. But such a purpose ignores the distinction drawn earlier between prescribed and emergent structures. Configurations of decoupling are not intended to catch the order, or sequence, by which design arrangements become decoupled. Do prescribed frameworks, in total or in part, drive changes in emergent interaction, or is it *vice versa*? Do prescribed frameworks and emergent interactions change in tandem? Does the order of change matter for the success or otherwise of attempted transformation? These are the kinds of questions addressed later when the focus is upon the *sequence* of decoupling. First, however, there is the primary concern with tracks as configurations of interpretive decoupling.

Configurations of Interpretive Decoupling

Organizational design archetypes cannot be self-evidently listed in advance of empirical investigation. The number and form of design archetypes within a population of organizations can only be ascertained through close attention to the meanings which organizational actors give to their situation, the connections made between those meanings and organizational arrangements and the historical context of ideas and legitimation processes operating upon them (Hinings and Greenwood, 1988). However, examples can be given of design archetypes and attempts to move organizations between them.

Barrett and Cammann (1984) in describing the National Steel Corporation (NSC) say:

> The problems facing NSC are familiar to many managers in mature industries. The organization had grown and successfully matured over a period of decades. However, the environment in which it operated changed significantly. The very methods and approaches that had produced success in the past were now inhibiting the changes that were required. National Steel faced the challenge of changing from a corporation that could function effectively in the 1960s and 70s to one that would succeed in the 1980s and 90s. (p. 219)

The nature of the organization that functioned under these conditions was essentially a set of autonomous operating units with little corporate direction. With functional autonomy as a basic organizational principle, there were few mechanisms for coordination and communication between units. Competition and conflict between units was a fairly frequent occurrence. Essentially, in the past, they had operated as effective separate businesses. There was a general congruency between the value of operating autonomy and the structural form in both its prescribed and emergent aspects. In design archetype terms, the NSC could be thought of as autonomously organized.

In the face of an economic downturn in the steel industry in the USA decisions were made at the NSC to reorganize, a not uncommon response to economic difficulty. The principles of this reorganization were to achieve a more coordinated approach to the management of the corporation as a whole. This was to be done through the establishment of clear financial, technological and human resource objectives, by becoming more innovative in business planning, by introducing participative management and by achieving greater levels of coordination between senior managers. Thus, new values and new structures were emphasized leading to a different organizational design archetype of a corporate coordinated business.

As Barrett and Cammann (1984) point out this involved significant business, cultural and organizational change. The scale of change envisaged was major, involving a transformation mixing revitalizing and reorganizing. It was not a question of the NSC maintaining momentum within a given design type but of embarking on a track requiring a movement from one organizational design type to another, a reorientation. However, following that track is not a matter of moving from one design type to another in one fell swoop but involves a pattern of cultural and structural detachment.

Thus, we are suggesting that in this particular case there were two coherent design possibilities, one of which may be labelled the autonomously organized archetype, the other a corporate coordinated business archetype. Between these possibilities, however, are various non-coherent positions. For convenience, five possible positions can be contemplated which show a variety of deviations from two design archetypes.

1 In *archetype coherence* the structures and processes of the organization's design consistently reflect and reinforce one interpretive scheme. In a situation of two available archetypes (as in the example of the NSC) there would be *two* positions of archetype coherence.
2 In *embryonic archetype coherence* the structures and processes nearly consistently reflect the ideas and values of an interpretive scheme. In this position, however, organizations have structures and processes in which significant design elements are discordant. In a situation of two available archetypes there would be *two* positions of embryonic archetype coherence.
3 In *schizoid incoherence* structures and processes reflect the tension of the two contradictory sets of ideas and values. These analytical positions are represented in figure 2.1.

The study of organizational tracks becomes the mapping of movements between these five positions. Organizations that move from either of

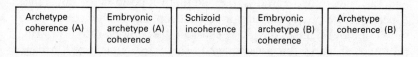

Archetype coherence (A)	Embryonic archetype (A) coherence	Schizoid incoherence	Embryonic archetype (B) coherence	Archetype coherence (B)

Figure 2.1 Archetype decoupling and recoupling

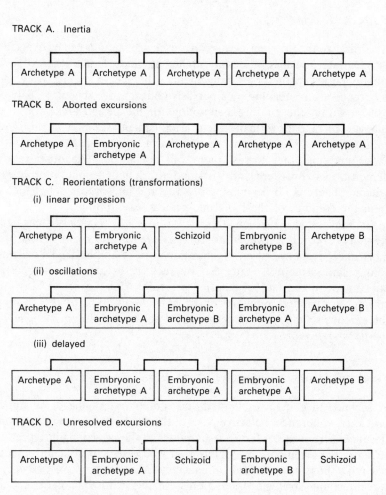

TRACK A. Inertia

Archetype A	Archetype A	Archetype A	Archetype A	Archetype A

TRACK B. Aborted excursions

Archetype A	Embryonic archetype A	Archetype A	Archetype A	Archetype A

TRACK C. Reorientations (transformations)

(i) linear progression

Archetype A	Embryonic archetype A	Schizoid	Embryonic archetype B	Archetype B

(ii) oscillations

Archetype A	Embryonic archetype A	Embryonic archetype B	Embryonic archetype A	Archetype B

(iii) delayed

Archetype A	Embryonic archetype A	Embryonic archetype A	Embryonic archetype A	Archetype B

TRACK D. Unresolved excursions

Archetype A	Embryonic archetype A	Schizoid	Embryonic archetype B	Schizoid

Figure 2.2 Configurations (tracks) of interpretive decoupling and recoupling. Each line joining the boxes represents one time period.

the coherent positions experience the process of interpretive decoupling and, as they move towards the alternative position of coherence, experience the process of interpretive recoupling. The possible permutation of movements is obviously considerable; however, four principal prototypical tracks can be envisaged. These are summarized in figure 2.2 and are discussed in turn below.

Track A: Inertia

According to the previous discussion most organizations can be expected to gravitate towards a design archetype and remain there for a lengthy period. Structural arrangements will develop a consistency and coherence given meaning by a pervasive interpretive scheme. Changes will be within the guiding assumptions of the design archetype, i.e. changes will take the form of structural adjustment. Changes inconsistent with the logic of prevailing meanings will not exist or will be suppressed. Over time, in other words, there will be inertia. The organization demonstrates consistent and sustained attachment to one interpretive scheme. There is no decoupling of structural and processual elements from the confines of the basic interpretive assumptions.

Starbuck et al. (1978) in their study of Facit, Handelstiftung and Kalmar Verkstad in Sweden argue that, even in the face of crisis, the most likely response of an organization is to re-emphasize its existing values and structural patterns. In such cases there is structural adjustment in the face of external pressures, but the broad range of structural attributes remains consistent with the logic of the existing interpretive scheme. In our terms, this track is one of *design archetype inertia or retention*.

Track B: Aborted Excursions

A second track involves limited and temporary fraying of an initial structural coherence. Selective parts of the structure or systems become decoupled from the ordering assumptions of the prevailing interpretive scheme. For example, an organization whose structural arrangements resemble those of a machine bureaucracy (Mintzberg, 1979) and where the prevailing strategic orientation is in line with that of 'defender' (Miles and Snow, 1978) has, in our terms, design coherence. However, 'defenders' may experiment with new structures (e.g. decentralized research and development) which act to weaken internal coherence. Movement occurs to the embryonic archetype category (as in track B of figure 2.2). However, weakened structural coherence may produce declining performance which could push management to abort the experiment and reinstate previous arrangements. Movement away from the starting archetype is reversed (as shown in the third period of track B in figure 2.2). Because the fraying of the paradigm is followed by subsequent archetype retention the track may be labelled an *aborted or discontinued excursion*.

Aborted excursions are conceivable for at least three reasons. One is that organizations lose structural coherence by accident: for some reason structures develop out of alignment with the prevailing order but are recognized as deviations and adjusted. Such unintentional decoupling is more likely where considerable organizational 'slack' is evident, or where the institutionally prescribed form of organizing is ambiguous (Hinings and Greenwood, 1988).

A second reason for an aborted excursion might be politically motivated. Structures serve symbolic purposes and there are known examples of organizations finding it expedient to adopt the structural trappings of a fashionable organizational form whilst operating according to the principles of an alternative set of ideas and values (Meyer and Rowan, 1977). Subsequently, the structural trappings, or symbolic disguise, may become unnecessary and be cast off.

A third reason for an aborted excursion is the genuine experiment with new ideas and structures. For some reason, however, these experiments are often tentative and discontinued. An interesting example is provided by Hackman (1984) who indicates how People Express began to experiment with greater bureaucratization before reverting to original values and purposes. Similarly, in the accounting firms examined by Hinings et al. (1987) the experiment with modules ran counter to the prevailing norms in which partners selected and negotiated their support staff based upon experience and preference rather than formal structural location. The experiment did not sit easily and was subsequently ignored.

Track C: Reorientations (Transformations)

Where an organization leaves one archetype design, and ultimately moves to another, a design *reorientation* (or transformation) has occurred. Prevailing ideas and values have lost legitimacy and become discredited. In their place, an alternative interpretive scheme emerges carrying with it a different pattern of structural arrangements. Structures become decoupled from the old legitimating interpretive scheme and connected – recoupled – to a new one. A new design archetype is established.

An example of a reorientation is provided by Burns and Stalker (1961) who noted that some organizations, under pressure to move from mechanistic to organic structures as a result of market and technological changes, initially instituted 'pathological' responses that fitted uneasily and inappropriately with contextual pressures. For some organizations these responses proved so unwieldly and disruptive that the prevailing interpretive scheme was held less surely. The result was a dissipation of the scheme's constituting presence and force. Erosion and displacement of the prevailing ideas thus allowed further structural change and, ultimately, movement from one archetype (i.e. the mechanistic) to another (i.e. the organic).

This description of movement from mechanistic to organic forms is couched in terms of a linear progression from one archetype to another via the embryonic and schizoid categories. Track C(i) of figure 2.2 is drawn in this way. Thus, archetype A may be conceived as that of the machine bureaucracy which in the first period appears in coherent form. For some reason, however, changes may be introduced in period 2. Initially, changes may be modest and restricted, e.g. the creation of decentralized research units not subject to the detailed controls characteristic of the parent company. In period 2, therefore, the organization has reached an embryonic archetype position. But the success of the new structures may persuade senior management to extend the experiment to other departments and across wider aspects of the organization, e.g. recruitment and incentive systems may become tailored to support the emerging conception of the organization as an entrepreneurial innovative company. In period 3, as a consequence, the organization has achieved a reorientation to an alternative archetype.

A rather similar progression occurred in the NSC. Its starting position was in one archetype (the autonomously organized): its aim was to move to another. In the early stages of the NSC change, a Steel Group was created 'that required managers to coordinate with and assist each other much more than in the past' (Barrett and Cammann, 1984, p. 222). This made managers uncomfortable. The underlying interpretive scheme of autonomy remained the same but a structural change was introduced which deviated from those values. The process of decoupling had begun. An embryonic autonomous position was being developed.

Subsequently, a mission statement was developed and task forces set up to work out how to implement that statement. According to Barrett and Cammann (1984) the task forces 'increasingly ran into problems with the organization's structure' (p. 229). While task forces, integrating mechanisms and corporate values were in place in some parts of the organization, in other parts structures and values 'did not give managers the freedom to make business decisions independently, and the reward structure put them in conflict with other managers' (p. 229). Two different sets of assumptions and structures were at work, i.e. the organization had moved to the schizoid position.

As a consequence, further organizational redesign occurred with the aim of institutionalizing the new culture. An overall strategic planning and policy formulation unit was introduced together with five operating units as separate profit centres. A new senior management group was instituted, designed to function as a team with decisions often made in a collaborative way. The aim was to institutionalize the new culture. But as Barrett and Cammann (1984) point out,

> The new organizational structure is now in the early stages of implementation. . . .A strategic planning process still needs to be put in place. Reward systems, both formal and informal, still need to be realigned for consistency with the mission. New communication flow patterns and information and reporting mechanisms will be needed. (p. 231)

This suggests that the NSC had reached the embryonic corporate coordinated business. The new interpretive scheme was in place together with most of the prescribed and emergent structures necessary to support that interpretation. But, at the time of Barrett and Cammann's account, there were still structural elements to be put in place to achieve a complete reorientation. However, the NSC seems to be a case of successful movement along the track set for itself between one archetype and another.

Linear transition from one archetype to another, however, as in track C(i) is only one of several possible reorientation tracks. Temporary reversals of direction could occur and/or categories be omitted. Furthermore, it is not difficult to envisage an organization whose reorientation track involves *oscillations*, as in example C(ii). *Delays*, or lags, may also occur, as in example C(iii). That is, an organization may stay for a short or long period in a particular position. Incremental movements, e.g. from one transitional position to another, may require varying amounts of time in the push towards reorientation.

An example of a non-linear reorientation is to be found in the work of Burns (1977) on the British Broadcasting Corporation (BBC). Burns charts the change from a 'creative' archetype, a form of professional bureaucracy with a highly segmented organization operated by creative and professional staff, to a corporate form of organization. The latter form is characterized by strong central departments concerned with personnel, finance and strategic planning. However, the process of interpretive decoupling and recoupling in the BBC was not straightforward. The initial introduction of staff grading systems, central financial controls and a managerial hierarchy (part of an embryo corporate form) was not smooth and led to the subsequent withdrawal and rethinking of structural devices. The professional system reasserted itself. However, because of financial pressures on the BBC corporate systems were reintroduced and reinforced and over time became the established ways of operating.

We could find only rare documented examples of this track. We suspect, however, that these non-linear tracks are much more common in practice than is evident from the literature. It is possible that *planned* organizational change, which has been the focus of much interest amongst organizational theorists, is more likely than not to display the characteristics of linear transformation. Much change, however, may be unplanned, occurring in response to task exigencies that are ill-understood. As a consequence, change may be fitful and replete with oscillations and delays rather than ordered and consistent revolution.

Track D: Unresolved Excursions

All the above tracks accept the assumption that archetypes exert a gravitational pull towards structural and processual coherence. Intermediate categories, whether embryonic or schizoid, would, according to that assumption, detract from operational performance by creating stresses and strains resolved only by coherence. However, an organization could become locked between the gravitational pulls of competing interpretive schemes if both are articulated within the organization itself (Ranson et al., 1980). This is track D of figure 2.2. Failures to obtain coherence – or *unresolved excursions* as we would term them – involve sustained movement from a coherent archetype without attaining a reorientation. Incompleted decoupling occurs without completed recoupling. These tracks are examples of *failed* or resisted attempts at reorientation. And, despite the attraction for researchers of studying *successful* change, the study of organizational tracks, as we suggested earlier, has to encompass aborted and unresolved excursions in order that the play of determinant factors may be understood. Certainly, much of the contingency theory literature reveals that as many organizations did not align their structures to the exigencies of the organizational setting as did. Similarly, Miller and Friesen (1984) cite five configurations (covering over one-third of their sample) that lacked coherence. Unresolved excursions are thus important and, hitherto, largely neglected tracks requiring examination.

Sequences of Decoupling

In examining the idea of decoupling prescribed frameworks and emergent interactions from one interpretive scheme and the substitution of another, the question is raised of the sequence in which this may occur. Do changes in interpretive schemes *precede* structural alterations or can the reverse sequence occur? Do prescribed changes *drive* emergent interactions, or can a reorientation occur from an emergent perspective? These are the kinds of questions to which we now turn. We shall discuss various possible sequences that might be involved in tracks B to D, i.e. those involving strategic change.

Sequence I: Simultaneous Detachment

One 'revolutionary' track occurs where a reorientation involves a virtually simultaneous change in interpretive schemes and the prescribed and emergent frameworks. The frequency of such design archetype revolutions is an empirical question but the likelihood is that they will be less common than tracks that move through various stages or in some sense stall in the process. Our survey of the literature failed to yield a clear example of such a revolutionary track.

Sequence II: Prescribed Emergent Detachment

More common is the situation where revitalizing (the reconstruction of necessary values and purposes) and reorganization (the reconstruction of systems and structures) go hand in hand, especially at the prescribed level. That is, new missions and strategies are developed, which mean new interpretive schemes, together with what are regarded as the appropriate prescribed structures and systems.

This sequence, in which prescribed reorientation precedes and acts to reconstitute emergent interactions, may occur for at least two reasons. One is that novel ideas and interpretive schemes are unfamiliar and the detailed organizational implications both unclear and unknown. Prescribed frameworks are established but in loosely specified form and it takes time for managerial appreciation to transform emergent working practices.

Examples of inadequate managerial appreciation of new arrangements are given by Clark (1972) in his study of educational institutions. According to Clark, newly appointed managers adjusted the prescribed structure in an attempt to signal shifts in top level values and expectations. The prescribed framework, in short, was used to symbolize the importance and priority of new sets of meanings. These meanings were embraced by existing staff but their organizational implications imperfectly understood. Not surprisingly it took time for the new values to become translated into emergent practices.

Alteration of the prescribed framework in order to precipitate change at the emergent level is not only a consequence of planned change coupled with imperfect understanding of emergent structural implications. A second possibility is that prescribed change as a forerunner of emergent change may indicate resistance to design alteration. Disagreement may exist concerning the appropriateness of alternative schemes with the result that the prescribed framework may reflect the ideas and values of a dominant coalition intent upon change, and the emergent structure the ideas and values of those resistant to change.

Indeed, several writers (Zaltman et al., 1973; Kimberly et al., 1980) have suggested that change may occur at the prescribed level rather more easily than at the emergent level, and that the aspirations of those wishing to secure a reorientation of design might be frustrated. This literature, with its emphasis upon the difficulties of the implementation of change and the problems of coordination that arise from complexity and diversity, indicates that frequently the fundamental resistance to change expresses itself in emergent interactions rather than in the prescribed framework. The prescribed framework may be amenable to transformation but not the emergent interactions. The pattern of emergent interactions is seen as *more fundamental* in generating resistance to change and in demonstrating that change in the prescribed framework can be more apparent than real.

The Ford Motor Company in the 1960s provides an interesting example of a prescribed framework altered in the face of resistance. At the beginning of the decade the overseas facilities of the company essentially operated as 'autonomous divisions, each producing its own line of cars . . . and submitting, sometimes reluctantly, to . . . coordination of export markets outside the three companies' defined domains' (Livesay, 1977, p. 439). Henry Ford II set about redefining the international domain on a more global basis, in line with his beliefs about the need for a product line of nationally interchangeable parts coupled with the creation of local manufacturing facilities. The new strategy involved substantial restructuring. European divisions were integrated in a single unit producing a single line of cars assembled from common parts flowing from all over the region (Livesay, 1977). Restructuring at the prescribed level was not difficult, given the personal authority of Henry Ford II. The new strategy and structure represented his ideas, beliefs and philosophy, and he was able to put them in place. But local resistance was overcome only by the replacement of higher-level European executives. Livesay reports that reorganization was achieved despite the objections of many of Ford's subordinates. The prescribed framework was reconstituted in line with a new or modified interpretive scheme and used to drive changes in emergent practices.

The NSC shows a similar sequence of altered prescribed frameworks meeting resistance at the emergent level, although steps were taken further to add the necessary emergent aspects. Initially there was the development of a new mission, i.e. statement of purpose and values, by the chief executive and senior management, followed by changes in the prescribed framework of operation emphasizing integration. As with the accounting firm, this provoked a reaction because of both the lack of general support and the lack of understanding of the relationship between the prescribed framework and emergent interactions. This in turn led senior managers to reassess the nature of the organizational devices and engage in a further reorganization that recognizes the importance of emergent practices.

A somewhat different sequence is provided by Burns and Stalker (1961). They noted that mechanistic organizations were ill-suited to handle rapid market and technological change. However, instead of developing new missions and strategies and the inculcation of appropriate values (interpretive schemes), pathological responses were developed in line with existing interpretive schemes. Structures were grafted at both prescribed and emergent levels that fitted uneasily and inappropriately within the rest of the organization.

Two prescribed pathological devices described by Burns and Stalker are the 'mechanistic jungle' and the 'supra-personal system'. The former is the creation of new jobs and departments whose existence depends on the perpetuation of the difficulties they are supposed to solve. The latter is the setting up of a permanent committee structure. An emergent interaction was the development of an 'ambiguous figure system'. This is the existence of a non-officially-recognized system of pair relationships between the chief executive and some dozens of people at different positions below him in the management structure, alongside the official hierarchy.

Pathological responses of this kind move an organization from its coherent state. If the responses are sufficiently disruptive to the prevailing orientation they may prove unwieldy, causing the prevailing interpretive scheme to be held less surely. The constituting presence and force of the interpretive scheme may dissipate and new interpretive schemes develop. Pfeffer outlines this sequence of erosion and displacement:

> Meanings are not questioned and thrown out all at once. Rather, actions are taken, often within the dominant paradigm, to solve some small problem, which in turn leads to other problems, other actions, and finally, the unravelling of the old system of revolutionary change or adaptation . . . and its replacement with an alternative paradigm. (1982, p. 233)

The sequence here, then, is from prescribed framework to emergent interactions to new interpretive scheme. The fundamental resistance to change expresses itself in emergent interactions and interpretive schemes. The pattern of emergent interactions and underlying meanings is seen as more fundamental in generating resistance to change.

Sequence III: Emergent Prescribed Detachment

A further possible sequence in a track is led by emergent interactions. Here, the emergent structures become decoupled from the prevailing interpretive scheme and operate within a prescribed framework that remains a reflection of that scheme. An example occurred in British local authorities in the early and mid-1960s (Greenwood and Stewart, 1971). Structured to handle a series of discrete activities – schooling, meals on wheels, road construction etc. – the organization came under increasing pressure as environmental and social problems were increasingly redefined and identified. Issues such as inner city decay, ethnic mixes, vandalism etc. could not be considered exclusively within the terms of reference of any single part of the existing departmentalized structures.

As a result of these developments, emergent networks arose linking school teachers, social workers, housing officers, environmental health officers etc. as responsive individuals sought to overcome the deficiencies imposed by the prescribed design. Along with these emergent patterns came new interpretive schemes, the product of new ideas about the role of the local authority and the nature of the tasks it faced. Conceptions of corporate planning were becoming part of the local government debate. It was only after the emergent interactions and their supportive values became established that prescribed frameworks were subject to alteration.

The local authority is an example of a sequence of changed emergent interactions producing new interpretive schemes leading, in turn, to changed prescribed frameworks. Emergent structural alteration, as illustrated in the example, can bring with it a questioning of prevailing ideas and beliefs and a rethinking of ideas, values and beliefs. Once the process of questioning happens the result may be a recasting of the prescribed framework.

Clearly, there is a whole series of possibilities. At this point there are no strong reasons for further amplification of the possible sequences that might exist. The aim has been to illustrate the issue and provide a framework for subsequent analysis. The full details of the sequences involved within organizational tracks cannot be anticipated. Their mapping is a matter of empirical observation.

The theory of strategic organizational design change developed in later chapters is essentially an attempt to explain why and how particular organizations move along particular tracks. In short, organizational tracks are the dependent variable and encompass the possible variations (successful, unsuccessful) of strategic change and strategic inertia. The important thrust of the argument is that organizations move along tracks exhibiting varying degrees of inertia and reorientation and that the study of organizational design change should be the tracking of the combinations of design arrangements that alter as the process of interpretive decoupling and recoupling takes place. In this chapter we have identified four primary configurations of tracks and, in addition, noted a significant subsidiary issue, i.e. the sequence in which interpretive schemes, prescribed frameworks and emergent interactions alter.

The next chapter turns to the explanation of why different tracks are followed or resisted. What, in short, are the *dynamics of change* and how do they operate?

3 Understanding Change and Stability

Introduction

The idea of tracks presented in chapter 2 suggests that some organizations manage to achieve major transformations and reorientations, some show stability and some oscillate between archetypes. The issue now becomes one of *why* these different tracks appear. What, in short, are the dynamics of inertia and change and how do they operate?

The approach developed in chapter 1 towards the study of design archetypes is holistic, emphasizing the congruence of values with prescribed and emergent structures and systems. Our approach to understanding movement or lack of it is similarly holistic. The basic idea is deceptively simple: organizational design is a process of constrained choice. Managers face pressures from the environment in which they operate. In the case of Chrysler and The Bay it was primarily collapses in markets. In the British Broadcasting Corporation one sees changing technologies at work, together with new ideas about the role of a government corporation and new competitive elements from the Independent Television Authority. The case of the Canadian accounting firm also shows a mixture of potential environmental effects. The local office faced a worsening economic situation coupled with the behaviour of a national office producing new mission statements and beginning to emphasize business planning. In ICI there was a dramatic worsening of business performance due to high interest rates and the rising value of sterling. At Cadbury's economic pressures came from the intensification of competition in a saturated market.

All these situations show the potential importance of movements and changes external to a particular organization. However, the assumption cannot be made that change is a simple matter of adjustment to external pressures. Certainly, they act as constraints and produce pressures to which there has to be a response. But such contextual features have to be recognized and responses have to be worked out by the members of an organization. A prime managerial function is the interpretation of an organization's environment and of determining an appropriate response.

Even those studies which essentially take the position that changes in structure can be understood as a process of adaptation to environmental shifts (e.g. contingency theory) illustrate the limitations of this view. The basic model is structural functionalism. What the empirical studies show is that while one can get relatively high correlations and r^2 values between context and structure, there is always a considerable amount of unexplained variance. That is, at any particular time there are organizations which are 'wrongly' structured, i.e. where the relationships between contextual features such as environmental uncertainty, size and technology are not as predicted. At the very least there must be a time lag in the effects of context; more likely is that internal structures and processes *as well as* organizational environments have to be taken into account in designing organizations. Donaldson (1985) puts the position well:

> Study of effective structures requires concern for functional imperatives or systems needs. This does not imply that they work in some metaphysical way. The political actors through their acts alter the structures and consequent functioning, and do so wittingly or unwittingly, and with a variety of purposes in mind. (p. 147)

Of course, there are studies which attest to the importance of internal processes. Starbuck et al. (1978) show that the difficulties Facit, Handelstiftung and Kalmar Verkstad had in adjusting to a changed environment derived from the re-emphasizing of *existing* values and structural patterns by *existing* managers and technical experts who were the ones who had to interpret the meaning of the environmental changes. Were the changes important? Did they pose a threat to continued operations? What kind of a response, if any, was necessary? These are the questions that all managers have to ask when faced by a changing environment. The answers that they will give will derive, at least in part, from the values espoused within the organization, within the section of that organization in which managers are located and within the occupations of which he/she is a member.

Thus, while environments present real situations and challenges to managers within an organization, these situations and challenges have to be interpreted and given meaning. But there are further processes which are important in determining the direction and pace of change, namely power and commitment.

In the case of ICI, Pettigrew draws a picture of a powerful figure, the chief executive, interpeting the situation and developing the need for change. His interpretation of that situation and his ideas about organizational solutions are, in one sense, authoritative and as such have to be listened to because of the hierarchical base of the firm. But there is still the need to generate commitment from the rest of top management to the chief executive's interpretations and solutions. The description by Pettigrew (1985) demonstrates the importance of this even within a clearly hierarchical organization.

Warren (1984) shows that the power of the president is much more circumscribed in an educational institution, Antioch College, than in a business organization. The process of developing a common interpretation of the environmental situation is very difficult. It was only when the situation reached a *financial* crisis point that he was able to take action. A somewhat similar state of affairs is illustrated by Hinings et al. (1987) in an accounting office, where the partnership basis of the organization produced a highly decentralized and deconcentrated authority system.

We are suggesting, then, that to understand both stability and change it is necessary to examine the interpenetration of organizational contexts and internal organizational arrangements and processes. Steel companies, retail outlets, universities, municipalities, school districts, airlines etc. are not just 'set' in contexts. Their initial and continued existence depends to a greater or lesser degree on their responding to those contexts. Their purposes and strategies are about dealing with an environment. But such contexts are not abstract features devoid of meaning. Processes of interpretation about what is important and meaningful in the environment have to take place. Values are an important base for interpretation. However, not all the espoused values in an organization are equal; the power of the holders of different values becomes a consideration. Power holders in organizations (usually, but not always, senior managers) set up organizational design arrangements according to *their* interpretations of environmental pressures. Through power holders organizations generate and re-enact the contextual situation in their internal design arrangements. But through the particular mixes of value commitment, interest satisfaction and power they also provide the conditions under which a potential transformation can take place. Thus, there is a constant interplay between external and internal features of organizations.

To develop this argument further, it is necessary to articulate more fully the basic analytical concepts which underlie our view of the dynamics of stability and change. These are

1 *situational constraints* which are inherent in the context of the organization,

2 *interpretive schemes* created by organizational members and articulated as 'values' and 'interests',

3 *interests*, i.e. the motivation to enhance or sustain shares of scarce and valued resources,

4 *dependences of power* and domination which provide for the resolution of conflicts over value preferences and sectional interests, and

5 *organizational capacity* which enables appropriate competences and capabilities to be brought to bear.

Initially each of these will be dealt with separately. But, because of the emphasis we place on their interpenetration with each other, we will return in subsequent chapters to the ways in which they are interdependent. For the moment, our concern is to define the manner in which the dynamics are conceptualized and used. In doing so they may be conceptualized as belonging to three categories. One category consists of the *constraints* that derive from the situational context or contingent circumstances. A second category consists of the patterns of value commitments and degree of satisfaction with interests; these represent elements of *strategic choice*. These first two categories have the capacity to place pressures on an organization for change or for inertia. The third category consists not of precipitators but of *enabling factors* that can facilitate or impede the scale of change. Thus, the structure of power dependences will not precipitate change but it can enable change efforts to be successful or halt their progress. Similarly the presence or absence of organizational capacities will affect the progression and conclusion of change.

Situational Constraints

There is, of course, a considerable body of organizational literature referred to as 'structural contingency theory' which has emphasized the idea of organizations adapting to pressures from contingent or situational circumstances. It is not our purpose here to review this literature and its attendant critiques. This has been done more than adequately elsewhere (cf. Child, 1972; Schoonhoven, 1980; Pfeffer, 1982). Rather, we wish to take and use the idea of features within an organizational context acting as *constraints* and as *pressures* upon processes of design choice.

Empirical studies of the relationships between context and organizational design have demonstrated strong connections. In the main, three particular situational circumstances have been dealt with, namely environment, technology and size (cf. Pfeffer, 1982). While there are problems of definition and measurement with each of these, there has been sufficient theorizing and empirical work to establish them as the initial basis for theories of organizational design. That is, organizational structures, to be effective and efficient, have to 'fit' this context. Within this notion of 'fit' are contained the separate, if independent, ideas of constraints and pressures.

The idea of context as *constraining* can be shown through a consideration of size. As Pfeffer (1982) says, 'Size is one of the most prominent characteristics of organizations, and the effects of size have been investigated in numerous studies' (p. 148). In particular, size has been shown to be related to the extent of the division of labour and the existence of impersonal control mechanisms (cf. Pugh and Hickson, 1976; Pugh and Hinings, 1976). Larger organizations have more extensive specialization of functions and personnel and more formal control systems. Child (1974; 1975) has shown that these organizational forms are related to performance.

What these (and other) analyses show is the constraining nature of organizational size. An organization such as ICI, which employs many thousands and has hundreds of top managers, *has* to be structured in a way which is different from a jobbing manufacturer of a particular speciality product with a hundred or so employees, if it is to remain efficient. It uses different kinds of systems, having formal employee appraisal systems, documents for communicating decisions, computer-based applications for manufacture and so on. The *size* that an organization has reached at any particular time puts it into a category for which a particular design archetype is appropriate. Attempting to change the design type without recognizing the limitations derived from scale will produce a decrement in performance.

The same kind of argument can be put forward for the other two aspects of context, namely technology and environment. Interestingly, here one sees the impact of the underlying subconcepts of *uncertainty* and *complexity*. The nature of the product and production process is an organization, and the kind of environment in which it operates, can be classified as more or less complex and uncertain, i.e. organizations vary according to whether there is greater or lesser surety of knowledge about the technology used and/or the predictability of the environment. The presence of certainty allows more systematization and formalization of structure and process. McDonalds is an excellent example of a company working with a technology that is simple (and hence highly predictable) in an environment that is also well structured; as a result a McDonalds' franchise can be organized as an efficient machine bureaucracy.

The point being made is that an organization of a particular size operating with a particular technology and in a particular environment is constrained in terms of the organizational design options available for efficiency. At any historical point an organization is 'caught' and constrained by its context.

Another important, and often neglected, element in an organizational environment is what Staw and Szwajkowski (1975) have identified as the relative scarcity or munificence of resources. All organizations require a flow of money, people and equipment (the economist's factors of production). The source and relative importance of these varies across organizations. Each one can produce a pressure on an organization. An example of such a pressure in a private sector company would be where a manufacturing subsidiary's cash is immediately claimed by a parent company to deal with a debt load or a strategy of diversification, leaving the subsidiary continuously squeezed. In a public sector organization which is dependent on another governmental organization for grants to carry out its functions, fiscal pressures can arise if there are major changes in the size or formats of those grants.

Other contextual features could be added to the prime three. The form of ownership or accountability is one (Hinings et al., 1975; Donaldson, 1985). Private and government-owned firms are different in their organizational design because their ownership is different. The particular impact of ownership is on the internal authority system and on the extent to which an organization can decentralize (Pugh et al., 1969; Donaldson, 1985). Another feature suggested by Hinings and Foster (1972) and Hinings et al. (1975) is that of ideas. This whole notion of organizations being constrained by ideas external to them is taken up by the institutional school of organizational analysis (Meyer and Rowan, 1977; Meyer and Scott, 1983; Zucker, 1984). Organizations have to adapt to ideas about their appropriate roles and forms of organization. This may be particularly the case where measures of performance are problematic. In such a situation, e.g. schools, churches and sport organizations, having a particular organizational design legitimates operations.

The role of institutionally prescribed and legitimated ideas about appropriate ways of operating, we are suggesting, may be an important constraint upon the choice of organizational arrangements, especially in non-profit organizations. The particular form that institutional prescriptions take, however, will probably vary from institutional arena to arena. At this stage, therefore, we should note the ideational environment as being potentially important; in chapter 5 we shall elaborate upon the *nature* (i.e. the structures of dissemination) of the institutional arena of the organizations under examination and upon the substantive content of the ideas prescribed as legitimate within that arena during the research period.

What we are saying, then, is that the existing context constrains an organization because of technical reasons to organize in particular ways. However, when that context changes it becomes a *pressure* on an organization. The extent of the pressure depends largely on the extent of the contextual change. Most of the macro-change literature is about the response of organizations to such changes; in the case of business organizations this may often initially be perceived through performance problems. Many of the examples that we have been using throughout this book are of this kind. The Chrysler company had been losing money due to falling market share and was in a critical cash-flow situation by 1978. Later the Iranian situation caused a major market shift in product preference for which the company was not prepared. Cadbury's was faced with the consequences of a successful competitor entering its market with new production techniques and different marketing approaches.

Market shifts and technological innovations may be important contextual changes for business organizations, but rather different pressures may operate for organizations not directly subject to markets.

Table 3.1   Situational context and tracks

Track		Degree of organization/situational context alignment	
		T_1	T_2
A	Inertia/retention	Good	Good
B	Aborted excursion	Mainly good	Good
C	Reorientation	Poor	Good
D	Unresolved excursion	Partial	Partial

In the case of British local authorities a political decision was made by a controlling organization (British central government) to redraw geographical boundaries, redistribute functions between types of local authority and increase the scale of the units in the system. Through legislation, changes were made which became pressures on the new local authorities. In the case of Antioch College, the pressures derived from changes in its cost structure, the result of the twin influences of increased inflation and energy costs on the one hand and declining enrolments and federal support on the other.

Whatever the nature of the contextual factors critical for an organization, the point that has to be grasped is that changes in those factors, of a scale that causes an organization to be out of fit with the exigencies of its technical context, become *pressures* in the sense that they produce the need for a response by an organization. As the quote from Donaldson (1985) used previously in this chapter points out, what that response will be is not automatic or mechanical. Responses will be mediated by the 'strategic choices' that are made by organizational members and, in particular, by those members who hold power. However, according to the logic of contingency analysis a broad set of associations between tracks and situational contexts may be anticipated, as summarized in table 3.1

Table 3.1 suggests that an organization which follows the inertia track will have a 'good' alignment between the existing organizational design and its situational context at the beginning of, and throughout, the research period. As long as that alignment holds there will be no pressures from the situational context for organizational change. The other tracks, however, are of organizations which do experience pressures deriving from the situational context. Thus, for example, the reorientation track is characterized by a poor initial alignment at time period T_1 and, at the end of the period T_2, a good alignment. The assumption is that organizations adjust structures in the face of situational pressures in order to secure alignment.

Before leaving the discussion of situational constraints a number of points should be made. First, table 3.1 refers to the situational context as though it were a homogeneous phenomenon. In fact, it is not necessarily the case that organizations face circumstances which 'require' the same form of structural response. There could be inconsistencies of contingency pressures. We might anticipate that the existence of inconsistencies in the pressures emanating from the situational context would lead to oscillations in structural design as the organization periodically attempts to resolve different sets of pressures arising from its heterogeneous environment. Second, table 3.1 is constructed as though organizations may be out of alignment with their situational context and, as a consequence, move towards a better fit. The logic of contingency analysis, however, means that the nature of the situational context can change, creating misalignment. Therefore, in studying the relationship between organizational design and situational context the researcher is looking not simply at how the organization obtains alignment with its context but, perhaps, at how the organization is chasing a moving context.

Interpretive Schemes

If the historical context in which an organization is placed acts as a constraint, and any changes in that context produce a pressure for organizational redesign, then an understanding of how and why a *particular* response is produced is necessary. Cross-sectional studies of the relationships between design options and situational constraints often show high, but not perfect, correlations (Pugh and Hinings, 1976; Donaldson, 1985). In the short run, at least, considerable discretion remains with organizational members, and especially with senior managers, in choosing which constraints and pressures to respond to and which design options to develop.

The Hudson's Bay Company has been clear, in general terms, that it faces a crisis. It faced the constraint of its own history as a Canadian institution and its status as a blue-chip company. Surely it was impossible for The Bay to go under! The pressures to act were strong as sales fell and competition in the retail sector became stronger. The whole position of department stores in the retail market has come under question. But what was the response to be? One response was to remodel stores making more intensive usage of floor space. Another response was to fire the chief executive and replace him with a three-person committee-in-charge, not one of whom would be more senior than another. Another response was to restructure, altering the responsibilities of vice-presidents.

The question that arises is why these particular responses (as well as or rather than many others)? If contextual changes produce pressures to act, what are the 'springs of action', the bases on which responses are presaged? A major one is the pattern of commitments by members of an organization to prevailing and alternative interpretive schemes.

The examples we have given in this and previous chapters have illustrated how structures are derivative of underlying ideas and beliefs. But beliefs about what? We suggested in chapter 1 that interpretive schemes, as they relate to organizational design archetypes, shape prevailing conceptions of what an organization should be doing, of how it should be doing it and of how it should be judged. It is the shared background of mutual understandings about these issues which constitutes what Brown (1978) has called 'the "agreement" between members that enables the orderly production of roles and rules' (p. 374).

To understand what track an organization might follow in the future it is therefore necessary to analyse the *current* nature of commitments to the prevailing or alternative interpretive scheme. Four generic patterns of commitment can be identified:

1 widespread commitment to the existing interpretive scheme (a *status quo* commitment);
2 widespread commitment to an alternative interpretive scheme (a *reformative* commitment);
3 low commitment to prevailing and alternative interpretive schemes (an *indifferent* commitment);
4 substantial commitment to two or more interpretive schemes (a *competitive* commitment).

Commitment which is *status quo* oriented is likely to be a necessary condition for an inertia track. Miller and Friesen (1984) argue that inertia, or momentum within a design archetype, is the most common track followed by organizations. In terms of the commitment to prevailing interpretive schemes, this view is also put forward by Starbuck (1976; 1983), Miles and Snow (1978), Weick (1979), Hedberg (1981), Meyer (1982) and Kimberly (1987). Interpretation of events is in terms of prevailing references and orientations. As Miles and Snow (1978, p. 156) put it,

> Because the search for solutions to new problems does not extend much beyond already known solutions, the organization is motivated to transform ill-defined problems into a form that can be handled with existing routines.

Reformative commitments, on the other hand, are liable to lead towards a track of reorientation transformation because of the commitment to an interpretive scheme in opposition to the officially prevailing one. There is a sense in which some level of reformative commitment is built into organizational tracks through the turnover of personnel. New people will bring different ideas to bear on the appropriateness of domain, form and performance criteria. Starbuck et al. (1978) from their case analysis of three Swedish companies argue that the replacement of top managers is essential to achieve a reorientation in an organization. The function of the replacement is to put in place an alternative interpretive scheme because of the inertial properties of whichever scheme is currently in place, a very common organizational event when major reorganizations and transitions are planned. The business magazines are full of stories of changes in senior personnel when companies are, for example, repositioning themselves in a market because this involves management rethinking the business of the firm. Of course, for it to be a reformative commitment the new ways of thinking about domains, forms and performance have to be widespread in the organization.

Both of the situations outlined envisage committed groups and individuals. But it is possible that an organization may operate without too much commitment on anyone's part. Inertia and a *status quo* commitment can drift into low commitment and indifference because of its taken-for-granted nature. The process of revitalization and change may well be an explicit recognition of the *lack* of commitment to anything substantial within an organization. Similarly, a structural reorganization may take place not because of any external stimulus but because of a need felt by senior management to shake up an organization, to move it from indifference and apathy.

A situation of indifference will probably be associated with an inertia track, especially in a possible subform of drift, rather than directed momentum. However, because of the lack of commitment an organization may find itself on a track towards an unresolved excursion as changes are made without any secure rationale or legitimation.

A more usual situation for many organizations is that of competitive commitment where there are different ways of conceptualizing an organization's business. Indeed, much of the work on differentiation and conflict in organizations (Lawrence and Lorsch, 1967; Nystrom, 1986) shows how technical boundaries between departments and sections are reinforced and buttressed by cognitive boundaries. The same point is made by studies of organizational climate and culture (Pugh and Payne, 1977; Schein, 1986). Any organization has within it the seeds of alternative ways of viewing the purposes of that organization, the ways in which it might be appropriately organized and how actions might be evaluated.

Child and Smith (1987) in their analysis of Cadbury's, the chocolate giant, talk of 'Cadburyism' as 'a strong ideology in the consciousness of family members, managers and workers' (p. 32). This ideology covered the nature of the firm, how it should be structured and so on. Because of its institutionalization in the firm's long history it became a benchmark against which any effort to change the firm would be measured. Again, to quote Child and Smith, 'As a benchmark it provoked key change agents deliberately to set out their case against the fundamentals of the tradition' (p. 32). The Technical Director articulated an alternative interpretive scheme, putting forward proposals which directly challenged the traditions by suggesting (amongst other things) that the Bournville works, the epitome of the Cadbury approach, should be shut down.

The existence of competitive commitments will act to destabilize organizational arrangements – the bases of legitimation are supported but under challenge. Such a challenge may result in a reorientation *if* the challenging interpretive scheme becomes dominant. However, the track followed may be that of an aborted or unresolved excursion if the supporters of the prevailing interpretive scheme successfully resist change.

The probable associations between tracks and patterns of commitment are summarized in table 3.2.

Table 3.2 Association between tracks and patterns of commitment

Track	Patterns of commitment
A Inertia/retention	*Status quo*–indifferent
B Aborted excursion	Competitive–indifferent
C Reorientation	Reformative–competitive
D Unresolved excursion	Competitive

Interests

Organizations, it was pointed out earlier, may be conceptualized as political systems in which advantaged groups jostle with disadvantaged groups to sustain patterns of privilege. Organizational subunits, i.e. functionally differentiated agencies, are not neutral and indifferent to the existence of other groups. Instead, each group has a distinct set of *interests* which are frequently at odds with the interests of other groups; consequently the interactions that occur between technically interdependent groups can assume the stance of disruptive competition or deliberate conflict. Each group competes within the organization to translate its interests into favourable allocations of resources.

The notion of interests is an 'incorrigibly evaluative' one (Lukes, 1974) in that it refers both to the distribution of scarce resources and to the ineluctable orientation and motivation of members to maintain and enhance their sectional claims. Within the organizational literature the notion of interests has appeared only sporadically. Selznick (1949) and more recently Pettigrew (1973), Pfeffer and Salancik (1974; 1978), Laumann and Pappi (1976) and Benson (1977) have pointed to the way that the structure of an organization represents a differential of functional tasks from which, crucially, there flows a distribution of scarce resources. The process of functional specialization distinguishes one set of organizational incumbents from another by differentially affording them scarce wealth, status and authority; built into the organization is a structure of advantage and disadvantage (Benson, 1977; Walsh et al., 1981).

There has been considerable debate concerning objective and subjective definitions of interests. In its Marxian roots, the concept refers to material advantages, to the scarce resources available in a society and to the demonstrable stakes that different groups have in their distribution (Stolzman, 1975). Similarly, Alford (1975) in his work on health reform in the USA defines interests as the consequences of policies for the distribution of resources between groups. It is in the interests of a group to have resources distributed in its favour.

Both Alford and Stolzman, however, also recognize the potential relevance of subjective interests. The difficulty lies in avoiding a definition that is equivalent to wants or likes, without any materialistic base to the definition. The idea of objective interests faces two main objections: (1) people act on the basis of their subjective interpretation and (2) it puts the analyst in the position of moral arbiter. But both the objective and subjective aspects of the concept are needed. The structuralist critique of action concepts of power argues that given systems of domination institutionalize a particular distribution of material advantage; they favour some rather than others. An examination of objective interests tells us who gains and who loses in material terms from a given organizational system. It tells us who has the demonstrable stakes in the organization and what the consequences are of the particular organizational structure. But it does not tell us why certain groups and individuals do not act in terms of their objective interests. For that we need both the concept of values as a definer of ends and preferences and that of subjective interests.

However, the crux in dealing with interests, as Stolzman (1975) suggests, is the interplay between the objective and the subjective in concrete situations. For this, subjective interests cannot be equated with any statement of wants or likes, e.g. a desire for more autonomy, but have to have a materialistic base. So, for us, interests refer to the relationship between an individual or group and the distribution of organizational resources. Interests are concerned with the aims of functionally discrete groups to secure a sufficient and fair share of organizational resources. Interests are expressed through a motivation to enhance or defend a particular distribution of organizational resources.

Defining interests in this way directs attention to the motivations, or lack of them, that they provide to action and to the commitment to change or the *status quo*. It is also important to underline that there are competing interests within an organization. Alford (1975) draws a useful distinction between dominant, challenging and repressed interests. Dominant interests are those engrained in the structure; such interests are served by being taken for granted as legitimate and

Table 3.3 Association between tracks and patterns of interests

Track		Patterns of interest
A	Inertia/retention	High satisfaction–no change
B	Aborted excursion	Modest satisfaction–high satisfaction
C	Reorientation	High dissatisfaction–satisfaction
D	Unresolved excursion	High dissatisfaction–no change

questions about them rarely arise. However, at particular points of change they may be challenged to the extent that alternative definitions of interest may have to be taken into account, i.e. they get on the agenda and motivate new patterns of action. Repressed interests are those of which, objectively, the structure takes no account.

This image of an organization as an aggregation of groups locked in battle for scarce resources can be overstated. There are always circumstances that limit, or hold in check, the nature of the struggle. But organizations are composed of groups with their own perceived interests which motivate them to struggle for a favourable pattern of resource allocations. And the intensity of the struggle and the pressure for change in existing allocative mechanisms will be a function of the amount of dissatisfaction with the share of resources going to particular groups. The number of dissatisfied groups and the intensity of their dissatisfaction can be a critical dynamic of change.

The relationship between satisfaction/dissatisfaction with interest and organizational tracks is summarized in table 3.3. The problem with table 3.3, of course, is that it treats interests as an analytically discrete dynamic, whereas it is closely locked into other dynamics. For example, interests are related to the ideas and values within an interpretive scheme. Given that choices can be made between interpretive schemes, and that each will not serve the interests of all groups equally well, groups will 'value' sets of ideas differently. Groups within organizations are receptive to particular ideas and not others. What they value depends to a considerable extent upon their interpretation of the congruence of their interests with the likely resource consequences of alternative ideas. Interests are inextricably linked to interpretive schemes, despite their analytical independence.

Dependences of Power

Organizational groups, of course, vary in their ability to influence the translation of their values and their interests into favourable organizational arrangements; they have differential *power*. Some groups and individuals in an organization are listened to more keenly than others. We have argued that organizational arrangements are constituted in accordance with members' interpretive schemes: more accurately, the act of organizational design is typically the privilege of *some* organizational actors. Organizations are typically composed of a number of groups, initially divided on vertical and horizontal task lines, but then underpinned by alternative conceptions, value preferences and sectional interests – i.e. organizations are political units. The relations of power and domination which enable some organizational members to constitute and recreate organizational structure according to *their* preferences thus becomes a critical point of focus.

While structural change is likely to be initiated by a contextual change and filtered by prevailing interpretive schemes and satisfaction or dissatisfaction with interest, it is the relative abilities of groups to express and protect those meanings and interests in structural and processual terms that is an important piece in the jigsaw of understanding change and stability. Power is a capacity to determine outcomes (Hickson et al., 1971; 1986) and structures are used to obtain and utilize power (Pfeffer, 1981). As Pettigrew (1985) has said in his study of ICI,

> The possibilities and limitations of change in any organization are influenced by the history of attitudes and relationships between interest groups . . . and by the mobilization of support for a change within the power structure at any point in time. (p. 27)

Starbuck et al. (1978), in their study of Facit' Handelstiftung and Kalmar Verkstad, show that existing powerful groups are frequently tied to prevailing interpretive schemes and structural arrangements because these are the basis of their power. Even when contingencies change powerful managers often remain committed to prevailing interpretations and structural responses because doing so serves their interests. Hence, the power structure can act to override the impulse for change created by pressures from a changed context.

The commitment of senior executives to the *status quo* may or may not be politically motivated. One interpretation is that managers act to maintain their interests which are well served by prevailing arrangements. Others would conclude that managers become captured or caught by prevailing modes of thought. Both of these interpretations can explain why organizations may pursue the inertia track despite lack of alignment with contextual factors. More importantly, both interpretations touch directly upon the importance of power and the ability to control decision premises as a key dynamic or suppressor of change.

The way in which we shall use power as a dynamic of change rests upon the distinction between the extent to which power in an organization is relatively dispersed between a multiplicity of groups, rather than focused and concentrated within a narrowly drawn coalition or elite. This is the distinction between a *concentrated* power structure and a dispersed one. Thus

> *Concentrated power* is characterized by organizations with restricted access to key decision processes and information sources. The routing information, the right to be involved and the opportunity to shape decisions is limited to a small group of senior executives towards the top of the organization. Power is concentrated in the hands of an elite.

> *Dispersed power* is characterized by organizations with open access to key decision processes and information sources. The routing of information, the right to be involved and the opportunity to shape decisions is not restricted to elite groups. Power is distributed amongst a variety of groups.

This distinction is based on the extent to which influence and power is concentrated in the hands of a small centralized set of actors, or dispersed either horizontally across agencies or vertically across hierarchical levels. Iacocca, in his experiences at Chrysler, describes the latter arrangement:

> Before the day was over, I noticed a couple of seemingly insignificant details that gave me pause. The first was that the office of the president . . . was being used as a thoroughfare to get from one office to another . . . then there was the fact that Riccardo's secretary seemed to be

spending a lot of time taking personal calls on her own private phone!
(1984, p. 52)

After a couple of weeks on the job Iacocca had come to his diagnosis
of the power structure of Chrysler and its problematic state:

> I soon stumbled upon my first major revelation: Chrysler didn't really
> function like a company at all. Chrysler in 1978 was like Italy in the
> 1860s – the company consisted of a cluster of little duchies, each one
> run by a prima donna. It was a bunch of mini-empires, with nobody
> giving a damn about what anyone else was doing. What I found at
> Chrysler were thirty-five vice-presidents, each with his own turf. (p. 152)

While this is not written in the language of the academic student of
power structures, it paints a graphic picture of an organization with a
dispersed power structure acting to maintain the organizational *status
quo*. What this situation had produced was a track of unresolved
excursion with competitive commitments to alternative interpretive
schemes, particularly between emphasizing engineering or marketing
as the principle domain, design and performance features of the
company.

The 'historic' concern of organizational theorists with
bureaucrat–professional conflict is similarly based on the impact of a
dispersed power system on the maintenance of competing interpretive
schemes (cf. Hall, 1977). Hinings et al. (1987) and Blau (1984) show
in professional accounting firms and architectural practices, respectively,
how the partnership form of ownership makes strategic change difficult.
As Hinings et al. (1987) put it in describing an attempt to change the
design archetype,

> . . . implementation was difficult because of the individualized, auto-
> nomous nature of authority. The question of responsibility for
> partner–client relations was difficult to tackle because of its sacrosanct
> status in the culture of the profession. Without the enthusiastic
> commitment of the powerholders, namely the partners, a diffuse body
> of 23 people in this particular office, implementation was bound to be
> difficult. (p. 25)

The power structure is important especially where there is a
competitive commitment to alternative interpretive schemes. The
interpretive scheme reflected in the organization will be consistent with
the ideas and beliefs of the elite where there is a concentrated power

structure. In such an organization the power structure acts as an instrument of the elite facilitating maintenance of the *status quo* despite opposition. We might also anticipate that a concentrated power structure would enable the elite at least to begin the process of reorientation. A dispersed power structure, however, would not lend itself to an imposed choice. Archetype reorientation would be unlikely to occur unless there was a widespread commitment to an alternative interpretive scheme (i.e. the reformative commitment).

In other words, the two power structures described here do not have opposite consequences. It is not the case that a concentrated power structure facilitates change whereas a dispersed power structure is obstructive. A concentrated power structure can facilitate imposed change *or* obstruct change; which it will be is dependent upon the commitment of the elite to particular interpretive schemes.

A dispersed power structure, however, can obstruct change but cannot facilitate change in a situation of competitive commitments. Under a reformative commitment, by contrast, a dispersed power structure or a concentrated power structure will facilitate change. In short, the role of the power dependences depends upon the pattern of commitment within the organization.

Organizational Capacity

The ability to achieve transformational change will be influenced by the capabilities and competences of an organization in two distinct and related ways. Put simply, in order to change from one archetype to another, an organization has to have sufficient skills for the generation of commitment and excitement over the prospect of change and have an understanding of what it wishes to do (i.e. the nature of the changes to be obtained). These two ideas can be discussed in terms of

(a) the extent of *transformational* rather than *transactional* leadership,
(b) the extent of expertise in the design of an alternative archetype or what might be termed *a capability in the architecture of archetype design*.

Capability in Transformational Leadership

One of the more interesting developments in organizational analysis over the past few years has been the 'rediscovery' of leadership as a phenomenon of relevance to structural theories of organizations. It is a rediscovery in the sense that some of the early writers on organizations defined the essential role of management as leadership (cf. Barnard, 1938; Selznick, 1957). Writers who have suggested that leadership requires a place in analysing change and culture are Kanter (1983), Peters and Waterman (1982), Romanelli and Tushman (1983), Tichy (1983), Tichy and Ulrich (1984), Pettigrew (1985; 1988), Tushman and Romanelli (1985) and Schein (1986). While the specific details of their positions differ, they have similar overall thrusts which are important to our approach as follows.

1   Senior managers in organizations are defined institutionally as leaders by virtue of their responsibility for an organization and its direction.
2   Leadership is a matter of defining overall values, strategic directions and internal organization and mobilizing commitment to those directions.
3   Leadership is crucial in organizational transformations because they involve restating values, directions and organizational forms.

The concept of a design archetype gives a strong role to values and their relationship to elements of organizational form. Institutional leaders play a key role in developing, maintaining and altering the interpretive scheme of an organization. It is, in fact, in this context of strategic change that the rediscovered notions of leadership have been most developed. Tichy and Ulrich (1984), for example, emphasize the role of leadership in revitalizing organizations. They draw on the work of Burns (1978), distinguishing between transactional and transformational leaders. The transactional leader manages exchanges within a basically stable and knowable framework – in our terms, the kinds of leadership which would support an inertial track and possibly an aborted or unresolved excursion. This is in sharp contrast with the transformational leader who is required to move an organization from one design archetype to another. The transformational leader is 'one who commits people to action, who converts followers into leaders, and who may convert leaders into moral agents' (Tichy and Ulrich, 1984, pp. 240–1). Such leaders are required for a reorientation.

Thus different tracks require different leaders. And perhaps more importantly, in the light of what has been outlined in chapter 2, changing an organization from one design archetype to another requires a special kind of leadership. However, it is important not to adopt too romanticized or heroic a notion of leadership. One of the strengths of an institutional approach is the way in which it starts from a positional concept. Meindl et al. (1985) and Meindl and Ehrlich (1987) have shown how leadership is given a strong value as a causal attribution by organizational members, essentially because 'it reduces and translates (organizational) complexities into simple human terms that they can understand, live with, and communicate easily to others' (Meindl and Ehrlich, 1987, p. 92). It is this which they label a romanticized conception of leadership because it is underpinned by a faith in the centrality of leadership in explaining the functioning of organizations.

This caution has been echoed by Pettigrew (1988) who suggests that leadership is an important ingredient in understanding major transformations, 'but only one of the ingredients in a complex analytical, political, and cultural process of challenging and changing the core beliefs, structure, and strategy of the firm'. For Pettigrew, and Romanelli and Tushman (1983), leadership is both context and time sensitive and has to be seen as part of a more general theory of organizational evolution. While executive leaders (to use the phrase of Romanelli and Tushman) have a *symbolic role* as emphasized by Pfeffer (1982) and Schein (1986), providing explanations, rationalizations and legitimization, they also have a *substantive role*. They have to engage in decisional activities which involve concrete outcomes of structure, workflow, careers, products, markets, acquisitions etc.

Peters and Waterman (1982), Kanter (1983; 1984), Tichy and Ulrich (1984) and Schein (1986) put particular emphasis on the exchange of values, culture and the symbolic functions of senior management. This is because they are dealing with the issue of moving an organization from one design archetype to another, a reorientation track. However, underlying this view is a very prescriptive view of leadership functions. As Tichy and Ulrich (1984) rightly point out, transactional leaders are engaged in exchange but such a person ' "*merely*" exchanges such things as jobs, money and security for compliance' (p. 241, our italics). This is a deliberate downplaying of the functions of leadership in an organizational situation where stability is the prime condition and the organization is on an inertial track.

These distinctions are clearly important to our formulations but we are interested not in making a prescriptive distinction between transformational and transactional leaders but in making a descriptive and analytical one. Schein (1986), while primarily focusing on the links between culture and leadership in situations of organizational change, discusses the different relationships between these two at different stages of an organization's life. As he puts it, 'Leaders create culture, but cultures, in turn, create their next generation of leaders' (p. 313). In the early founding stages of an organization it is the leader, the owner/entrepreneur, who is significantly involved in creating the culture of his/her organization. However, once an organization has a history (of what duration is not empirically clear, although Schein suggests 'substantial'), culture becomes more cause than effect which leads to the issue for a mature organization of 'breaking' an existing culture.

Again, this analysis suggests that the maintenance of a particular design archetype requires a transactional approach, whereas movement away requires transformation. This approach is also echoed by Kimberly (1987) and Kimberly and Rottman (1988) in their notion of organizational biographies. Kimberly suggests that, when an organization is founded, the leaders make decisions, perhaps unthinkingly, about the domain to be served, the nature of organizational governance, the kinds of people required and the form of organization to be adopted. This is the act of leadership, creating a design archetype. Once decided, however, the organization acquires momentum and those initial decisions 'capture' the organization as they are institutionalized into a series of normative propositions about the 'correct' way of doing things. As such they produce a particular leadership which will be oriented towards an inertial track.

From our point of view the important feature of these discussions is that all senior managers are exchanging cultural values, interpretations and meanings whether it be in a knowing transformational way through mission statements, visioning etc, or in an unknowing transactional way through rewards, job descriptions, routine decision making etc. The exercise of leadership to maintain or transform a design archetype is not just a matter of disseminating meanings in a symbolic sense. Kanter (1984) makes the point that

> . . . values do not exist independently of rewards; preferences do not exist independently of political signals from power holders; expectations about activities do not exist independently of action vehicles or programs permitting the activities. (p. 196)

To summarize, senior managers are put into positions where they are responsible for the formation, evolution, transformation and destruction of provinces of meaning; they become leaders in so far as they recognize this responsibility and exercise it in a conscious way. As Schein (1986) states,

. . . [a] leader needs insight into organizational culture and its role as aider or hinderer, and intervention skills for change. (p. 320)

But, in carrying out that symbolic leadership function, an executive is involved in introducing and implementing substantive decisions which shape the direction and form of an organization.

Capability in Archetype Design

Important components of the exercise of leadership are *knowledge* and *skills*. Schein (1986) recognizes this point when he states that a leader requires insight into organizational culture and also intervention skills for changing that culture. However, this statement is a limited one in two ways. First, it focuses only on knowledge and skill concerning culture. Second, it fails to recognize the collective nature of leadership in organizations, a collectivity which represents an important organizational capacity.

To maintain, alter or transform an organization those in positions of leadership require knowledge and skills other than cultural, such as those suggested by Romanelli and Tushman (1983); that is, they must have knowledge concerning the organizational structures, systems and processes that they are introducing or maintaining. Moving an organization from one design type to another requires not only the mobilization of commitment to symbols but also the mobilization of expertise on the technical details of the new system and on the processes of change. Child and Smith (1987) in their analysis of transformation at Cadbury's examine 'the market for the transfer of design concepts and technical knowledge required to effect the transformation of a firm's products, processes or organizational mode' (p. 19).

Lee Iacocca in reorganizing Chrysler recognized the need for symbolic actions and the importance of interpretive schemes. However, he was also able to see the importance of engineering and manufacturing working together and saw it as a major problem that they were not talking to each other (Iacocca, 1984, pp. 152–3). Not only could he recognize the problem but he was able to visualize solutions himself and, perhaps more importantly, mobilize the necessary organizational systems to produce solutions.

Similarly, H.M. (Pete) Love, the chairman and president of the NSC, not only saw himself as changing the culture of the organization and developing new strategic directions but as designing a new organization and mobilizing new kinds of expertise (Barrett and Cammann, 1984). 'As a result, Love *with the advice and consultation of several of his key managers*, created an entirely new structure for the company' (Barrett and Cammann, 1984, p. 229, our italics). Love required a knowledge of organizational and system possibilities but more importantly he required skills in bringing together the expertise of others to form a collective leadership.

Leadership has to be related to power, structure and the mobilization of groups into coalitions. Leadership in most organizations, and in particular in larger organizations, is not a matter of individual action. Child (1972) in his seminal article on strategic choice wrote of 'dominant coalitions' making decisions about the structure of an organization. He suggests

> . . . when incorporating strategic choice in a theory of organization, one is recognizing the operation of an essentially political process in which constraints and opportunities are functions of the power exercised by decision-makers in the light of ideological values.

While the language is somewhat different from that used by contemporary writers on leadership, the thrust is similar and its importance lies in bringing a directly political and power focus to the discussion. Dominant coalitions are structures of leadership; they identify a group of people, usually managers, who are making choices and directing an organization. To translate values into the actions of others, not only do leaders have to obtain this political commitment to the values *per se* but also they have to ensure that necessary knowledge and expertise is present and/or developed. Coalitions have to be more than value based.

Kanter (1983; 1984) makes somewhat similar points from her work with Honeywell, Defence Systems Division (DSD), when she uses the term 'prime movers'. For her an important potential problem when dealing with an organizational reorientation is the abdication of managerial responsibility. Prime movers are senior people who take responsibility for the change, build the coalitions and mechanisms necessary for successful outcomes and demonstrate the power commitment of the organization to the particular change process. In doing this an organization ensures that there is an understanding of what is needed to effect the change. In Honeywell, DSD, 'the vehicle for doing this was a top-management steering committee, composed of representatives of all major functions and facilities, chaired personally by the general manager' (Kanter, 1984, p. 204).

Child and Smith (1987) show the importance of knowledge and skills in eventually achieving a reorientation at Cadbury's. When, by the late 1970s, the 'Mars model' was adopted for Cadbury's new production rationalization philosophy learning was required 'to shift from one sector template to another' (p. 19). One way was to recruit staff directly from the competition ('the men from Mars'). 'Another was to rely on a transfer of advanced production technology through the medium of equipment suppliers. . .who had developed and tested new equipment in other chocolate making firms' (p. 19). In addition, during the 1950s and 1960s Cadbury's had recruited graduates who had followed professional careers within the firm. As they moved into senior positions, so they were able to articulate different and new strategic visions for the company and exercise their power to have them implemented. Apart from the symbolic effects of these visions, the actual basic technical knowledge of engineering and marketing was necessary.

In addition, having experienced previous major change was important. 'The prior experience of the major agents of Cadbury's transformation in managing previous new projects and/or major changes appeared to give them a determination to stick by their visions and lent a sense of urgency for their implementation once this threshold had been achieved' (Child and Smith, 1987, p. 36). Knowledge and skill were present which made leadership commitment easier. They were able to avoid Kanter's problem of abdication of managerial responsibility, a key component of institutional leadership.

In order to reorient, or to remain on an inertial track, an organization has to have the necessary knowledge and skills about organizational solutions to issues and problems. This involves leaders ensuring that there is sufficient knowledge in the dominant coalition about the desired end point that it is trying to reach and something about the skills required to get there. Of course such resources may already be in place because of the historical experience of an organization. However, it is in the nature of a transformation that new ideas requiring

Table 3.4   Organizational capability and tracks

Track		Leadership	Knowledge
A	Inertia/retention	Transactional	High
B	Aborted excursion	Transactional	Low
C	Reorientation	Transformational	High
D	Unresolved excursion	Transactional	Low

new structures, systems and processes are being introduced. Leadership of a purely visioning and cultural kind is not enough. There have to be members of the organization who understand and can design and operate those new structures and systems. Thus, in a transformation it is necessary for the collective leadership to have a real understanding of the substantive aspects of organizational design and, more particularly, to ensure that there is the necessary expertise in the organization.

Organizational Capability and Tracks

Taken together, the nature of leadership and the existence of particular and specific knowledge and skills form what we have called the capability of an organization to achieve a transformation successfully. This suggests that different kinds of capability are appropriate to different tracks. Table 3.4 summarizes the potential relationship between the two aspects of capability and tracks.

Once again, then, we emphasize leadership in an organizational setting as an institutionally derived position and an organization as having a leadership *structure*. Leadership is *organized* as well as *exercised* and it is organized and exercised in different ways in different tracks. As such, the specific styles and activities of leaders are important in understanding why organizations follow particular tracks. But all the leadership in the world will not overcome an absence of knowledge and expertise. Taken together we can begin to characterize the capability of senior management to undertake a reorientation.

Summary

The theory presented in this chapter is that of constrained choice through the interpenetration of situational context, interpretive

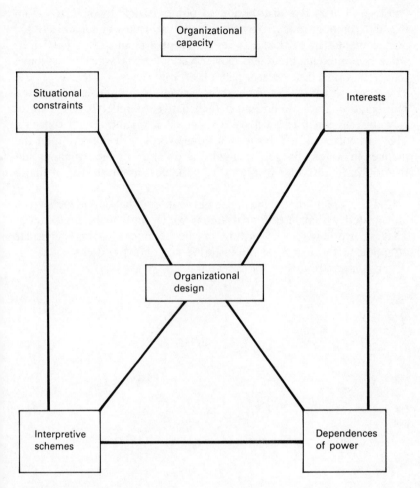

Figure 3.1 The dynamics change

schemes, interests, dependences of power and organizational capacity. The framework conceives of organizational archetypes being held in place or destabilized by one or more of the five dynamics of context, interpretive schemes, interests, power and capacity. But it is the *interplay* between these that will determine the particular track followed by an organization. Contingencies do not operate independently upon structural arrangements but are interpreted through filters of meanings and aspirations. The distribution of power is not disconnected from the environment nor from interpretive schemes or organizational arrangements. In particular, where there is a competititve pattern of value commitments the role of power will determine which interpretive scheme is utilized to order structural arrangements. Furthermore, the extent to which a destabilized organization progresses along the reorientation track or becomes stuck between archetypes (the unresolved excursion track) will be a function of organizational capacity. The particular tracks followed, in other words, will depend upon the manner in which changes occur in one or more of the dynamics and the triggered response in the other variables, as illustrated in figure 3.1.

Chapter 4 picks up the idea raised in chapter 1 that design archetypes are located within institutional arenas which have to be understood. That is, we discuss the setting of the research, paying particular attention to the nature of the institutional context and characteristics of the temporal basis of the research.

4 Institutions, History and Starting Points

Introduction

Chapters 1–3 have elaborated the nature of macro-organizational change and stability through the concepts of design archetypes, the interacting dynamics of interpretive schemes, interests, power and contextual pressures and the structures of institutional leadership. The theory presented in those chapters is that of constrained choice through the interpenetration of context, interpretive schemes, interests, power and organizational design archetypes bound together by the strategic actions of senior managers. The framework conceives of organizational archetypes being held in place or destabilized by a combination of the precipitating and enabling dynamics of change (Lundberg, 1984), with the interplay between these determining the particular track followed by an organization. Contingencies do not operate independently upon structural arrangements but are interpreted through filters of meanings and aspirations given form and action through structures of power, leadership and knowledge. The distribution of power is not disconnected from the environment nor from interpretive schemes or organizational arrangements. The particular tracks followed will depend upon the manner in which changes occur in one or more of the dynamics and the triggered response in the other variables.

While these concepts have been elaborated by reference to current theoretical developments and case study material has been widely used to illustrate their utility, more systematic development and testing is required. This is the purpose of chapters 4–10. Drawing on a ten year study of a reorganization of British local government between 1972 and 1982, the theory is elaborated and the nature of tracks and the dynamics of change and stability demonstrated across a sample of organizations. More details of the study and its empirical details and procedures can be found in chapter 5.

This chapter will begin the process of systematically examining our theories of macro-organizational change by establishing the existence of design archetypes in a particular setting in a particular place at a particular time.

The first task is to establish the existence of design archetypes and describe their overall form, i.e. the particular connection between interpretive schemes and structural forms. As we pointed out in chapter 1, organization theory has long been concerned with the search for generic types. However, our concept of design archetype argues that coherence comes from the relationships between ideas, values and beliefs *and* structure *and* systems. Not only this, but our approach through interpretive schemes gives an initial primacy to values and their implications for organizational form. This means that not all possible organizational elements are equal. Thus, organizations cannot necessarily be typed according to a set of scores on, for example, specialization, standardization, formalization and centralization. It is *what* is specialized, standardized etc., and *how* that relates to the value premises of the archetype.

As a result of this, we have a general hypothesis that different design archetypes will exist both within and between institutional spheres. The initial task is to isolate and describe what design archetypes exist in the particular setting under study.

The Organizational Situation

The concepts and theoretical dynamics outlined have to be located within a concrete setting. Of particular importance in understanding tracks and their dynamics is establishing the existence of design archetypes and the starting point of organizations in relation to them. We argue that there are ranges of normative prescription, the narrowness of the range differing from organizational sphere to organizational sphere. At different times, different organizational sectors are more subject to both general and particular institutionalization than others. Chandler (1962) shows how at particular historical times manufacturing industry in the USA was subject to pressures, initially contextual but increasingly institutional, to move to specific organizational forms.

Other examples of what might be thought of as 'waves' of institutionalization can be found in three quite different organizational sectors. The debate and discussion over the past decade about the M form in manufacturing industry (cf. Ouchi, 1981) demonstrates the development of new organizational domains, forms and performance criteria in relation to contextual circumstances of changing markets and technologies, followed by the adoption of that form by a wide range of other organizations because of its perceived success and subsequent legitimacy. Tolbert and Zucker (1984) in their study of state and local government in the USA similarly demonstrate that the adoption of 'reform' structures and criteria initially develops in relation to specific environmental pressures. Once adopted by a few cities and states there is a dramatic 'take-off' as other governmental jurisdictions adopt the new form on the basis of its legitimacy.

A further example comes from amateur sport in Canada (Hinings and Slack, 1987; Slack and Hinings, 1987). In 1983 the Federal Government, through its sports directorate, Sport Canada, introduced a planning process to cover 36 Olympic national sport organizations. Each of these organizations had to produce a plan to ensure a 'best ever' performance in the 1988 Summer and Winter Olympic Games. This plan involved moving the domain of these organizations increasingly towards high performance elite sport, it involved the development of new organizational forms emphasizing the role of full-time professional staff rather than volunteers, and it involved evaluating performance on the basis of outcomes in one major event. Some organizations had already adopted these approaches prior to the Sport Canada initiative but many had not formally dealt with these kinds of issues even if they had been generally drifting in that direction. The planning cycle institutionalized and legitimated specific notions of domain, form and performance for all 36 organizations.

We can take this kind of argument a stage further and examine it more systematically in the context of attempting to change the domain, form and criteria of performance in local authority organizations in England and Wales. Again, there is an initial evolutionary process as new ideas and ways of organizing are developed in individual organizations in relation to new problems. This evolutionary process is then followed by a more rapid rate of adoption which was given a legitimating push by governmental institutions. Our initial aim is to outline the design archetypes present in local government at the beginning of the 1970s.

Design Archetypes in Local Authorities[1]

Services which are, or have been, the responsibility of local authority organizations in Britain include engineering, housing, pollution control, land use planning, transit services, education (including higher education), industrial development, recreation, social welfare, sanitation and water, public health, tourism development, libraries, museums and art galleries, street lighting, emergency planning, highways, country parks, airports, racetracks, probation services, police, fire, ambulances, hospitals, dog licences, auto licences, shops and offices inspection etc. The list could be extended.

What this list serves to show is the diversified nature of local authority responsibilities and the conglomerate form of the institution of local government. The range of responsibility does not show an overall integrating task logic. Indeed, more apparent is the centrality of a political logic in that services are allocated to local authorities based on the judgements of those *not* directly in the system (Foster et al., 1980). Institutionally a local authority becomes defined as an organization providing a loosely connected or unconnected set of services to a given geographical area.

As a result, the domain of a local authority consists of a diverse array of services and activities provided for an equally diverse array of clienteles within the local community. It is a domain that cannot be easily altered or escaped in that the tasks and responsibilities are substantially dictated by a higher level of government and legislation. However, this is not to say that the exact nature of the domain is not subject to debate, nor does it deny disputes over how tasks and responsibilities should be organized. Indeed the research reported here was monitoring a major attempt both to redefine the nature of a local authority's legitimate domain and to introduce a model of organization consistent with that redefinition.

By the early 1970s there were two design archetypes available to local authorities in England and Wales, each with its own definition of appropriate domain, form and criteria of performance. These were the *heteronomous professional bureaucracy* (Scott, 1965) and the *corporate bureaucracy* (Greenwood and Stewart, 1971).[2]

The Heteronomous Professional Bureaucracy Essentially the traditional definition of a local authority's domain considers the organization to be an agency with a set of responsibilities each of which may be planned for, and provided, with little reference to the other services. As a result they require minimum coordination. The common organizational framework provides the opportunity for economies of scale of an administrative kind, but for any other purpose the services are planned and provided as separate. The definition of a local authority's domain is strongly associated with the organizational form of an heteronomous professional bureaucracy.

Reviewing the attempts to reform and reorganize British local government, Dearlove (1979) uses the interrelated phrases 'old orthodoxies' and 'traditional administration', phrases which capture an accepted legitimate view of the institutionally prescribed organization of British local authorities. Given a set of ideas which emphasize the individuality and autonomy of services, it follows that the basic organizational pattern should be one of high differentiation of departments. Each service is organized as a separate organizational unit. It is seen as desirable to separate services, organizationally, and to staff each differentiated unit with appropriate professionals. There is no concept of general management; only fully fledged professionals can rise to the top and there is a career progression tied to professional qualification. The combination of departmental and professional boundaries produces high differentiation (Lawrence and Lorsch, 1967).

This administrative task structure is paralleled at the political level in a system of committees through which elected representatives are intended to control policy formulation, exercise resource allocation and initiate the monitoring of performance. As Alexander (1982) put it, 'the internal organization of local authorities has always entailed the maintenance of parallel structures, loosely identified as the member side and the officer side'.

The heteronomous professional base is further underscored by the absence of any officer, administrator or manager with clear responsibility for the total organization. Responsibility for overall coordination rests with the majority political party, supported by various functional officers such as the treasurer or legal services officer (the clerk). The coordination that does occur is through central allocation of the resources of money and personnel rather than through the central or joint direction of policy.

This low level of structural integration means that policy development and review occurs within individual departments in which professional judgement is the instinctive and preferred method of analysis and choice. There is likely to be an incremental budgetary system which allows allocations across services through negotiation and opportunism (Wildavsky, 1975; Greenwood, 1984). There is no extra-professional analysis of base budgets.

The heteronomous professional bureaucracy is based on two important beliefs central to the overall interpretive scheme. The first belief is that local authorities administer a set of services that have little or no connection with one another. As a result, little value is placed on searching for connections between issues and using joint decision making. Rather, emphasis is placed on establishing the boundaries between issues so that responsibilities can be clearly allocated to the relevant committee and department. This is Mintzberg's (1979) idea of the pigeon-holing process necessary to a professional bureaucracy which functions to enable the application of the professional's standard programmes.

The second belief underpinning the legitimacy of this particular design archetype is that demonstrated professional competence is crucial to operation and performance. As new problems emerge, existing professional groups embrace them or new professions arise and in turn become institutionalized into the organizational structure. The professional basis of local government organization has been so powerful and institutionally entrenched that new groups could only establish their claims to resources, and gain access to power, by establishing their professional status and having it enshrined in an organization through a separate department with an attendant career hierarchy. Perhaps the major example of this process over the past two or three decades has been the emergence of social services departments and the development of the social work profession.

It is a strong part of such a design archetype that the basic criteria of performance are laid down by professionals and that standards arrived at professionally become the accepted way of evaluating activities.

Until the late 1960s the heteronomous professional bureaucracy dominated local government thinking. A comprehensive national survey conducted in 1965 concluded

> One of our criticisms of the present internal organization of local authorities is that it is bound too much by a present pattern. . .(para. 132). Stress is laid on the absence of unity in the internal organization of a local authority which is the result of close association of a particular service, the service committee, the department concerned and the hierarchy of professional officers. The separateness of the committees

contributes to the separateness of the department, and the professionalism of departmental staff feeds on its separateness (para. 224). (Committee on Management of Local Government, 1967)

The Corporate Bureaucracy Alford (1975) suggests that within any organizational system there will be challenging or repressed interests in addition to those that are currently dominant. In the health service in the USA, the administrators represented the challenging interest to the dominant medical view. Alternatives to the institutionalized design archetype will be available if circumstances allow them to be put forward. In her discussion of civil service reform, Zucker (1984) suggests that new organizational practices are likely to be introduced as a reaction to new needs. Putting these two views together, there have to be both pressures for organizational innovation arising from considerations of task performance, and the existence of alternative schemes for organizing.

Greenwood (1984) states that the idea of corporate planning as an alternative organizational design archetype emerged in the late 1960s as a response to a task concern with the deteriorating social and urban infrastructure and the interrelated nature of the problems facing an urban local authority. Government-sponsored studies such as the Sunderland Report (Department of the Environment, 1973) emphasized the need for new approaches to issues of urban deprivation.

Complementary to this there arose ideas stressing the role of local authorities in 'community governance'. As Greenwood (1984) puts it,

> In place of administering services a local authority should assume responsibility for the well-being of the local community, examining the impacts not only of the local authority's services, but those of other tiers of government (Stewart, 1971). Services should be planned as interdependent means of addressing community problems and opportunities. Redefinition of the local authority's domain (toward the community as a whole rather than service recipients) and its guiding strategy (*community governance rather than service administration*) held implications for modes of organizing and budgeting. (p. 292)

Hedberg (1981) and Miller and Friesen (1980) both suggest that some form of performance failure is necessary to institute organizational change of a design archetype kind. Because of the forces of inertia and momentum a crisis in the affairs of an organization has to be perceived to produce major strategic change. In the case of the organizations under consideration here, the initial crisis was that of urban problems, in particular the physical, social and economic decline of inner cities.

Those organizations which faced severe problems of urban deprivation, such as Coventry, Bradford, Hull, Sunderland, Oldham and a variety of London boroughs, began to recognize that they were operating with a form of organization (the heteronomous professional bureaucracy) in which it was difficult to deal with complex problems cutting across professional boundaries. If an environmental problem is defined as 'urban deprivation', it is not immediately clear to which professional department it should be assigned. Indeed, the process of redefining the role of the local authority in terms of dealing with one task, urban deprivation, made the existing organization problematic. Such a redefinition was at odds with the notion of a structure and systems which presumed little need for integration between departments over service development, service implementation, policy analysis and review or resource allocation. Organizations based on a high level of professionally located differentiation and a low level of task integration were seen as inappropriate.

Not only was the structure deemed inappropriate; underlying processes were critically appraised, especially their reliance on professional judgement. What was needed (in terms of the emerging design archetype) was the application of universal criteria within a framework of explicit analysis of local authority wide goals, political preferences and policy effects. Policy options would be analysed in terms of goals and domains wider than professional priorities and budget allocations would be reviewed in terms of performance attained (Greenwood, 1984). This approach suggests analysis and decision making based on interprofessional operation with the possibility of clearer controls of professional activity.

Because of the problems of agreeing on problem definition and solution, those interests challenging the dominant heteronomous professional bureaucracy archetype required external validation for the acceptance and diffusion of a new corporate design archetype. This came in a series of central government appointed committees (the Maud Committee (1967), the Bains Working Group (1972) and the Wheatley Committee (1973)) and a Royal Commission (1969) (Redcliffe–Maud). Two consistent themes came through all these reports: first, the requirement for larger organizations to achieve economies of scale and allow the recruitment of more expert staff and politicians because of the greater challenges and rewards; second, the need for local government organizations to break from the professional mode of operation in favour of an integrated structure which operated on the basis of a more managerially rational analysis of objectives, activities, outcomes and performance. All these bodies recommended organizational structures which were clear departures from the dominant design archetype.

One result of these pressures was a reorganization of the local government system in England and Wales that took effect on 1 April 1974, and in Scotland on 1 April 1975. Each of these reorganizations reflected the themes identified. Existing organizations were combined to produce larger local authorities (in England and Wales a reduction from almost 1500 organizations to 422). The report of the Bains Working Group and that of the Wheatley Committee, which were circulated to all politicians and senior managers, extolled the virtues of corporate working and produced organization charts depicting corporate organization structures. The corporate organizational design archetype was legitimated; what remained was its implementation.[3]

The corporate organization design archetype conceives the role of local authorities as encompassing 'community governance' and a concern with effective problem solution. Local services could be treated as strands of a strategy for managing and influencing the nature of the local authority's community. The role of the authority was not administrative, implementing legally prescribed services, but governmental, combining packages of services and intervention in strategic fashion.

This alternative conception of purpose and domain (governance rather than local administration) was connected to significantly different ideas about how the local authority should evaluate its effectiveness in discharging its role. The corporate model emphasized the value of analytical appraisal and rigorous assessment of programmatic (i.e. interservice) performance. Clear statements of purpose would be made, targets established and performance monitored. Attention would focus upon the interactive effects of services upon client groups. Appraisal of performance would be the responsibility of senior management. This contrasted sharply with the professional bureaucracy model with its heavy regard for the values of professional autonomy and judgement as critical. The driving criterion of performance in the latter model was professional competence within each service area and good performance meant good professional practice as defined by professionals. In the corporate model, moreover, the structure of accountability transcended professional jurisdictions and imposed analytical rigour and clarity of performance targets. In the heteronomous professional bureaucracy, in contrast, accountability was within professional jurisdiction and professional judgement as to good practice was the permitted mode of evaluation.

Structurally, as already noted, the professional bureaucracy exhibited high differentiation and low integration, combined with high specialization. Services were organized as separate units which became highly specialized as professional competences were developed. Recruitment and career development systems emphasized the importance of professional qualification, which meant that all department and unit heads would be professionals rather than general managers: 'administrators' would be of low status and position. Compensation and appraisal systems focused upon performance of professional activities and, perhaps most important of all, the resource allocation mechanisms (and the underpinning information system) were arranged in terms of Wildavsky's (1975) incremental model of budgeting – a model suited to the values of the professional bureaucracy (Greenwood, 1984).

The corporate bureaucracy had a rather different organizational framework. It emphasized the use of integrative devices, such as a chief executive officer, management team, programme directors and central analytic capabilities superimposed across service departments. Recruitment at the very highest levels would emphasize general management competence combined with professional experience. Incentive systems would reward corporate rather than professional contributions. Career structures would facilitate movements across professional boundaries, e.g. by secondment to central agencies or through membership of interdisciplinary project teams. Resource allocation mechanisms would encompass rigorous programmatic – as well as professional – review. Allocations reflected corporate goals and subordinated professional to managerial judgement (Skelcher, 1980).

The principal aim of the discussion thus far has been to establish the existence of design archetypes in a particular setting. The two alternative possibilities of the heteronomous professional bureaucracy and the corporate organization have been outlined. These two sets of ideas and values, with their structural implications, represent the dominant 'gestalts/archetypes' relevant to the organizations under examination. In this sense, the archetypes are constructs, uncovered

Table 4.1 Contrasts between two archetypes relevant to the institutional arena of the study

	Archetype 1 Corporate bureaucracy	Archetype 2 Professional bureaucracy
I Interpretive scheme		
A Domain	Community governance	Local administration
B Principles of organizing	Based on integrative devices of corporate form	Based on professional differentiation
C Evaluation criteria	Analytical appraisal by transjurisdictional management	Professional practice defined by intrajurisdictional professionals
II Organization design		
A Structure of roles and responsibilities	Modest differentiation: high integration	High differentiation: low integration
B Decision systems	Non-incremental resource allocation system	Incremental resource allocation system
	Centralized bureaucratic control system reporting to chief executive	Decentralized clan control system
C Human resource systems	Recruitment and promotion based on professional and managerial competence	Recruitment and promotion based on professional competence

by the researcher, towards which particular organizations may approximate. They are summarized in table 4.1.

It has been suggested that there were strong pressures on this set of organizations to move from one archetype, the heteronomous professional bureaucracy, to the other. Indeed, these organizations have been subject to pressures for functional and managerial change for the past two decades. During the 1960s and the early 1970s the domain and organization of local authorities were in flux. At the same time, the corporate planning model of organization (how to cope with the domain) was being viewed as an increasingly legitimate way of running the affairs of a local authority organization.

On 1 April 1974, 422 new local authority organizations were created, arising from the demise of almost 1500 predecessors. Many of the new authorities were large in scale, the majority serving populations of more than 100,000 and a substantial number serving over 250,000 people. The largest local authorities, with responsibility for education, employed up to 50,000 people. More importantly, from the point of view of the theoretical thrust of this book, a report was prepared (Bains Working Group, 1972), which outlined and recommended to all local authorities the organizational structure for corporate management. This report was sent to all elected politicians and all senior managers in the new organizations and was intended to assist them in designing management structures and systems. The report became the handbook of organizational change, challenging the professional archetype, and achieved widespread legitimacy (for details on the Bains Report and its impact on local government reorganization see Greenwood et al., 1980a, and Alexander, 1982).

The organizations upon which we report in subsequent chapters, therefore, have to be understood in the light of two points. The first is that during the 1960s they had been, and during the 1970s and into the 1980s were to continue to be, subject to large schemes of organizational change. The system was one in flux. Major change was defined as institutionally legitimate and was widely accepted as necessary. The second point is that the corporate organization archetype had begun, by the early 1970s, to supplant the heteronomous professional bureaucracy as the legitimate method of organizing.

The Fiscal Setting

The previous section pointed out the prevailing sets of ideas concerning organizational archetypes that exist within the institutional context during the period of study. A second important feature of that context was the nature of the fiscal environment. At the outset of the research we had little intention of paying especial attention to the fiscal context. The organizations to be studied had not experienced serious problems of revenue generation for almost three decades. Spending and revenues had grown, annually, almost as a fact of life. Stewart (1980) documented the rise in employment in local government over the period, showing that in 1952 there were 1.45 million local authority employees, representing 6.2 per cent of the working population, rising to 1.82 million (7.3 per cent) in 1962, 2.56 million (10.4 per cent) by 1972 and 2.9 million (11.3 per cent) in 1975.

It became apparent early in the research that the fiscal context was becoming a crucial element within the institutional context (Greenwood et al., 1980b; Greenwood, 1984). Restraint, urged and promoted by the central government, came as a shock to a system of local government which was organizationally and conceptually geared for growth. Underlying the organizational arrangements of local government authorities was the assumption of growth. Yet, within two years of the 1974 reorganization, annual cutbacks in government grants were introduced and sustained into the 1980s. Furthermore, the procedures for distributing grants to local authorities were altered to tie them into specific and different spending targets established by the central government for each local authority. Such changes produced major pressures on almost every organization, pressures that demanded an organizational response (Hinings et al., 1980).

The importance of fiscal pressure has been noted elsewhere. Hedberg (1981), for example, has pointed out that organizations learn from the emergence of performance failure:

> Organizational unlearning is typically problems triggered. Funds shortages, falling revenues, actual losses, diminishing popular support, or public criticism from evaluation are some examples. These triggers cause hesitancy and build up distrust in procedures and leaders. Ultimately the world view and the standard operating procedures break down. The organization has unlearned its yesterday and finds itself either paralyzed or busily relearning. (p. 18)

The same point has been made by Miles and Randolph (1980) in their study of business firms: 'the stress produced by negative performance feedback is an important condition for organizational learning'.

Miller and Friesen (1980; 1984) take the notion of performance impairment a step further. To them, organizations become locked into a way of doing things: a 'momentum' is established which is difficult to deflect until performance is very seriously damaged. Initial negative information is ignored or reinterpreted by the 'self-sealing' train of thought which serves to justify continuation of existing patterns (Mitroff and Emshoff, 1979). Change will occur only when there is 'encompassing remediality', i.e. failures 'so devastating that they provide a crisis that simply cannot be explained away as a fleeting condition or as an insignificant anomaly' (Mitroff and Emshoff, 1979, p. 608). However, change is unlikely when organizations are performing well: 'Success breeds somnolence' (Hedberg et al., 1976, p. 49).

Translating this general level of analysis to the present discussion implies that prevailing systems will be 'unlearned' if the organization is faced with serious external problems, such as dramatically falling revenues, not easily handled by existing procedures (Tung, 1979). Some evidence in favour of Hedberg's view is provided by David and Kantor (1980). Reviewing the changing political and economic circumstances of New York from 1945 until 1980, these authors note that incrementalism was characteristic of the city's budgetary process as long as the political context was stable and the resource base of the city expanding. Removal of either condition created problems which triggered alterations in the pattern of budgeting. Similar conclusions have been reached by Wildavsky (1975), who outlined the limiting conditions of relative wealth ('largesse') coupled with predictability of available resources and spending demands. Schick (1980) has also constructed a taxonomy of conditions restricting the relevance of various systems of budgeting, anticipating that incrementalism would be appropriate under conditions of 'chronic scarcity', i.e. where there are sufficient resources 'for limited program growth, but not enough for substantial program expansion' (Schick, 1980, p. 120). 'Relaxed', 'acute' or 'total' scarcity, however, would require different budgetary arrangements.

Falling revenues are one example of changes in the environment that have serious performance implications and compel organizations to question the relevance of prevailing modes of operation. Confronted with serious performance impairment the organization begins to question the ideas and values ordering the pattern of events and decision processes. The hegemony of ideas is shaken and there is a very real possibility that the structure of interests and power will be redrawn as, and if, the dominant coalition fails to control the new strategic contingency (Hickson et al., 1971).

The point being stressed is that the period of study was one of an intruding deterioration of the fiscal environment. The deterioration affected all organizations in that the pressure upon spending was applied to all organizations, although not equally, and no organization could be unaffected by the vocabulary of restraint that was imposed upon the public sector. Any understanding of how local authorities changed or did not change their organizational arrangements has to embrace, in short, the manner in which they interpreted the institutional prescriptions for the corporate archetype *and* for fiscal restraint.

Conclusions

A central point of our analysis is that an understanding of strategic organizational change has to take account of the institutional and temporal context. We have identified two very significant streams of events flowing around the organizations under investigation. One stream was ideational, in that the organizations were being urged to adopt a particular form of organization. The other stream was partly ideational, in that it represented a belief in the importance of cutting public spending, and partly fiscal, in that resources were less readily available. The pressure on resources demanded an organizational response.

Chapter 5 begins the description and analysis of how far and in what manner these organizations responded or reacted to these pressures for change and managed the competing ideas and values over appropriate organizational arrangements and the need for restraint.

Notes

1 This chapter draws heavily on Hinings and Greenwood (1988) and Greenwood and Hinings (1988).
2 The two design archetypes were 'uncovered' by the researchers through a multiplicity of approaches. A major approach was the analysis between 1967 and 1970 of key documents (e.g. national reports, reports from individual authorities, consultants' reports, etc.) combined with semi-structured interviews with 200 senior local government managers from over 40 organizations. This analysis permitted identification of two dominant interpretive schemes, with their organizational implications, which had widespread currency within this institutional context at the time.
3 The sheer force of the new ideas led one leading commentator to become apprehensive of their wholesale adoption by local authorities: 'There is, thus, a danger of new orthodoxy' (Chester, 1968, p. 296). It illustrates how the legitimating influence of central networks was known to operate.

5 The Research Design

Introduction

Chapters 1–3 established a theoretical framework for examining the nature and dynamics of strategic change. In developing the rationale and concepts of that framework case studies and more wide-ranging empirical analyses were drawn on to support the conclusions being made. Chapter 4 then introduced a particular historical and institutional setting, that of British local government from the late 1960s to the early 1980s, to illustrate the existence of design archetypes. That chapter established the presence of two design archetypes in local government by the beginning of the 1970s. The two alternative possibilities were the heteronomous professional bureaucracy and the corporate bureaucracy. It was suggested that there were strong pressures on local authority organizations in Britain to move from the one archetype, the heteronomous professional bureaucracy, to the other, the corporate organization.

These pressures for functional and managerial change had been evident for more than two decades. In the 1960s and the early 1970s the domain and organization of local authorities was in flux. The government of London was reorganized in the mid-1960s. Local government outside London was reorganized on 1 April 1974. This reorganization resulted from a variety of reports and recommendations. In 1967 the Committee on Management of Local Government reported on the need for new management structures and systems in local authorities. This was followed by the Royal Commission on Local Government, which reported in 1969, recommending a root and branch functional and geographical reorganization of the system. As a result, in 1972 a new Local Government Act was passed which restructured the system (although it was not restructured along the lines recommended by the Royal Commission).

This legislation created 422 new local authority organizations which came into existence on 1 April 1974. These 422 were the result of amalgamations among the approximately 1500 predecessor local authorities. There were four kinds of local authorities created, all of which were very large in scale when compared with most organizations.

1 *Metropolitan counties*: these were completely new to the system. There were six of them, responsible for strategic functions in the six major metropolitan areas outside London. They served populations from 1.5 million to 3 million and employed between 10,000 and 15,000 people. They were abolished in 1985.
2 *Metropolitan districts*: these were the 36 service delivery authorities within the six metropolitan counties, including most of the large cities in England. They served populations from slightly under 250,000 to just over 1 million. Because of their major functions of education, highways and transportation, housing and social services, they employed from 10,000 to 50,000 people.
3 *Shire counties*: these were the 47 historic successors to the county councils and were both strategic planning and service delivery organizations. They served populations ranging from 120,000 to 1.4 million. They supplied education, highways and transportation and social services to their populations, so their employee numbers ranged from 10,000 to 55,000.
4 *Shire districts*: these were service delivery authorities with a limited range of functions (housing, environmental health, engineering, planning) within the shire counties. They were by far the most numerous organizations, there being 333 of them, and they ranged in scale from serving a population of 35,000 to some large free-standing cities which served populations of more than 300,000. Their employee size ranged from 300 to 5000.

Of central importance from the point of view of issues of organizational transformations, a report was prepared by a committee, at the same time as the legislation, which outlined and recommended to all local authorities the organizational structure for corporate management. The report (Bains Working Group, 1972) was not given legislative status, but it was sent to all elected politicians and senior managers in the new local authorities to assist them in designing management structures and systems. The report was the handbook of organizational change and it had a major impact on local government reorganization (Greenwood et al., 1975; Alexander, 1982).

As a result, then, it became possible to design a long-term research project, examining processes of strategic change, that took advantage of a major natural field experiment. This experiment was to take 422 organizations and change them all in the same direction by introducing a common approach to management, that of the corporate bureaucracy. Yet it was known that only a small number of these organizations were already going in that direction. Clearly this was fertile and exciting ground for studying the dynamics of change.

The Research Design and Sample

The detailed empirical analysis on which the following five chapters are based comes from data collected on 24 local authorities in England and Wales over a period of ten years between 1972 and 1982. The government of London, having been reorganized earlier (in the mid-1960s), was excluded from this study. The design and sampling was based on the two features of (a) the pressure on these organizations to adopt a corporate mode of organizing, and (b) the functional and contextual differences between types of local authorities.

After the Report of the Working Group on the New Local Authorities (the Bains Report) was published in 1972, and consequent upon the passing of the Local Government Act, 1972, all the 422 local authorities that were to come into existence on 1 April 1974 set up working parties to consider their organizational arrangements. All these organizations were contacted by the researchers and asked for copies of the reports that they were producing that described the management structures they would introduce on 1 April 1974. Material that could be analysed was returned by 304 organizations, a response rate of 72%. The reports, stating what organization these local authorities would put into place when they officially came into existence, were analysed around the twin concepts of differentiation and integration using the notions of corporate management and professional bureaucracy as templates. Of course, the data that could be culled from these reports centred on issues of structure such as number and type of departments, number and type of committees, the existence of central planning and controlling units etc. Very little was said about systems and processes. However, there was material, of a value kind, stating their commitment to corporate management. Greenwood et al. (1975) give details of the actual variation for these organizations on the measures used.

In order to capture the corporate management–professional bureaucracy difference, the 304 organizations were classified as being high or low on differentiation and, similarly, high or low on integration. (Of course, there were many that were neither high nor low on either dimension.) Having done this we then selected authorities which fell into the four categories that are constructed by combining the two values, high or low, of the two concepts. That is, we have organizations that were highly differentiated and highly integrated (a potential corporate matrix), highly differentiated and lowly integrated (a potential professional bureaucracy), lowly differentiated and highly integrated (a potential corporate monocracy), and lowly differentiated and lowly integrated (neither archetype).

To deal with the second sampling issue, the functional and contextual differences between organizations, we ensured that the three major types of local authority (metropolitan districts, shire counties and shire districts) were represented in the sample. Metropolitan counties were not included because they were so few in number, they had very different purposes and functions to the others and, importantly for our research design, they had no predecessor organizations. In choosing the sample organizations we also ensured that there was some variation on other variables. We have large districts as well as small; we have authorities that are predominantly urban, as well as those that are mainly rural. We have authorities in relatively affluent areas as well as in less-privileged ones.

As a result of these deliberations we had a sample distributed as in table 5.1.

While the selection is balanced between types of local authority, it is not balanced between types of organization. Given that the institutional thrust was towards corporate management away from a professional bureaucracy it was necessary to ensure a good representation of the former type. In particular, the category of low differentiation and high integration is the one which is furthest from that of the professional bureaucracy. Thus this gave us a set of organizations which were likely to be strongly reorienting and so more organizations were included in this category. However, the low differentiation and low integration category is non-archetypical and of

Table 5.1 Distribution of the sample by local authority type differentiation and integration

	High differentiation, high integration	High differentiation, low integration	Low differentiation, high integration	Low differentiation, low integration
Shire county	2	2	3	1
Metropolitan district	2	2	3	1
Shire district	2	2	3	1

less interest in the general research design and so fewer organizations were included.

It is important to reiterate that the sampling was carried out on the basis of what these organizations said their structure would be on 1 April 1974. So we were sampling on the basis of a *desired* outcome of organizational planning. It was possible that on that commissioning date a somewhat different structure would be implemented.

Of course, because this was a study of strategic change, a longitudinal design was adopted. Given that we were sampling on the basis of a planned organization, it was necessary to establish a real starting point for the analysis and to see in what archetype (if any) these 24 organizations were prior to producing their reorganization report. The beginning of 1972 was chosen as such a point because it was before the Local Government Act had been passed and the Bains Report published. A series of interviews were carried out in 1973, establishing the organizational structure and systems in the middle of 1972. In those cases where amalgamations of local authorities were taking place, it was possible to establish a dominant predecessor organization, either through its sheer scale and importance or, if there was no such obvious domination, through an examination of which predecessor local authority was supplying most of the appointments to senior management. This first data point, then, was chosen to establish an archetypal starting point for the 24 organizations.

The second point chosen was the middle of 1975, with interviewing continuing until the end of that year. This was chosen to give the reorganization some time to settle down. Being about 15 months after reorganization there had been an opportunity for any new structures and systems to be tested. At this point the aim was to examine the dynamic processes of change as well as to establish where the organizations were archetypal. Thus, in 1975, we have a picture of structure, systems, context, values, interests, power and capacity.

The third data point was the middle of 1978, again with interviewing going on until the end of the year. The basic rationale for this point was that it was a further three years on from the second point, which had been three years from the first point. Again, as in 1975, the aim was to examine both where the organizations were in archetypal terms as well as the dynamic processes of change. Thus, in 1978, we have a picture of structure, systems, context, values, interests, power and capacity.

The final data point for structure and systems was the beginning of 1982, slightly more than the three year period established previously. 1982 was the outcome point, so data was only collected on archetypal position, i.e. structures and systems.

Methods of Data Collection

Four formal methods of data collection were used in the study: interviews, questionnaires, documents and observation. Informal data collection was also important.

For the 1972 point, data were collected on structure and systems through interviews (carried out in 1973) with the chief executive and whoever else might be necessary. Also, documents such as budgets, procedural manuals, position statements and corporate reports were collected and used for the analysis.

For the 1975 point, data were collected on structure, systems, context, values, interests, power and capability. A major method of data collection was a focused interview with the senior managers in each of the 24 local authorities. Senior managers were the chief executive and each chief officer reporting to him (all chief executives were male), i.e. a senior manager responsible for a major function such as education, housing, finance etc. In addition there were usually a number of functional heads who were not in such senior positions but whose role in the organization was important from a design perspective, e.g. corporate planning officers, personnel managers, budget officers, project coordinators, executive assistants etc. Normally each interview lasted two hours although it was not unusual for them to be longer. In the smallest local authority this involved ten interviews; in the largest, 26. Altogether 384 interviews were carried out in 1975.

Again, documents were collected (usually in profusion as many of these organizations produced considerable numbers of reports about their organization and their environment; corporate management encouraged them to do this). Also, opportunities were taken to attend meetings in these authorities, such as management teams and project groups. This was possible as to carry out the interviews it was necessary to be in the organization for at least three days, and more usually for at least a week. This also meant that informal methods were important. The formal interviews frequently developed into informal discussions over coffee, lunch and dinner. Without exception we were given full run of the local authority and spent time 'wandering around', a very valuable way of collecting information.

A further method used in 1975 was the distribution of a questionnaire to all those interviewed, plus those managers who reported directly to the chief officers responsible for major functions. This varied from two managers reporting to a senior manager to nine. Altogether 765 questionnaires were distributed and 551 returned, a response rate of 72 per cent. This questionnaire covered commitments to professional and corporate values, satisfaction with resources, power structures and perceived effectiveness.

This pattern of data collection was repeated for the 1978 data point. 368 interviews with senior managers were carried out along the same lines as 1975. Documents were collected, meetings attended and the questionnaire distributed again. This time 724 questionnaires were distributed and 486 returned, a response rate of 67.1 per cent.

In 1982 the data collected were structural and systemic as it was the final design archetype outcome point. The data were collected by means of a mailed questionnaire, followed up by telephone interviews with the chief executive officer of the organization where necessary.

We have mentioned informal methods in the context of coffee, lunch and dinner. However, there is a much more important aspect to this. The research was carried out from the Institute of Local Government Studies at the University of Birmingham. Inlogov is a unique institution that has an almost symbiotic relationship with the world of local government. It had a highly successful ten week residential executive development course which ran three times a year, educating 150 senior local government executives each year between 1965 and 1972. After a break for the period of local government reorganization it started a six week course of a similar kind. In addition there was a constant stream of one, two and three day seminars for local government managers both at the Institute and in particular local authorities. There were a number of consequences of this for our research.

One consequence was that access to research sites was excellent. To gain access to our 24 organizations we had to approach 25; only one turned us down. Inside each of the 24 organizations there were graduates of Inlogov's ten or six week courses who were willing to devote large amounts of time to our concerns. Information was freely and willingly given. A further consequence of the uniqueness of Inlogov was the constant flow of senior managers through the place. Thus, without exception, we were able to keep in contact with our 24 organizations because senior managers came to the Institute for courses. We always took the opportunity to interview them. Also, all of the courses used speakers from local government. Again, many managers from the organizations we were researching came to the Institute to speak about activities in their authorities. We always attended their talks and also spent time on another interview.

It is difficult to underestimate the importance of these kinds of linkages. It gave us continuing contact with our research sites. It meant that we could always telephone and get information. In addition, the Institute was an amazing repository of information about local government in general and specific local authorities in particular. Fifteen of the 24 organizations in our sample were involved in other data-gathering activities by the Institute during the ten year period of study. Many were the conversations that took place between staff members not involved in our study and ourselves, about Wool City, Steeltown, Milltown, Rootley, Midland City, Commuter County and others. Overall, then, there was a vast amount of data and information over the whole ten year period even though we concentrated on four data points for manageability and rigour of analysis.

Measures

There are six conceptual areas which were subject to measurement, namely organizational design archetypes, interpretive schemes, situational context, interests, dependences of power, and organizational capacity. Each of these will be discussed in turn.

Organizational Design Archetypes

Table 4.1 outlined the organization design characteristics for the two archetypes of the heteronomous professional bureaucracy and the corporate bureaucracy. Of course, these are observer-generated ideal types. Three general categories were dealt with, namely the structure of roles and responsibilities, decision systems, and human resource systems. Our measures deal with the first two of these categories but not the third.

The rationale for not dealing with human resource systems primarily comes from the national nature of the local government system in Britain and the consequent small variation in the way such human resource systems are structured. The terms and conditions of service, i.e. hiring and firing practices, compensation packages, general evaluation and even education and training, are laid down and controlled through a central body, the Local Authority Conditions of Service Advisory Board (LACSAB). There is no freedom for individual local authorities to vary salaries and very little flexibility in job gradings for various levels of post. Local authorities as a whole act as a national career system, with officers moving readily from one part of the country to another, carrying their seniority and benefits packages with them. For this to happen there has to be a high level of standardization of human resource systems. As a result we did not include this aspect in our operationalizations. However, this is something which would require study in other institutional populations and it also requires further examination in this population.

As a result, seven dimensions of organizational structure and systems, prescribed and emergent, were used to describe a particular organization's position *vis-à-vis* an archetype, using the categories of roles and responsibilities and decision systems. Table 5.2 outlines the measures used. The measures were, in the main, institutionally specific to the local government sector, derived from the large literature on corporate management (Greenwood and Stewart, 1974).

Prescribed differentiation is measured by a count of the number of departments (functional units reporting to the chief executive) and committees that an organization has. The greater the number, the greater is the extent of prescribed differentiation.

Prescribed integration is measured by a count of the number of committees and subcommittees specifically charged with integrating functions such as budgeting, policy and resource allocation, central

Table 5.2 Organization design measures

	Prescribed	*Emergent*
A Structure of roles and responsibilities	Differentiation integration	Integration
B Decision systems	Decision-making pattern Decision-making criteria	Decision-making pattern Decision-making criteria

land management, personnel matters etc. Added to this is a count of the number of coordinating executive functions such as corporate planning, research and intelligence, project coordination, personnel, financial planning etc. The greater the number, the greater is the extent of prescribed integration.

Emergent integration is measured by a count of the number of officer working groups that cut across departmental boundaries and the number of politician panels with similar cross-cutting purposes. They are emergent because the particular groups come and go. The greater the overall number, the greater is the extent of emergent integration.

Prescribed decision-making pattern is a measure of the openness and inclusiveness of formal decision making in an organization. It is made up of a number of items, including the inclusiveness of the membership of the management team (from all chief officers to a small minority), the membership of corporate groups (generally all departments represented to just those concerned with the issues), the attendance at policy committees (all chief officers to just those concerned with a particular item), and whether there is a 'Whitehall' form of governance (whether officers deal only with members of the majority party or whether all parties can be dealt with). The series of rating scales for each of these are summed for an overall score with the greater the score the more inclusive the prescribed decision-making pattern.

Emergent decision-making pattern is measured by the routing of issues through a single or multiple channels. It is made up of three items: whether all major policy and resource issues go through the policy committee to council (one channel) or directly from programme committees to council (multiple channels); whether all major policy and resource issues go through the officers management team or independently from each senior manager to a programme committee; whether corporate groups report through the management team or to individual chief officers. These items are then summed and the higher the score, the stronger the system of routing.

Prescribed decision-making criteria are measured by the existence of a system which formalizes issues for examination. It is made up of three aspects: whether there is a system to search actively for policy and resource issues (anticipatory) or whether policy making is reactive, whether there is a meta-policy-making system (Dror, 1978), i.e. procedures for deciding what is or is not a policy issue; whether there is a system which attempts to define comprehensively issues for organizational attention, or whether it is essentially single-issue-based. Responses to these questions are summed and the greater the score the more prescribed are the decision-making criteria.

Emergent policy-making criteria are measured through two scales, patterns of budgeting and modes of analysis. Patterns of budgeting deals with the parameters of budgetary review, such as examinations of base, committed and growth expenditure, the discretion available over different kinds of expenditure, the use of programme reviews and 'value-for-money' audits etc. Modes of analysis examines how far there is an attempt to carry out a strategic analysis of policies and expenditures via the use of tools such as profiles of the social, economic and physical circumstances of the organization, preparing position statements, carrying out community reviews etc. Together, the higher the score on these scales, the wider the range of emergent policy-making criteria.

Having established the basic operational dimensions, the next task was to describe the position of an organization in terms of its relationship to the two design archetype. A professional bureaucracy would score high on prescribed differentiation, low on both prescribed and emergent integration, low on prescribed and emergent decision-making pattern (i.e. low levels of inclusiveness and multiple channels of decision making) and low on prescribed and emergent decision-making criteria (i.e. no anticipatory or comprehensive policy-making systems, no meta-policy making and no systems of budgetary or policy review). A corporate bureaucracy would be the opposite.

All seven measures were scored so that a high score is corporate and then standardized so that comparisons could be made across measures. To be in either design archetype an organization had to have a score of a least one standard deviation above the mean on all seven dimensions. To be in an emergent category, scores on one or two dimensions had to be one standard deviation below the mean for the corporate bureaucracy or one standard deviation above the mean for a professional bureaucracy. There are two ways of being in a schizoid category. One is to have scores on three or four dimensions below (or above) the mean and three or four above (or below). The other way is to have all seven scores around the mean, i.e. to be indeterminate.

Interpretive Schemes

Given the design archetypes underpinning the study, two sets of values were measured: commitments to professionalism and commitments to corporate management. The basic measures were threefold.

1 In the interviews respondents were asked directly (and indirectly) about their own commitments and those of other senior members of the organization.
2 The questionnaire had a set of five items on each value area with a five point response scale.
3 Documents were subjected to latent content analysis to establish the overall position of the organization.

Three stages were then followed to establish the nature of commitment, i.e. *status quo*, competing, indifferent or reformative. First, the interview data and the questionnaire data were aggregated (separately), compared with each other and with the documentary analysis. This analysis showed a high degree of correlation between the measures. Second, a distinction was made between the responses of chief officers (the elite) and other managers (the sub-elite). Third, the position of each of these groups was compared with the design archetypes. From this an overall scale was produced. For example, if both the elite and the sub-elite had the same high commitment to a set of corporate values and not to professional values, but the structure was professional, embryonic professional or schizoid, then that would be a reformative commitment. If the commitment of both the elite and the non-elite was the same, and in line with the structural position, then that is a *status quo* commitment. If the elite was committed, but the sub-elite was anti, then that would be competitive. Similarly the sub-elite could be pro, but the elite anti, which is competitive, but of a rather different form. In other words the measure of interpretive schemes was in terms of what the commitments of two separable hierarchical groups were and how these were related to the current organizational structure and systems.

Situational Context

Situational context has two general elements: task environment and fiscal pressure. Task environment is measured by combining three measures. One is the complexity and variability of the environment. This is measured by examining the population make-up (percentage under age 5; percentage over 65; percentage foreign born), the socio-economic characteristics of the area (percentage in professional occupations; percentage unemployed), the population density and the physical make-up of the area (percentage industrial hereditaments; percentage in public housing). From these a score of complexity–variability was produced. The composite score changed only marginally over the research period.

The second measure for task environment was that of the range of tasks performed by the organization. This goes with type of authority. Metropolitan districts have the most wide-ranging tasks, followed by shire counties, with shire districts having a relatively narrow range. These did not change at all during the research period. The third measure was the scale of the authority, in terms of both population served and number of employees. These are very highly correlated. Again they did not change significantly over the period although there was some marginal downsizing.

These three measures were combined for an overall measure of task environment which showed almost no variation over the ten year period.

Fiscal pressure was measured in two different ways over the research period. In 1975 it was the average expenditure growth in percentage terms since the fiscal year preceding reorganization. This was because this was a period in the life of the local authority system as a whole where the main problem that was being perceived by the middle of 1975 was that of 'runaway' expenditure growth: the higher the growth, the higher the pressure. By 1978, such growth had come down sharply, but central government, the major source of funds, still saw expenditures as too high. Its approach to controlling that expenditure was to produce its own figures for the expenditure levels of each local authority. From this it produced a figure of whether a particular local authority was overspending or underspending and by how much. We adopted this measure, with more fiscal pressure coming from higher levels of overspend. Fiscal pressures did change markedly over the research period.

Interests

The measures for interests came from the interview data. Three resources were examined, namely financial (budgets), people (establishment) and status. For each one, the senior manager was asked his level of satisfaction with the provision for his department and his response was scored on a five point scale from very satisfied to very dissatisfied. The responses to all three were summed across organizational units to give an overall level of satisfaction with interests.

Dependences of Power

The measure for power came from both interview and questionnaire data; structural and substantive dimensions were used. Structurally, a distinction was made between the centralization of power and the coherence of power. Centralization is a measure of the hierarchical locus of power. Coherence can be separated from this, being the extent to which decisions are made by a small number of people or units rather than by large number. In principle an organization could be centralized and non-coherent, i.e. power rests at, say, vice-president level, but with each vice-president making a distinct set of decisions. Similarly an organization could be decentralized and coherent, with power resting in the hands of a small set of operational managers. Substantively a distinction was made between power over general policy making and power over resource allocation.

Data on centralization were collected primarily by questionnaire using a Tannenbaum (1968) format. For each organization in the sample a list was compiled of the primary organizational units and respondents were asked to rate their power separately for policy making and budgeting on a five point scale from 'a very great deal' to 'very little'. From these responses a mean score for the organization was computed, aggregating the two decision-making arenas. Similar information was collected from interviews and served to validate the questionnaire responses.

Data on coherence was collected from interviews. Respondents were asked about the extent to which power over budgeting and policy making resided in particular bodies or individual departments, such as the policy and resources committee, the chief executive, the management team, the finance department or particular service departments. A five point rating scale was used to classify the responses which ranged from highly coherent to highly non-coherent.

The measures of centralization and coherence were then combined under the general rubric of concentration to produced an overall threefold classification into concentrated, intermediate and dispersed power structures. A concentrated power structure is one which is both centralized and coherent. A dispersed power structure is one which is both decentralized and non-coherent. There are two somewhat different kinds of intermediate: decentralized and coherent and centralized and non-coherent.

Organizational Capability

Organizational capability has two aspects to it: the nature of leadership and the knowledge and expertise available to an organization. Data for both of these were collected from interviews.

A threefold classification was used for leadership: transformational, transactional and in-between, or a mixture. There are no formal measures for this kind of leadership so it was a matter of inter-interviewer rating and agreement. First of all transformational leadership was measured on a collective basis; that is, it is the extent to which certain approaches to managing strategic change are shared by all the dominant elite. Those approaches included elements of an articulated vision (a future to which an organization was moving), an understanding of the nature of the change being undertaken, culturally and behaviourally as well as structurally, some degree of thought being given to processes of change which go beyond the technical designing of systems to behavioural processes and some abilities to gain the commitment of other members of an organization to the new direction. Essentially, transactional leadership is where these visions, understandings and skills are not present and change is seen in technical design terms.

Knowledge and expertise were measured in two ways. The first way was through the presence of people in the organization skilled in corporate management. This was done through the interview process, but then backed up by getting expert opinions from those members of the staff of Inlogov responsible for compiling a nationwide register of corporate planning in local authorities. The second way was to examine retrospectively the history of corporate planning in each organization over the previous time periods. The two measures were combined for an overall measure.

Conclusions

Describing research designs, techniques of data collection and operationalization of variables gives a much neater and tidier picture of the research process than was actually the case. With a cross-sectional design it is not only possible but necessary to keep a tight hold on one's approach. But in a study in which it took ten years to collect the data and a further six years to analyse and write up, there is no possibility that ideas will stand still. The ideas of design archetypes and tracks were not part of that original 1972 design, nor was the concept of organizational capacity. But because of the flexible open-ended nature of data collection information was available to support these ideas as they developed.

It was a very important part of this project, as it must be of any long-term project, not to have the ideas and data 'written in stone'. When the project was designed, the whole situation of local government was one where there had been continued expansion of services and growth in expenditures for a decade. Reorganization was presaged on the continuance of that situation. But within a year of that reorganization the fiscal environment was changing and it continued to worsen throughout the whole period. Examining the impact of fiscal pressure was not part of the original design, although the general task environment was. The concept and measurement of fiscal pressure had to be added. This kind of development is inevitable in a longitudinal design. An important part of the theoretical dynamic is the notion of continuously changing circumstances and their unanticipated consequences. The researcher is caught by this dynamic also, having to modify theoretical frameworks during the life of the project. We think that this is a very important element in longitudinal designs that requires much more recognition and discussion.

6 Organizational Tracks: An Overview

Introduction

The task of this chapter is to establish the tracks followed by the 24 organizations under study. We have already outlined four generic tracks in chapter 2, namely reorientations, inertia, aborted excursions and unresolved excursions. The starting point for the present chapter will be to examine the relative incidence of these tracks. That is, we ask how many of the 24 organizations moved along each track. Subsequent chapters will focus on a particular track, looking at the dynamics of the processes involved.

This chapter, in other words, examines tracks at a general level. In particular, it looks at two aspects, or dimensions, of tracks – firstly, the *incidence* of the generic tracks and, secondly, the *periodicity* of tracks.

The incidence of generic tracks refers to the frequency at which the four generic tracks occur. That is, the question posed is: What tracks occurred? There are a number of general hypotheses that can be raised about the tracks that we should anticipate. The first of these concerns the likelihood of archetype coherence itself. An assumption of the holistic approach is that organizations will exhibit structural and systemic coherence, which means that over any given time period a substantial majority of organizations will travel along the inertia and reorientation tracks and (possibly) the aborted excursion track. The unresolved excursion track, characterized by incoherence, will be much less common.

A second general hypothesis, again to do with the incidence of tracks, is that far more organizations will pursue the track of inertia than any other track, and certainly far more than either would achieve a reorientation or would remain between archetypes (unresolved excursions). Given the 'gravitational pull' associated with archetypes it follows that inertia will be the more common. However, in examining this hypothesis we have to be aware of the particular institutional location of this empirical study with its strong pressures to change from one archetype to another. Because of the pressures for change we might anticipate occasional and modest fraying of coherence (aborted excursions) *towards the corporate bureaucracy* – this is the third hypothesis. In other words, the general hypotheses have to be qualified and made more specific in order to accommodate the detail of the institutional and temporal setting.

The periodicity of tracks is to do with the scale of change as reflected in the *routing* through transitional or intermediate positions between archetypes. That is, periodicity is about questions such as: Do organizations move incrementally through nearby positions towards a further archetype? Is movement to another archetype only to be accomplished swiftly, adjusting simultaneously many aspects of design? Is movement gradual and linear, or do delays and/or reversals occur? What proportions of movements towards another archetype eventually culminate in a reorientation?

What Tracks Occurred?

The number of organizations following each of the generic tracks is given in table 6.1. In looking at the data the hypothesis raised earlier should be considered. The first hypothesis was about whether organizations do, or do not, tend to operate with design coherence. Do they, in other words, operate within the framework of an archetype? It was hypothesized that of the four tracks identified earlier that of an unresolved excursion, in which organizations operate between archetypes and thus without coherence, is the least likely. Therefore, the greater the number of organizations following such a track, the less support there is for the hypothesis.

According to table 6.1, four organizations operated with the same set of structures and systems for the whole of the twelve year period. In these organizations there was no alteration of the underlying set of ideas and values. Seven other organizations (those undergoing an aborted excursion) were, for the most part, within or closely attached to a particular archetype. In fact, all these seven organizations were

Table 6.1 Frequency of generic organizational tracks, 1970–1982

Track	No. of organizations	Percentage
A Inertia/retention	4	16.7
B Aborted excursion	7	29.2
C Reorientation	7	29.2
D Unresolved excursion	6[a]	25.0
Total	24	100

[a] This figure includes four organizations that were outside an archetype throughout the full period and two that were within an archetype at the beginning of the period but between archetypes thereafter.

inside an archetype for at least ten of the twelve years, which indicates a lengthy period of retained coherence.

To these organizations may be added four of the seven organizations that moved between archetypes (reorientation). Analysis of the data indicated that these four organizations had coherence in 1972 but had moved to a new coherence by 1975; significantly the new coherence was sustained for the remaining seven years of the period. In other words, these four organizations had design coherence for *more* than seven of the ten years of the research period, but not the same design. The other three of these reorienting organizations, however, had coherence only at the very beginning (in 1971) and the very end (1981) of the period. It took these organizations longer to move between archetypes.

We conclude, then, that 15 (62 per cent) of the 24 organizations demonstrated design coherence as the more usual state of affairs over the twelve year period. (These are the 11 organizations which exhibited either inertia or aborted excursions, plus four of the reorienting organizations). This contrasts with nine organizations (37.5 per cent) with a clear *lack* of design coherence for all or most of the period covered. In other words, the organizations examined here were significantly more likely to exhibit design coherence than they were to experience incoherence. In fact, this degree of support is even more significant when the institutional context, with its tremendous pressure for change, is taken into account.

The second hypothesis was that for lengthy periods most organizations will remain within the same archetype. In our terms, it means that the retention or discontinued excursion tracks will be more common than either the reorientation or unresolved excursion tracks. How far was this the case?

Table 6.1 indicates that 54 per cent of the organizations examined (13 of the 24) did *not* experience stability of attachment to any one archetype. Thus, the proposition is hardly supported. However, it is important to refer back to the nature of the institutional context which, as we have stressed, was unusually destabilizing. In chapter 5 it was pointed out that the organizations under examination were subject to institutionally legitimated pressures for large schemes of change.

The pressure to adopt corporate structures and processes was considerable. Indeed, such was the growing legitimacy of the corporate model that, when the reorganized local authority organizations came into existence, 95 per cent appointed a policy committee to oversee the general direction of the organization (in 1970 the figure was less than 50 per cent), 98 per cent appointed a chief executive officer to oversee the management of the organization as a whole (again, in 1970 the figure was less than 50 per cent and 98 per cent set up a management team of the most senior managers (Greenwood et al., 1980a). As Greenwood et al. put it, 'the net effect (of these and other changes) is that the extent of structural integration in 1977–78 was noticeably higher than that of 1967–74' (p. 86). The important point is that the flux and ferment of ideas was unusually high and no doubt contributed to the relative instability of organizational archetypes in the period pictured in table 6.1.

We can add to this suggestion. Following the logic of Meyer and Rowan (1977) the considerable pressure upon local authority organizations to exhibit integration *structures* may have been particularly significant because local authorities are organizations where perform-ance is operationally difficult to demonstrate. Therefore, conformity with institutionally expected structural characteristics can become a symbolic way of achieving credibility and legitimacy.

It may well be that the results reported here provide support for the complementary analytical thrusts of Tushman and Romanelli (1985) and of Zucker (1988). Tushman and Romanelli suggest that organizations evolve through a series of lengthy stages of design convergence (in our terms, organizations pursue the design retention track) punctuated by dramatic and concentrated upheavals or 'metamorphoses' (i.e. the reorientation track). Tushman and Romanelli present their thesis in terms of individual organizations rather than populations or classes of organizations but Zucker's work indicates that within institutional sectors new forms of organizational arrangements, once legitimated, would be rapidly adopted by the majority of organizations within the same institutional sector. This seems to be what has occurred for the sample of organizations examined here. Prior to 1967 few of the organizations operated with the corporate bureaucracy archetype and few had reviewed their overall design arrangements systematically (Greenwood et al., 1969). However, by 1972 the corporate archetype had become articulated and legitimated as the appropriate model for the challenge of the post-reorganization era – hence the apparent instability and reorientations reported in table 6.1.

In other words, the data in table 6.1 do not support, in themselves, the idea contained within the archetype thesis that organizations essentially retain a given archetype once it is established. However, we are suggesting, following Tushman and Romanelli (1985) and Zucker (1988), that the hypothesis as originally formulated may be too simple, ignoring the periods of upheaval that occur as institutionally prescribed interpretive schemes are radically rescored. Our data are reflecting a period of upheaval rather than of convergence sandwiched, possibly, between periods of stability and convergent inertia.

This issue of coherence, stability and the institutional pressures to change can be looked at in a slightly different way. We argued in chapter 5 that all these organizations were under pressure to move away from the heteronomous professional bureaucracy archetype towards the corporate bureaucracy, even if this did not mean complete reorientation. Thus, the tracks can be examined in terms of how far there was movement away from the 'traditional' archetype to the newly legitimated one. Thus, there should be inertia or discontinued excursions on the part of those organizations which started the period as corporate bureaucracies. Reorientations should be from the heteronomous professional bureaucracy to the corporate bureaucracy. Table 6.2 shows the distribution of archetypes, at the start of the research period in 1972, by subsequent track.

Of the 24 organizations, 20 started the period set within a design archetype, which suggests that prior to 1972 the total system was in a very stable state, mainly travelling on the inertia track. Furthermore, 15 of the organizations were within the historically institutionally approved archetype, namely the heteronomous professional bureauc-

Table 6.2 The incident of archetypes

Track	Archetype
Inertia retention	2 Heteronomous professional bureaucracies 2 Corporate bureaucracies
Aborted excursion	4 Heteronomous professional bureaucracies 3 Corporate bureaucracies
Reorientation	7 Heteronomous professional bureaucracies
Unresolved excursion	2 Heteronomous professional bureaucracies 4 Unresolved designs

racy, and only five were corporate bureaucracies. The data in table 6.2 thus raise two points which are worth making about the relationships between the particular archetypes and the tracks subsequently followed.

First, reorientations, as a class of organizations, are different from the other three tracks in that transformations were all in the *same* direction. The directional currents within this track were consistent. No organizations moved from a corporate to a professional bureaucracy. As a result, by 1982 there were 12 organizations operating with the corporate bureaucracy archetype (an increase of seven) and only six as heteronomous professional bureaucracies (a decrease of nine), a major turnaround. The figures for reorientations, in short, clearly reflect a response to the strong institutionally legitimated pressures, thus supporting the hypothesis.

In sharp contrast, however, there were still six organizations at the end of the twelve year period (two on the inertia track and four on the aborted excursion track) which had managed to resist the pressures to change to become corporate bureaucracies. This shows very strong inertia as they managed to retain an archetype which was under attack. This is an inertia of the kind that Starbuck et al. (1978) describe with regard to Kalmar Verkstad and Facit, where an organization resists external pressures to change and continues to reiterate its known but criticized practices. Of course, the fact that four of these professional bureaucracies experienced discontinued excursions demonstrates the pressures for change.

Pulling together the above analysis we can reach the following conclusions. First, the organizations examined here illustrate the strong tendency to operate with archetype characteristics, i.e. arrangements of structures and systems that exhibit coherence. Second, there is no evidence that inertia (archetype retention) is the usual course of events, unless as a phase of convergence punctuated by periods of instability and change. Each of the four generic tracks was found in the sample of organizations covered and, of these tracks, the inertia track was the *least* common. Third, there is strong evidence of institutional pressures legitimating and prescribing choice of alternative design archetypes and overriding the pressures for archetype inertia.

The Periodicity of Change

The idea of organizational reorientation or transformation often carries with it the notion of a single revolutionary event, of an organization moving from one state to another in a short period of time. Such an event would seem to have both a beginning and an end. But this is a mistaken view. In actuality, as Meyerson and Martin (1988) point out, a transformation may come about through monolithic and revolutionary changes, by differentiated, localized and incremental changes or by diffuse, invisible and continual changes. Quinn (1982) suggests that many strategic changes come about by a process of 'logical incrementalism'. Child and Smith (1987) and Pettigrew (1985) emphasize both the radical and incremental elements in an organizational transformation. Indeed, theoretically and empirically there seems to be an increasing consensus that organizations go through long periods of incremental and inertial change within a design archetype, punctuated by revolutionary change (Miller and Friesen, 1984; Pettigrew, 1985; Tushman and Romanelli, 1985; Child and Smith, 1987).

The approaches of these researchers illustrate and focus the issue of *periodicity* in organizational change. The concern with transformations, which at first glance seem to be revolutionary in nature, has led scholars to begin the process of adequately mapping the pace and sequence of changes in organizational arrangements. Questions such as 'What organizational elements change, in what order and at what rates?' are perceived as crucial. As Greenwood and Hinings (1988) have put it, 'the study of macro-organizational change is the tracing of the parts and combinations of design arrangements that alter, the sequence in which they alter and the overall pattern of the routes taken' (p. 49).

The examination of the periodicity of change, we would suggest, involves three issues.

1   The *pace of change* focuses upon the speed at which transformations/ reorientations occur. This issue is about whether radical change occurs incrementally over a period of time, or is revolutionary and concentrated within a small time period.
2   The *sequence of change* focuses upon *what* changes. This issue contains two possible approaches. Earlier we referred to interpretive decoupling and recoupling. One approach would be to observe whether organizations which reorient tend to alter their prescribed framework first or are they emergently led? A second approach is to observe which aspects of design (differentiation, integration etc.) are altered first. Do organizations in aborted excursions change certain structural elements, whereas reorientations follow from changes in other organizational elements? These questions are to do with the sequencing of change.
3   The *linearity of change* focuses upon the extent of directional consistency. That is, one conception of change would anticipate a cumulative momentum or 'roll' from one archetype to another. An alternative conception would perceive the organization as pulled and tugged between competing interests and, as a result, characterized by disjunctions, oscillations and temporary reversals or delay in the overall movement towards a different archetype.

In this section we examine the pace, sequence and linearity of change involved across the four generic tracks. But a cautionary note should be made. Periodicity refers to change *from* a particular archetype. By definition, therefore, the four organizations which followed an inertia track do not have change of this kind, so they do not figure in the ensuing discussion. However, this does not mean that they are not subject to change. Indeeed, Miller and Friesen (1984) and Greenwood and Hinings (1988) both argue that inertia involves momentum and the heightening of archetypal qualities. The extent of *intra*-archetype change in the inertia track could be considerable but will be taken up in chapter 7 when we examine the dynamics of that position.

A central issue in examining the timing and content of change in the three tracks of aborted discontinued excursions, unresolved excursions and reorientations is the extent by which the reorientation track differs from the other two. Arguments from a variety of theoretical perspectives suggest that successful organizational transformations are difficult and implicitly require quite different management of the change process from those which are unsuccessful (cf. Starbuck et al., 1978; Kanter, 1983; Tichy, 1983; Tichy and Ulrich, 1984). These differences could be to do with the timing and content of the change, the dynamics of the process, or both.

Therefore, it makes sense to compare the periodicity of change of organizations which successfully achieve reorientation with that of organizations that do not. Are there factors in the pace and sequencing of events in the organizations that move along the reorientation track that distinguish those organizations from others moving along different tracks? And do these factors give clues as to the characteristics of successful attempts at achieving organizational transformation?

The Pace of Change

The relevant data on the *pace* of change are given in table 6.3, which shows, for each track, the mean numbers of changes in each time period for each track. (For example, in the early phase (1972–5) the average amount of design change in those organizations moving along the reorientation track was 4.29, compared with an average of 2.67 in the unresolved excursions.) By reading across the table some overview can be obtained about the timing of changes (did they occur in particular phases?). By reading down the columns comparisons can be drawn across the tracks.

What table 6.3 shows is that reorientations exhibit a relatively high incidence of change in the first period (4.29), compared with discontinued (3.14) and unresolved (2.67) excursions. This suggests that organizations which are going to transform their archetype successfully have to produce considerable and early change activity to overcome inertia. Unresolved and discontinued excursions, it would seem, never manage to produce that critical mass of action.

Here, then, is a possible clue to why some organizations are able to achieve full reorientation whereas others are not. There appears to be the need for an initial critical mass of change effort in order to break from the inertia track and to sustain movement towards an alternative

Table 6.3 Periodicity of change

Track	Early phase changes	Middle phase changes	Late phase changes	Total
Aborted excursion	3.14	2.71	4.71	10.57
Reorientation	4.29	1.86	4.43	10.57
Unresolved excursion	2.67	0.83	3.00	6.50
All	3.40	1.85	4.10	9.35

Scores indicate the average amount of design change for the particular category of organizations; a score of 3 for an organization indicates that it changes its position on three of the seven design characteristics.

design archetype. That is, the *pace* of change in the reorientation case is similar to and different from other cases. It is similar to that of the discontinued and the unresolved excursions cases in that there is more change at the beginning of the process of upheaval than in the subsequent phase. All three tracks show this pattern of higher effort at change in the first phase relative to the second. But reorientations are different in terms of the sheer *amount* of change activity at the outset. The pace of change in the reorientation situation is noticeably quicker in that greater changes occur at the outset.

A second observation that may be drawn from table 6.3 is that for all three tracks there is much more change at the outset and at the end of the 12 years than in the middle years. This is consistent in part with the ideas of Miller and Friesen (1984), Pettigrew (1985), Tushman and Romanelli (1985), and Child and Smith (1987) who suggest that change occurs through the intermixing of periods of incremental change with 'revolutionary' jolts to the system. On this basis, given the strong institutional pressures for change in the period before 1972, it is not surprising that considerable change took place in the 'early phase' from 1972 to 1975. After the initial flurry of change a period of more incremental change occurred, from 1975 to 1978. However, the marked increase that occurred in the third period from 1978 to 1982 is more surprising. These findings suggest that the mix of external pressures and internal dynamics, especially as they unfold during the later phase of the research period, requires further examination. These changes will be examined in the following chapters.

Table 6.4 Changes in prescribed or emergent elements by time period

Tracks	Early phase		Middle phase		Late phase	
	Prescribed	*Emergent*	*Prescribed*	*Emergent*	*Prescribed*	*Emergent*
Aborted excursion	1.57	1.57	1.26	1.42	2.71	2.0
Reorientation	1.85	2.28	1.14	0.7	2.57	2.0
Unresolved excursion	1.16	1.5	0.3	0.5	2.0	1.0
All	1.8	2.1	1.1	1.0	2.88	2.0

Table 6.5 Focus of design changes in the early phase (1970–1975), by track

Track	PD	ED	PI	EI	PDR	EDR	PCs	EmCr
Aborted excursion	8.1	0	10.4	15.4	12.8	13.7	6.6	7.3
Reorientation	4.7	0	22.0	15.8	15.4	21.0	12.0	14.9
Unresolved excursion	4.0	0	9.5	10.8	16.2	16.3	5.8	11.8
Total (N=20)	5.7	0	14.2	14.2	14.8	17.1	8.3	11.3

Table 6.6 Number of oscillations, by track

	Number of oscillations	
Track	Average	Range
Aborted excursion	6.43	4–8
Reorientation	5.71	3–11
Unresolved excursion	4.00	2–6
All	5.45	2–11

The Sequence of Change

Does it matter *which* elements of design arrangements are first altered? Put another way, are successful reorientations commenced by redesigning particular parts of structures and systems, or does it not matter? Data on these issues are given in tables 6.4, 6.5 and 6.6.

Table 6.4 summarizes the sequence in which prescribed and emergent design elements were altered. More specifically, it shows whether the changes introduced at the beginning, in subsequent or in later periods were concentrated at the prescribed and/or emergent level. In presenting the data in this way we are returning to the issue raised earlier as to whether strategic change is more usually driven by prescribed restructuring or builds upon emergent practices. As expected – given the discussion of the material in earlier tables – the unresolved excursion track is characterized in the early phase by little change (compared with the other tracks) at either the prescribed or the emergent level and, as is clear from table 6.4, the fraying of the design coherence is as likely to occur at either the prescribed or the emergent level. But in the organizations undergoing a reorientation there is a tendency for more change to occur in the early phase at the emergent level combined with significant change at the prescribed level. In other words, the characteristic that separates those that secure a reorientation from those that become 'stuck' between archetypes is that there is a greater initial pace of change (noted earlier) *and* a greater tendency for change to originate at the emergent level. One might argue that a successful organizational transformation is less likely to follow an imposed alteration of prescribed frameworks than the development of systems of operation which become part of day-to-day activity and are then consolidated and furthered by revision of authoritative (prescribed) arrangements. This is not to imply that change is not 'managed': on the contrary, it means that the subject or focus of managerial effort should be upon emergent properties rather than aspects of the prescribed framework.

Indeed, there is the possibility, implied by the data in table 6.4, that the prescribed framework is very much a lever which is used to effect strategic change in a two-stage manner. Thus, in the first stage of the change process there has to be considerable attention to emergent practices (how this happened in these organizations is examined in detail in later chapters) with the prescribed framework being used to reinforce, nudge forward, signal and legitimate the direction of change. However, once the initial momentum for change has been released prescribed structures exhibit a 'catching up' with the emergent structure and assume a stronger directional role. That is, in the second stage of transformation there is a quickening, visible and increased usage of prescribed frameworks to consolidate and complete the evolution of emergent practices.

We can deepen this analysis of how the tracks differ by examining which particular elements of structure or systems are changed. So far we have noted whether it is the prescribed or emergent levels that alter first; now it is worth exploring whether it is the structure (e.g. extents of differentiation, integration) or systems (e.g. decision-making practices) that are manipulated. In effect, we are exploring whether there are differences between the tracks in terms of their focus upon what are increasingly referred to as high or key impact systems.

The idea of high impact systems is that in the majority of organizations there are aspects of organizational design which have a high impact in terms of the messages encoded within them and in terms of the extent to which they underpin prevailing ideas of purpose and organizational character. The high impact systems can vary from organization to organization. For example, in a university one of the critical high impact systems is usually the tenure and promotion system, which signals and controls the values of the organization. In the organizations examined here two of the high impact systems are (a) the *routing* of decisions through the system (indicating either the autonomy or the subservience of the professional department) and (b) the criteria used in decision making (indicating, again, the relative autonomy or otherwise of the professional department). Therefore, in an organization moving from the traditional heteronomous professional bureaucracy to the corporate bureaucracy, any alteration to the routing and/or criteria of decision making is highly significant both in signalling the transformation and in its implementation. What is interesting is to ask whether organizations that achieve a reorientation *use* these high impact systems as early symbols and levers of transformation.

Table 6.5 sets out which elements of organizational design were altered in the first phase of the research, by track. The question posed is whether the different tracks are characterized by differences of initial change focus. The figures refer to the average change in score in each design variable, by track. (For example, the average change in extent of prescribed integrative structures for organizations undergoing a reorientation was 22, compared with 10.4 in the aborted excursions.)

A number of interesting observations can be made. First, there was very little attempt across the organizations as a whole to effect change of altering patterns of structural differentiation. Much more attention was placed upon creating integrative structures of a prescribed form and, to a significant extent, upon altering the *routing* of decisions through the centralized structures and the criteria that would be used for making decisions. These directions of change occurred irrespective of subsequent track. But the organizations that eventually achieved a reorientation also tended to *emphasize* certain design features. Thus, the organizations on the reorientation track would

1   put in place (a) *more* prescribed integrative structures (almost twice as much change in this area than other organizations) and (b) more prescribed *systems* for introducing new criteria for decision making, and

2   have a strong emergent-led change in the routing of decisions through the integrative structures and the utilization of new criteria for decision making.

Our understanding of these statistics, in the light of the various interviews and discussions with managers in the organizations concerned, is that reorientations usually occur because there are individuals who have the skill to recognize emergent trends and to create those trends (see later chapters) at least partly by restructuring areas of the organization in highly symbolic ways. Thus, in order to move to the corporate bureaucracy several chief executives recognized the need to erect an array of integrative structures usually consisting of lateral devices (interdepartmental teams and task forces) that criss-crossed professional boundaries, combined with staff specialists (e.g. policy analysts, corporate planners, research and intelligence officers). These lateral devices and staff specialists provided three things: *visibility* to the new sets of ideas and values, *opportunities* for professional departments to participate in the teams and task forces and new *skills* for the development of new budgetary procedures and policy frameworks. Many of these arrangements were found in non-orientation organizations but not to the same extent. In particular, there was often a lack of worked out and workable ideas about how decisions were to be made, i.e. the criteria of decision making were not fully understood. In the reorienting organizations, however, there was considerably more change at the emergent and prescribed level on this critical aspect of organizational design.

Put another way, a movement from the heteronomous professional bureaucracy to the corporate bureaucracy requires a fundamental shift in the way that resources are allocated and policies framed. As such it strikes at the heart of political interests and motivation. Those organizations that achieved such a reorientation were much more likely than the others to have developed *early* change in decision systems. Such changes symbolize the coming transformation and act to make it happen. In our earlier terms, the high impact system is reconstituted in terms of the targeted values and beliefs and then serves as a reconstituting force on wider design activities.

The Linearity of Change

The linearity of change refers to the extent to which the change process is marked by movements that are consistently towards a new archetype or punctuated by temporary reversals of direction. The discussion thus far has created the impression that reorientations build up an initial momentum that helps break down the constraining assumptions of one archetype and propels the organization towards another archetype. The imagery would lead to the expectation of unbroken movement and the absence of reversals. Unresolved excursions, in contrast, might be expected to show oscillations (unlike aborted excursions) between archetypes as the tugs and tensions of competing archetypes fail to overcome one another. These issues are taken further in table 6.6.

The statistics in table 6.6 show the average number of oscillations experienced by organizations over the twelve year period. For example, organizations that followed by aborted excursion averaged 6.43 design changes that *reversed* the direction of the prevailing momentum. Thus, in one organization which began to move towards the corporate bureaucracy, three design elements moved towards that organizational model in the early phase of the period but *reversed* direction in the second phase (producing a score of three oscillations).

We draw two conclusions from table 6.6. First, and perhaps of greatest significance, organizations that achieve a reorientation do not usually do so without a number of oscillations. There are 'backtracks' and temporary 'reversals'. Why this should happen is not, at this point, entirely clear. It may reflect a lack of understanding by managers manipulating change as to the appropriate organizational design. Shifting from an established paradigm of ideas and structures to another is, by definition, a radical and thus imperfectly understood set of events. Hence, oscillations occur as second thoughts and rethinking take place. However, it may be that the oscillations reflect the accommodation of political interests which resist or only partially adopt the supplanting ideas and structures. Reorientations may well involve some structural backtracking in order to avoid the hardening of resistance.

Why oscillations occur may involve different answers depending on the particular track followed. These answers will be examined in chapters 7–10. For the moment the general observation has to be that strategic change, i.e. reorientation, does not occur as a series of unbroken movements towards a new state. Movement is halting and involves at least some reversals. But a closer examination of the organizations under scrutiny reveals a potentially important feature. We noticed earlier that in many ways the kinds of changes introduced along the discontinued and/or aborted excursion tracks tended to be

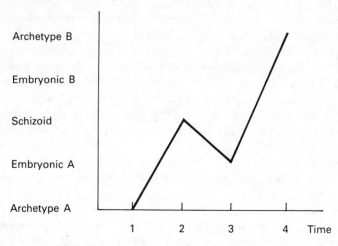

Figure 6.1 Typical oscillation along a reorientation track

structural in form, rather than the routing and nature of decision making. Reorientations, however, were equally concerned with decision making as with structures. Interestingly, many of the oscillations in reorientation tracks involved the systems and criteria of decision making. That is, in these organizations the tug and push of strategic change centred on the high impact system which embodied the core values of the organization. But, and this is, perhaps, the crucial point, the organizations on the reorientation track were able to take cumulatively large steps towards the new archetype (i.e. a new decision system) and relative modest regressions to the old archetype.

The latter point is illustrated in figure 6.1, which shows that in moving from one archetype (A) to another (B) the movement up to time 2 is strongly in the direction of a new archetype, reaching the schizoid position (in terms of decision-making criteria). But there is a fallback towards the original archetype between time 2 and time 3 before the resumption of movement towards the new archetype.

In summary, therefore, we can say that reorientations are not revolutions, in that they do not involve the change of all design components at the same time, that they are not smooth evolutions, in that some reversals and oscillations do occur, but that the central struggle focuses upon the high impact systems (i.e. those that mark starkly the difference between the old and new archetypes) which in net terms move cumulatively towards the new archetypes. How and why such movement is achieved in some organizations but not others is addressed in chapters 7–10.

Conclusions

This chapter has presented an overall view of the tracks followed by 24 organizations and of the differences between tracks. A number of observations have been made.

1 There is a strong tendency to operate with *design coherence*, i.e. to have structures and systems that 'hang together' as an archetype.
2 There is no evidence that inertia (archetype retention) is the usual course of events. Instead, there appears to be considerable movement between archetypes.
3 There is strong evidence of institutional pressures (a) legitimating and prescribing particular archetypes and (b) overriding pressures for archetype inertia.

The above observations are to do with the existence and stability of archetypes and of the movement of organizations between them. A further set of observations centred on the periodicity of tracks, identifying whether organizations that move along the reorientation track differ in their approach to change from other organizations. The observations were as follows.

4 Successful reorientations usually follow a significant and considerable initial change effort, which establishes a sustainable momentum.
5 Often the initial change effort in reorientating organizations is at the emergent level, which is subsequently and quickly embodied at the prescribed level as a means of furthering completion of the reorientation process.
6 Successful reorientations tend to have an early focus upon high impact systems, at both prescribed and emergent levels.
7 Reorientations are not free from oscillations (i.e. reversals in direction of particular design elements) which tend to centre on the high impact systems. But reversals are usually of lesser magnitude than changes toward reorientation.

These observations are producing a pattern of strategic change activity which gives the basis for a theory of tracks and transformation. In chapters 7–10 these ideas and observations will be taken further both in the sense of providing specific examples and discussion but, perhaps more importantly, by seeking to explain the dynamics that cause an organization to move along a particular track rather than another.

7 The Dynamics of Change and Stability: Retaining an Archetype: Inertia

Introduction

The aim of this chapter, and of chapters 8–10, is to explain why particular organizations follow particular tracks. It takes up the patterns established in previous chapters and demonstrates why they occur. This requires dealing directly with the interaction between design archetypes, context, values, interests, power and capacity. Our theory suggests that the particular design archetype (or lack of one) has an important effect on subsequent change. This will be even more so if there is a contextual change which requires evaluation by organizational members and which potentially challenges existing interpretive schemes. However, patterns of commitment to prevailing or alternative interpretative schemes have to be related to the power structure and the consequent structure of leadership and expertise.

In our theoretical argument, a central explanatory role is taken up by ideas of inconsistencies, incompatibilities and contradictions between the various conceptual elements. Organizations are conceptualized as having inherent tensions because of their basis in a variety of different interest groups, the processes of structural legitimation and their relationship to a problematic environment. The degree of tension engendered, and the ability to handle it, varies from organization to organization. In a situation of stability, all of these various elements will be within a *relative* equilibrium.

One must be careful with concepts such as equilibrium. While we argue that organizations may strain towards a balance amongst their internal characteristics (the idea of archetype coherence), and of those

Table 7.1 Inertia: compatibilities between context, choice, capabilities and design, 1975

Organization	Contextual pressures for change			Choice		Capabilities		
	Task/environment	Fiscal	Institutional	Values	Interest dissatisfaction	Power	Expertise	Leadership
Wool City	Low	Low	Low	Status quo	Medium	Concentrated	Medium	Intermediate
Home County	Medium	High	High	Status quo	Medium	Intermediate	Low	Transactional
Northern City	Low	Low	Low	Status quo	High	Concentrated	High	Transformational
Midland City	High	High	High	Competing	Medium	Concentrated	Low	Transactional

Table 7.2 Inertia: compatibilities between context, choice, capabilities and design, 1978

Organization	Contextual pressures for change			Choice		Capabilities		
	Task/environment	Fiscal	Institutional	Values	Interest dissatisfaction	Power	Expertise	Leadership
Wool City	Low	High	Medium	Status quo	Medium	Concentrated	High	Transactional
Home County	Medium	Low	Medium	Status quo	Medium	Intermediate	Low	Transactional
Northern City	Low	Medium	Medium	Competing	Medium	Concentrated	Low	Transformational
Midland City	High	Low	Medium	Competing	Medium	Concentrated	Low	Transactional

elements with external pressures, we are by no means suggesting that an equilibrium is achieved. Indeed, our analysis of the tracks of these particular organizations demonstrates that they can spend considerable periods of time in states of incompatibility. Because of turnover in personnel, changes in prevailing ideologies, developments of tasks and domains and so on, there are always more likely to be incompatibilities and contradictions together with a dialectical process, rather than stability and balance. As we have suggested previously, a key question becomes the degree of tolerance that can exist within an organization over the actual divergence between organizational elements.

While implicit in this approach are the ideas of appropriateness of structures and goodness of fit, the notion of *tolerance* suggests that organizations can live with a degree of divergence among, or contradiction between, these various elements. Thus, a key theoretical interest becomes the examination of the degree of contradiction possible without causing organizational change and, following from this, the necessary and sufficient conditions for the occurrence of change or stability in organizational design archetypes. Balance or fit between contingencies, values, interests and power means that the organizational processes for sustaining and reproducing a given structure would be strong. But, because the interpenetration of these effects is always less than perfect, an imbalance between reproduction and transformation pressures is produced. It is because of the likelihood of inconsistencies, incompatibilities and contradictions that change occurs.

In this chapter these issues will be examined in the context of the four organizations that, over the period of 12 years, followed an inertia track.

We propose to analyse, in some detail (and in greater detail than will be practised in later chapters), each of the four organizations in turn. In essence we will provide a case sketch of each of the four in order to give a feel for the kind of analysis being attempted. Rather more general observations will be drawn at the end of the chapter. The data on the dynamics of these organizations are summarized in tables 7.1 and 7.2. The first provides data on the precipitating and enabling dynamics of change as pictured in 1975; the second provides a picture of the situation in 1978.

Case 1: Wool City

It is worth repeating the basic thrust of the analysis. Design archetypes, it was argued in chapter 3, are held in place, or destabilized, by the relevance of the structures and systems to the circumstances of the situational context and/or by the congruence of the same structures and systems with the internal profile of values, interests and power. External and internal factors, of course, are interdependent in their influence upon structural form. Put simply, one would expect that organizations that follow the inertial track would have a 'goodness of fit' between their structures and systems and its external *and* internal circumstances. Furthermore, the role of leadership in this situation would be primarily *transactional*.

How far does Wool City fit this general proposition? In an effort to answer this question we will begin – purely for analytical purposes – with the degree of fit between the nature of its external and its organizational form.

During the first period of the research, Wool City faced an environmental situation of high complexity. Wool City is an old city which has been subject to considerable urban decay. It has a large new immigrant population, in particular from India and Pakistan. (Indeed, its inner city problems were recognized nationally when the City was given special status under the central government's programme for the inner cities.) The City's major industries such as the production of woollens have been in steady decline for a considerable time. The City was also involved in amalgamations with a number of other smaller local authorities to form the new Wool City. All this adds up to significant environmental complexity.

As a metropolitan district, the City was responsible for providing a wide range of services, *inter alia*, primary, secondary and tertiary education, social services, public housing, engineering, recreation, environmental health, refuse collection, land-use planning and so on. Metropolitan districts have the widest range of functions of any type of British local authority, indicating a high level of task complexity. Wool City was large in scale, serving a population of 460,000 and employing more than 24,000.

Increasingly, as noted in chapter 4, the range of problems confronting local authorities was regarded as less amenable to traditional 'solutions'. The differential and sometimes contradictory impacts of local services were recognized or ambiguously detected and the sureness of the professional response was questioned and became less confident. Urban problems, in other words, were seen as more complex and intractable: in Perrow's terms (1972) there was low *analysability* and thus heightened *task uncertainty* as the apparent links between services (solutions) and problems were perceived to be less sure.

These high levels of environmental and task complexity and uncertainty, together with the very large scale, produced pressures for a corporate bureaucracy archetype. In familiar terms of organization theory, organizations facing complex and uncertain environments, which are required to perform a complex set of tasks and which are large, require many lateral devices in order to carry out the necessary amounts of information processing (Galbraith, 1975) involved in the provision of interdisciplinary solutions to ill-understood problems and to provide the readiness to appraise and displace tried and inadequate approaches. In other words, the more complex and uncertain the environment and tasks of the local authority the more appropriate is the corporate bureaucracy archetype. The opposite is true for the heteronomous professional bureaucracy.

Wool City did, indeed, have a corporate bureaucracy format. In fact, it was one of the first local authorities to introduce a corporate form, in the 1960s. There was a 'fit' between the external context and organizational form at the beginning of and throughout the research period.

But environments and tasks only produce pressures that demand a response; they do not of themselves produce structures and systems. There are interpretive schemes held by managers which interpret the meaning of those pressures. In the case of Wool City a strong commitment to corporate planning (and anti-professional solutions) was in place throughout the ten years of study. This view was held widely in the organization amongst various levels of management and politicians. The pattern of commitments to values, in short, was one of supporting the *status quo*. While there was some dissatisfaction with interests, from time to time, it was never high enough to form the basis for any action away from the dominant archetype. In so far as such dissatisfaction was articulated it led to change *within* the archetype because of the fundamental interpretive commitment even when that change was to lessen the structural and systemic tightness of the archetype. That is, no group connected with its interest position to a competitive commitment. The power structure was concentrated throughout the period, with decision making in the hands of a small active group of senior managers, organized at the officer level around the chief executive and at the political level around the Leader of the

Council. There were strong relations between managers and politicians. This particular power structure meant continuing control of decision parameters by the organizational groups most committed to corporate bureaucracy. Not surprisingly, as a result of this sustained congruence between context, interpretive commitments, interests and the structure of power, the pressures against change were very strong.

Examining organizational capacity, in an inertia track we might expect that leadership would be of a primarily transactional form, concerned with the continued maintenance of existing structures and the reiteration and development of known expertise and knowledge. Surprisingly, the case of Wool City did not fit this anticipated mould. On the contrary, the chief executive in this organization was one of the more transformational leaders in the whole sample. Why was this the case?

One of the issues in studying change is selecting an appropriate starting point. Every organization has a history which has an important influence on its present and future direction (Kimberly, 1987; Kimberly and Rottman, 1988). While Wool City clearly followed an inertia track during the ten year period of this research, in the previous ten years it had undergone a reorientation, and was instrumental in working out the operational meaning of the corporate bureaucracy archetype. During this earlier period the chief executive officer had operated internally and externally on building commitment to the new archetype. Internally the major focus of effort was in ensuring that other senior managers were not only committed to a corporate approach but, equally importantly, that they *understood* the structures, systems and processes required to make it work. A collective leadership was established, together with the necessary expertise and skills.

Externally, the chief executive became a national figure in proselytizing the virtues of the corporate bureaucracy. This was done primarily through addresses to national meetings within the local government circuit. The chief executive's high profile culminated in an invitation to serve on the Bains Working Group which produced the influential report extolling the need for a move to corporate organizational forms. Such an external profile had positive effects internally as it enabled the senior officers within the organization to build up commitment to the corporate archetype because of their pride in belonging to a high profile organization. The same pride and commitment developed at the political level: politicians enjoyed the status of belonging to an oft-cited example of managerially innovative organization. Second, the external legitimacy being granted to the organization (paradoxically, partly created by the actions of the organization) made it much more difficult for any opposition to the new forms to be voiced.

As a result, although Wool City followed an inertia track from 1972 to 1982, there was always an air of being a pioneer and a feeling of the need to guard and push forward the organization. There was a strong commitment to programme and organizational innovation. So, maintaining the archetype was always a positive activity for senior management with leadership being much more of a transformational than transactional mode. This is important to reiterate: maintaining an inertial position may require considerable activity and directed effort.

The role of leadership within the inertially evolving organizations, then, is not straightforward. There are at least three factors that complicate it. There is, first, the history of the organization (i.e. where it has been) and how this relates to the institutional system as a whole. We are suggesting that, in 1972, Wool City was at the tail end of the reorientation and the practices of that track were still part of the organizational memory. But, more importantly perhaps, local authorities are part of a major institutional system which has a career system which operates across individual organizational boundaries. Because of its national nature there is a strong collective sense of history. In terms of the history of the system, even by 1982, the corporate bureaucracy was still seen and thought of as a 'new' organizational form. Ten years is a brief phase in terms of the historical sweep of the institution. As a result, while many of the particular organizational forms of the corporate archetype had been adopted the institutionalized cultural backing was much slower in taking root. Thus, inertial corporate bureaucracies – as exemplified by Wool City – felt their innovative status and the need to promote and'protect it.

A second reason which produces a requirement for transformational leadership activity within an inertial track also derives from this newness of the corporate bureaucracy. In 1974 the reorganization of the local government system created a set of organizations which adopted in principle the urgings of the Bains Report that they adopt 'the corporate approach'. But only a relatively small pool of experienced corporate practitioners was available. Wool City had developed its organizational capacity for corporate planning through both selective recruitment and internal training. The managers of the small number of organizations that had already adopted a corporate approach (and received wide publicity as a result) became a valuable and sought-after body of expertise. As a result, Wool City, as one of these organizations, continually lost staff to other organizations over the whole ten year period. Six of the senior officers of Wool City left to become chief executives of organizations attempting to develop the corporate model. So, over the period, constant education and training were required to cope with senior staff turnover in order to maintain the inertial track. Indeed, there was an active and large internal training system focused on supplying the needs of running a corporate system.

The third reason for the continued leadership activity aimed at maintaining the archetype was a consequence of the changing environment. As mentioned before, contexts are unlikely to stand still. In the case of the organizations examined here there was considerable general turmoil between 1975 and 1982. One source of turmoil was the introduction of restraint on spending referred to previously. The second source of turmoil in the environment was a deterioration in relationships between the central government and local government following the election of the Thatcher government in 1979. The central government developed new instruments of control and altered norms and understandings that 'governed' the interdependence of the two levels of government. The assertions and claims of local government's incompetence and mismanagement became more strident and a debate developed, again, as to the appropriate distribution of powers and functions. One casualty of the debate was the Greater London Council and the metropolitan counties which were eventually abolished in 1985, i.e. barely a decade after the previous reorganization.

In effect, the later period of the research was one of high contextual turmoil creating uncertainty about the domain, form and criteria of local government. The corporate bureaucracy archetype, which had been promulgated in the early 1970s and was strongly associated with the 1974 reorganization, was less wholeheartedly advocated. The moving context disturbed and undermined the ability of the corporate archetype to become grounded in tradition. As will be seen later, this weakening of the institutional prescription favouring the corporate archetype caused a retreat from it in some authorities, but *not* in Wool City, because of the transformational actions of the chief executive, in particular, but also through the actions of other informed senior managers.

The point we are making is that the inertial track followed by Wool City still required transformational leadership, partly because of the 'newness' of the corporate archetype, partly because of the need to continually socialize new entrants into the organization and partly because of the moving context of ideas which became less favourable. The way in which the chief executive promoted support for the corporate archetype in the face of the less favourable context of ideas was by stressing the effectiveness of the corporate approach in handling the pressures of financial restraint and cuts in government grants.

Wool City was fortunate in that its traditional spending patterns were modest relative to the expenditure targets imposed by the government. There was no sudden collapse of revenues. A study in 1978 (Jackman and Sellars, 1978) showed Wool City to be a slight *under*spender by government definitions of appropriate standards of service. Moreover, the City was able to secure additional monies from the government through special programmes such as those intended to support the deprived inner cities. Within Wool City these benefits were attributed to the corporate way of working. In effect, Wool City had a transformational leadership which continually stressed the advantages of the prevailing (but relatively new) corporate archetype. And to back this up there was a high level of corporate expertise. In addition the worsening financial context did less damage to the organization than to others. Hence, the archetype could not be challenged as ineffective. In Wool City, members of the organization began the period believing that their organization was reasonably effective. As the period of research developed the City was perceived to be highly effective. An organizational capacity of leadership and expertise had been built up, which actively kept the organization on an inertial track.

A counterpoint to Wool City was Home County which, by contrast, remained a heteronomous professional bureaucracy throughout the period. This organization was one of two to resist successfully all the institutional pressures to 'go corporate'.

Case 2: Home County

Home County shows many similarities to Wool City, and a significant difference. The similarities are in terms of the absence of incompatibilities between task context, the internal profile and organizational design. Thus, the environment and task were of medium complexity, which does not fit the corporate model. Home County had a population of 940,000 and a workforce of 32,000. The existing heteronomous professional bureaucracy was compatible with the task context.

Furthermore, throughout the research period there was a compatibility of values and interests with the prevailing archetype. All senior managers maintained a strong commitment to the interpretive scheme of a professional bureaucracy, i.e. the pattern of commitment was for the *status quo*, there were average levels of satisfaction with the distribution of resources and the distribution of power was decentralized into the professionally based departments.

The little centralization that did occur was administrative in nature, not strategic and directional, because the chief executive officer had his own functional responsibilities for the legal and administrative services of the organization. As a result, issues within the ambit of these functions came through him. He had no direct control over budgeting. Strategic planning did not exist. All this went hand in hand with a leadership pattern of dispersal of responsibility for functions and programmes to professional departments. Leadership was dispersed into many positions both because the professional interpretive scheme legitimized this leadership structure and also because of the high level of commitment in the organization to the *status quo*.

So far, in other words, we have exactly the same pattern as in Wool City – the inertial track was followed because of the congruence between situational context, organization archetype and internal profile. There were no precipitating dynamics for alteration of the *status quo* other than the institutional pressures in 1975 and fiscal pressure in 1978. But a noticeable difference between these organizations is that of the role of leadership and skill in Home County. Leadership was decidedly low key and transactional in kind. 'Visioning', in Home County, did not play a large role at the organizational level: it was much more important at the programme level with, for example, the chief education officer wanting to develop the best quality education service in the country. Thus, within the professional bureaucracy archetype a transactional style of leadership was possible. In addition, Home County had little or no experience or expertise amongst its staff in managing a corporate bureaucracy. Its organization and staff were geared to dealing with a professional structure. In other words, there was low organizational capability for developing a corporate bureaucracy mode of working.

But, the institutional environment for at least eight of the ten years produced pressures to move to a corporate bureaucracy, which Home County resisted, apparently without an overall pattern of *active* maintenance of the professional bureaucracy alternative. How was this possible?

One reason explaining the lack of need for active maintenance *at the outset*, despite the strong institutional pressures, was the combination of self-satisfaction within the organization with overall performance and the lack of disruption caused by the 1974 reorganization. Home County was one of only a handful of organizations which underwent either no or very slight changes to its boundaries, functions or population base in 1974. There was little change in staff at senior levels (unlike Wool City). When the chief executive retired in 1977 he was replaced by his chief administrative officer. Hence, there was no need to face the issue of amalgamating staffs from different organizations. In effect, what was, remained. And there was no apparent performance problem. The senior members of Home County saw the organization as relatively effective, and continued to do so. There was no motivation to question the appropriateness of existing ways of doing things. In an almost unique way Home County was insulated from many of the institutional trends causing disruption to other organizations.

Retention of the professional archetype without active maintenance was possible because of the same processes that affected Wool City. Like Wool City, Home County was in a good position to cope with the changing fiscal environment because up to 1978 it had not been an overspender or subject to major cuts. While its expenditure growth rate in 1975–6 had been very high this was a one-off phenomenon quickly brought under control in the following year. This ability to cope with the changing fiscal environment was attributed to the professional bureaucracy archetype. The flux occurring over the set of prescribed ideas, moreover, made it possible from 1977–8 onwards to defend increasingly and successfully that archetype in its own right.

Case 3: Midland City

Midland City was the second of the two organizations to retain the heteronomous professional bureaucracy archetype. But, unlike Home County, in this organization there were pressures from the situational context to develop a more corporate design. In many ways, the environment and tasks of Midland City resembled those of Wool City. It is a large organization, serving a population of 320,000 and having 14,000 employees, with a complex set of tasks within a complex environment. The area covered is run down, physically, with large numbers of immigrants, a poor housing stock, and declining industries. These are the contextual conditions which the proponents of corporate management and planning argued as necessitating the corporate form of organization.

Internally, however, the situation was not so clear cut; indeed the mark of Midland City, throughout the period, is one of competition and conflict over ideas of how to organize. There was a pattern of commitments characterized by sharp competition of views. The senior managers in the organization (the members of the management team responsible for strategic direction) were indifferent in their initial commitments. That is, they were not highly committed to either a professional bureaucracy or a corporate bureaucracy. The managers at the next two levels in the organization wished to see the organization change its structural form and systems to a corporate bureaucracy. But Midland City maintained a concentrated power structure so there were no prescribed or emergent channels through which less senior managers could make their options known. There was moderate dissatisfaction with the distribution of resources but this level of dissatisfaction was controllable by the elite coalition. However, all members of the organization interviewed and surveyed agreed that there were high levels of conflict.

Midland City, in short, had an external context appropriate for the corporate archetype, which was supported by middle managers. However, power was largely concentrated in the hands of senior managers who were *not* committed to the corporate approach and who were not unduly dissatisfied with the distribution of resources. Moreover, the organization was *not* perceived as being ineffective, despite the high levels of conflict between departments which the middle managers attributed as evidence of the need for a corporate approach. Movement towards a corporate approach was stymied at the outset not because those with power were positively against it or in favour of something else but because they were indifferent to it. Finally, Midland City suffered a lack of organizational capability for the practice of corporate planning. There was no 'champion' of the corporate approach with any positional authority or demonstrable expertise. There was no chief executive of the kind that drove Wool City. There was no reservoir of expertise in corporate management at any level. In effect, there was no articulate and visible focus clarifying and championing the case for a new archetype. There was only a widespread swell of belief at middle management level that 'what was' was not working and that 'the corporate approach', urged upon them by the outside world (e.g. the Bains Report), would be an improvement.

As table 7.2 shows, by 1978 Midland City was experiencing stronger pressure to change. The general environmental and task situation continued to produce pressure – in the form of visibly worsening urban problems and greater demands for action in the face of downward pressures on spending – for more integrated responses to problems of urban deprivation. In addition, despite a trend in expenditure between 1975 to 1978 substantially above the average growth in all local authorities' expenditure between 1975 and 1978, it was seen as low given the needs the organization was facing (Jackman and Sellars, 1978). Managers admitted that the performance of the organization was deteriorating. In other words, the lack of fit between the organization archetype and its task context was worsening and becoming reflected in poorer organizational performance. So why did the organization remain on the inertial track? What was going on *within* the organization?

To understand the nature of the internal situation it is necessary to distinguish between pressures for change and pressures against change. Where these are balanced there is a competitive situation which may lead to oscillation or stalemate. Our theory would predict that power becomes a crucial variable. Interestingly, as the research period developed the value situation within Midland City showed a marked transformation. Elite indifference to change gradually became a positive commitment to changing the organization towards a corporate bureaucracy and the power structure remained concentrated giving the elite the opportunity to implement organizational changes in line with their value preferences. But the other senior managers, who had supported the corporate approach, became more committed to the existing professional bureaucracy. In other words, two of the precipitating dynamics of change – task context and patterns of commitment – were acting as pressures for change. But by 1982 change had still not occurred. Why?

There were clear signs by the end of the final period (1982) that change was beginning to happen, although not necessarily in a coherent way. There was both a tightening and a loosening of the professional bureaucracy archetype. Change had taken Midland City to the edge of the archetype. In Midland City there was a real heightening of structural change in the 1978–82 period after five years of little change.

Indeed, the organization showed the most structural and systemic change in the third period of any of the organizations on inertial tracks. Levels of integration were increased at both prescribed and emergent forms. A central budget committee was established and began allowing groups of managers to meet to discuss integrated approaches to issues. The degree of routing of issues through the central management team was increased. However, the amount of formal and informal analysis of issues through the use of rational–synoptic processes decreased.

Midland City resembles an organization looking for structural answers to the pressures upon it. Indeed the emphasis was more structural than systemic. Two interrelated factors were in play here. First, there was no appreciable turnover in senior management and, therefore, no particular increase in the knowledge of alternative forms of management. Nor did Midland City make use of general management training, either internally or externally, which would have brought its officers into contact with the experiences of (say) Wool City. In such a situation where there is a lack of organizational capacity for change, it is easier to alter structures than to build new systems.

Second, leadership continued to be transactional in nature when a move to a more transformational form was required. Those wanting change were unable to articulate or champion an alternative way of operating, to develop a vision of what could be achieved. So piecemeal and limited change was taking place in the form of experimentation with poorly understood structures. On this basis we would predict a fraying of the archetype status and a move to some form of excursion. In other words, Midland City is an example of an organization following, for the moment, the inertial track not because of any commitment to the prevailing archetype but because it lacks the *understanding* of how to move to a more suitable and preferable archetype. Midland City was an organization that knew where it wanted to go, and ought to go, but did not know how to get there. One would predict continued change, breaking from the archetype.

Case 4:   Northern City

Northern City, the fourth inertial organization, also began to indicate that change was in the offing in the later period of the research. Early in the period, however, it 'fitted' the theory of stability arising from the absence of precipitating dynamics through inconsistencies and tensions. The initial contextual pressures were for a corporate form (high environmental and task complexity and uncertainty); the pattern of commitments within the organization were in line with this (i.e. a *status quo* commitment to a corporate bureaucracy archetype), the power structure was concentrated allowing the managerial and political elite to implement their preferences, effectiveness was not a problem, the managers in the organization had some experience and expertise at running a corporate organization and leadership was transactional in nature. The only feature not in line was a high degree of dissatisfaction with the distribution of resources, but this potential trigger for change could be 'capped' through the concentrated power structure and the widespread commitment to the corporate approach to resource allocation. The dissatisfied could not mobilize and remained a 'repressed' interest (Alford, 1975).

By the later stages of the research, Northern City was exhibiting tension between a continuing contextual push for a corporate organizational form and internal pressures for change towards a more professional archetype. That is, the elite wanted to change the organization – in this case towards a professional form – whereas the managerial non-elite wished to retain the prevailing corporate bureaucracy. In this organization there was some turnover of senior staff, including the chief executive. The power structure remained concentrated, giving the elite the instrument to implement their preferred options (which was to change). Interestingly, the elite wished to change despite a widespread belief that organizational performance was reasonable and despite a drop in the level of dissatisfaction with decline. The changes in the fiscal environment were not severe to Northern City and there was no sense of crisis. In other words, there was no obvious reason to justify removal of the corporate archetype other than the low commitment of senior managers to it.

In short, we would regard Northern City as an organization travelling along the inertial track because of events and personnel in the organization's history, not because of the committed support of powerful figures. Because the prevailing archetype was not connected to the structures of power we would regard Northern City as a candidate for subsequent movement off the inertial track. In this respect the period of research was possibly too short to show the impact of the altered pattern of commitments.

Northern City may well fit the Starbuck et al. (1978) and Hedberg (1981) models of an organization which reacts to changing external and internal conditions by re-emphasizing current structural and systemic patterns. Certainly, by 1982 it was in a situation where there were tensions developing between situational pressures and the dynamics of values, interests and power.

Conclusions

Chapter 3 raised a series of propositions concerning the association between the precipitating dynamics and the inertia track. These were (in a slightly rephrased formulation) as follows.

1 Organizations on the inertia track will have a compatibility of organization design and situational context.
2 Organizations on the inertia track will have a *status quo* pattern of value commitment or a pattern of indifferent commitment.
3 Organizations on the inertia track will exhibit a high measure of satisfaction with interests.

Essentially, these propositions have the same underlying theme, which is that organizational stability will only occur in the long term if there is a congruence between design form, situational context and the internal profile of values and interests. Incompatibilities between any of these dynamics for change and organizational arrangements will produce tensions and pressures that will destabilize organizational practices and precipitate change.

The small number of organizations examined so far makes it difficult to be definitive in drawing conclusions. However, some observations can be made concerning the above propositions. First, the proposition that situational context and design archetype will be in alignment within the inertia track is borne out by three of the four organizations. This suggests that the proposition has significance. The fact that the one organization out of alignment with its task context was experiencing pressures to move towards a new alignment may be further evidence of the 'influence' exerted over design arrangements by the task context. The second proposition, similarly, receives support both directly, in that all four organizations had a *status quo* pattern of value commitments in 1975, and indirectly, in that the loss of that pattern was associated with pressures for change. The third proposition is rather less well supported in that *some* dissatisfaction was evident in all four organizations. Dissatisfaction with interests may have low potency as a precipitator of change.

The logic of our approach, however, is that what matters is the interaction between the several dynamics and the substantive position and content of the interpretive scheme within the organization. We believe that the four cases of inertia illustrate the relevance of this form of analysis. We would suggest that there are two broad conclusions that can be discerned.

1 Organizations that have a congruence between the situational (especially the task) context, internal profile of value commitments, interests and power and organizational arrangements are likely to follow the inertial track.

Two of the organizations in this chapter – Wool City and Home County – had this degree of compatibility between context, internal profile and design archetype. There were no precipitating dynamics for change. Therefore, the pressures were for stability and inertia. Importantly, *no* other organization in the sample of 24 had this degree of fit between the dynamics of change/inertia and the prevailing organizational archetype, at the outset of the period. As will be seen later various organizations moved to such a position of congruence.

Organizations in the position of overall congruence, we would suggest, have a 'strong' attachment to the inertial track. However, a distinction should be drawn between organizations that require transactional or transformational leadership in order to sustain inertia.

2 Organizations that have adopted relatively 'new' sets of ideas about organizational form require an organizational capacity of transformational leadership, together with expertise in the new form, so as to sustain those ideas.

The scale of organizational capacity required to sustain organizational stability and inertia, especially that element which represents the difference between transformational and transactional leadership, indicates the importance of the immediate history of the organization and the relevance of a temporal base to the study of strategic change. An organization's past is a conditioner of the pattern of precipitating and enabling conditions necessary for continuation of current practices. Thus, in Wool City, transformational leadership was appropriate (as was the concentrated power structure which enabled a tight control to be maintained over decision processes) because the organization was operating with a relatively new archetype. The relevance of transformational leadership to sustain a new archetype, despite a congruence between situational constraints and organizational design, is further illustrated by Northern City where commitment slipped and made the inertial track rather fragile. In contrast, Home County did not exhibit or need transformational leadership because the prevailing archetype was long-standing and deeply rooted.

These cases illustrate how external contexts and inner profiles are in constant flux and that from a research point of view the location of an organization on a particular track is very much influenced by the particular organizational starting point and history. Any examination of change involves a relatively arbitrary starting and finishing point. Understanding change requires continuous study. Thus, one cannot understand the active transformational leadership in Wool City without knowing about its history of proselytizing the corporate bureaucracy. Similarly, an examination of Midland City and Northern City produces the prediction that, *ceteris paribus*, their archetypal position will break down and they will both begin excursions; that is, the examination of change leads to the issue of what next, why stop the story at that particular point?

The small number of organizations covered in this chapter make it rather presumptuous to comment too far on the relative importance of particular dynamics or relationships between dynamics. However, it is worth indicating two possibilities that can be considered in chapters 8–10 as the number of organizations added to the analysis increases. First, there is the possibly strong role of situational (especially *task*) pressures upon organizational design. In three of the organizations there was a compatibility between design and task context. In the fourth there were emerging pressures to move towards such an alignment. How far, in the long term, do organizations gravitate towards a fit? This is certainly an important question that will have to be addressed in later chapters.

A second, possibly important, issue is the necessity for a high degree of organizational capacity in order to change towards an institutionally novel archetype. Wool City and Northern City had such a capability and attained the new archetypal form: Midland City wanted the new form, lacked sufficient capability, and failed to move. We would expect, as explored in chapter 8, organizations which moved towards and/or attained the corporate archetype to have a substantial organizational capability.

In leaving these inertial organizations it is worth stressing again the format of the explanations being attempted. Our primary theoretical assertion is that the extent to which an organization engages upon the track of strategic reorientation or remains stable within a prevailing archetype is a function of the interaction of situational constraints and the profile of internal values, interests, power and capabilities. That interaction, we are now arguing, has to be understood within the biographical context of the particular organization. This is why the four organizations along the inertial track interpreted *differently* the same fiscal context to produce the same effect, i.e. stability.

The above themes will be developed and elaborated in chapters 8–10. We turn first to a discussion of the organizations that achieved strategic reorientations because they represent the sharpest contrast with the four organizations discussed so far.

8 The Dynamics of Change and Stability: Changing an Archetype: Reorientations

Introduction

The 24 organizations which form the basis of this study were part of an institutional population which was not only functionally and geographically reorganized but subject to a set of relatively novel ideas about management. Therefore we would anticipate that any reorientations would be away from the heterogeneous professional bureaucracy towards the corporate archetype. In fact of the 15 organizations that began in the professional bureaucracy archetype seven experienced reorientations; no organizations moved in the other direction. By 1982 only six organizations were in the heteronomous professional bureaucracy category, a major turnaround.

Chapter 6 showed that there were a number of distinctive characteristics of reorientations. One is that they show a high incidence of change early in the research period, and a relatively low one in the second. This suggests that in order to transform their archetype successfully organizations have to produce considerable activity to overcome inertia. Another characteristic is that not only do reorienting organizations get more change under way early but change is more emergent-led than the other tracks. A successful organizational transformation requires that systems of operation and process are put in place rather than remaining at the level of prescribed roles and relationships. Reorienting organizations show signs of their prescribed structure 'catching up' with their emergent structure in the third period of the research.

A further characteristic of reorienting organizations is a particular concern with the pattern and criteria of decision making. Again this presents a picture of organizations that successfully achieve a transformation by putting considerable effort into systems rather than structures; systems essentially differentiate the corporate and professional archetype. Those organizations which successfully manage transformations create a considerable level of initial change activity focused on actions which will produce behavioural changes. Such activity raises the possibility that organizational capacity may be an important ingredient.

However, this organizational reorientation or transformation is unlikely to be a single revolutionary event, with an organization moving from one state to another in a short period of time. Such an event would seem to have both a beginning and an end. Meyerson and Martin (1988), Quinn (1982), Child and Smith (1987) and Pettigrew (1985) emphasize both the radical and incremental elements involved in an organizational transformation. Oscillations certainly occur. Reorientation means, of course, that these seven organizations altered both their structures, introducing policy committees, chief executive officers, management teams, corporate groups etc., and their systems to carry out policy analysis across the organization and to deal with resource allocation. Also these organizations changed their underpinning interpretive schemes so that the structural and systemic changes were anchored in an appropriate set of values. The structural and systemic arrangements were altered in a manner consistent with the ideas and values of the new archetype. But none of them managed their reorientation without some form of oscillation, whether of a major kind as in the case of Hill County or of a more minor kind as with Cheswich. One of the tasks of this chapter is to examine that process of oscillation.

What produces this track of reorientation? In attempting an answer to this question a distinction should be drawn between the dynamics that precipitate and enable an organization to break from an inertial track and those that enable the completion of a successful reorientation. What we are pinpointing here is the difference between the pressures that may cause an organization to move away from its current archetype and those that may enable a successful reorientation. Part of the way of achieving this may be high levels of senior management change in order to change interpretive schemes, power and capacity. Reorientations may require new people embodying the ideas of the reorganization and understanding the new organizational forms and processes.

The Dynamics of Reorienting

The dynamics that might precipitate and enable an organization to move from one archetype to another, according to the logic of the conceptual argument developed in chapters 1–3, would be a series of consistent incompatibilities between prevailing organizational arrangements on the one hand, and, on the other, the situational context and internal profile of values, interests, power and capabilities. Such a degree of incompatibilities, however, is probably unlikely and, as indicated in table 8.1 is not characteristic of the seven organizations with which this chapter is concerned. For example, three of the seven had no pressures for change arising from the task situation.

In table 8.1, therefore, we should seek similarities between the seven organizations and differences between the seven as a whole and the characteristics of organizations that did not move (i.e. the inertia organizations). In terms of common precipitating events several patterns may be discerned. First, the task context was not one that demanded changes: in some cases it did and in others it did not. In fact, as with the inertia organizations of chapter 7 there is hardly any serious pressure for change that can be traced to the size or complexity of the organization or to its geographical context. At best these organizations operated in contexts which would support either archetype: at worst the contexts would be consistent with the heteronomous professional bureaucracy.

A much more evident precipitating factor is the extent to which people within the organization are committed to the new corporate approach. Indeed, five of the seven organizations had competitive patterns of value commitments (i.e. the elite wished to change whereas the middle managers did not) and one had a reformative commitment. In effect, these six organizations had values which were consistent with the institutional prescription which favoured change. Interestingly, the remaining precipitating factor – extent of dissatisfaction with interests – shows no apparent pattern. The precipitating factors for commencing upon a track of strategic change that eventually leads to reorientation, therefore, appear to be as shown in figure 8.1.

It is important to note not only that this combination precipitated movement but that the movement occurred despite the lack of substantial pressures from the task situation. That is, the role of legitimated strategic choice is acting to override the incompatibility of pressures arising from the task context (as at Churchtown, Cheswich and Valeden) or to provide direction to mixed or intermediate pressures. But there were other organizations that had the same combination of precipitating factors that *either* did not move from the prevailing archetype (e.g. Midland City) *or* moved out of the archetype but to a more modest extent and subsequently failed to complete the reorientation (e.g. Southton and Leafy County in the unresolved excursions). This implies that there were enabling factors at work.

The first enabling factor that should be considered is the structure of power dependences. Power might be expected to have been important because five of the seven organizations had competitive commitments – with the elite desiring change – and we have already suggested that a concentrated power structure permits the elite to establish greater control over the form of organizational arrangements. Perhaps surprisingly, only one of the five organizations with competitive commitments had a concentrated power structure. It is incorrect, in other words, to suppose that elites simply impose their views. Instead, the role of transformational organizational capacity seems more pertinent. Thus, the five of the seven organizations that have competitive commitments have a significant expertise in the architecture of corporate planning (either 'high' or 'medium') and in transformational leadership (either 'in-between' or 'high'). It will be remembered that the discussion in chapter 7 noted the inability of Midland City to break from the

Precipitating factors

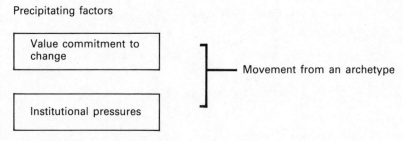

Figure 8.1 Precipitating factors and strategic change

Table 8.1 Reorientations: compatibilities between context, choice, capabilities and design, 1975

Organization	Contextual pressures for change			Choice			Capabilities	
	Task/environment	Fiscal	Institutional	Values	Interest dissatisfaction	Power	Expertise	Leadership
Hill County	High/medium	High	High	Competitive	High	Intermediate	High	In-between
Commuter County	Medium/low	Medium	High	Competitive	Medium	Concentrated	High	In-between
Garden County	Medium	High	High	Competitive	Low	Dispersed	High	In-between
Amalgam	High/medium	Very high	High	Competitive	Medium	Dispersed	High	Transformational
Churchtown	Low	Low	High	Competitive	Medium	Intermediate	Medium	Transformational
Cheswich	Low	Very high	High	Competitive	Low	Concentrated	Low	In-between
Valeden	Low	Low	High	Indifferent	Medium	Concentrated	Low	Transformational

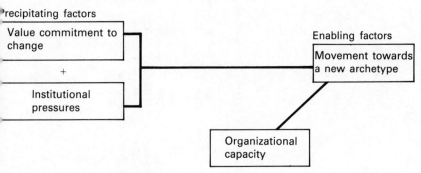

Figure 8.2 Precipitating factors, enabling factors and strategic change

prevailing heteronomous professional bureaucracy because of the organization's inadequate understanding of how to implement corporate planning. The five cases in table 8.1 further highlight the importance of this enabling factor.

In short, one combination of dynamics that creates the initial shift towards the new archetype consists of two precipitating factors (institutional pressures *and* a pattern of value commitments in favour of change) and one enabling factor (organizational capacity) (figure 8.2).

Table 8.2 gives an indication as to how this shift towards change might develop. Thus, despite the variance in the extent of fiscal pressure and the weakening of the institutional prescription for corporate planning, there is a modest strengthening of the power structure (i.e. it becomes rather less dispersed) and, in two cases, a strengthening of the commitment to the new values (a change from a competitive to a reformative commitment). We would suggest that the basic thrust of this approach, in other words, is for the initial movement towards a new archetype to become consolidated through a spreading of commitment to change and a gradual tightening of the power structure. The first of these trends – the spreading of commitment – reflects the success of transformational leadership in expressing the vision of the new archetype and the willingness of the elite to reinforce their values by adjusting power structures. There are, of course, variations within this basic format, but the first five organizations in tables 8.1 and 8.2 can be treated as a group. In order to illustrate this

Table 8.2 Reorientations: compatibilities between context, choice, capabilities and design, 1978

| Organization | Contextual pressures for change | | | | Choice | | | Capabilities | |
	Task/ environment	Fiscal	Institutional	Values	Interest dissatisfaction	Power	Expertise	Leadership
Hill County	High/medium	High	Medium	Reformative	High	Intermediate	High	Transactional
Commuter County	Medium/low	Low	Medium	Competitive	Medium	Intermediate	High	In-between
Garden County	Medium	Low	Medium	Indifferent	Medium	Dispersed	High	In-between
Amalgam	High/medium	Medium	Medium	Reformative	High	Intermediate	High	In-between
Churchtown	Low	Medium	Medium	Competitive	High	Intermediate	Medium	Transformational
Cheswich	Low	Low	Medium	Indifferent	Medium	Intermediate	Low	In-between
Valedon	Low	Low	Medium	Competitive	Medium	Intermediate	Medium	Transformational

general pattern in operation we will use Hill County and Garden County as examples. But the other two organizations – Cheswich and Valeden – are different and should be commented upon.

The interesting feature of Cheswich is that it began with a reformative commitment to change, some transformational leadership but low architectural capability. In other words, there was a strong precipitating factor for change but a weak enabling one. By 1978 (table 8.2), however, the level of commitment to change had weakened and it is puzzling that the organization completed its reorientation. That is, Cheswich runs counter to the patterns observed in other organizations and defeats our attempt to understand it. It is an unexplained deviant case. Valeden, on the other hand, is more understandable. It experienced a quickening of elite commitment to change (partly a consequence of the strong transformational leadership) and built up its expertise in the implementation of corporate planning. Valeden is thus an example of how completion of a reorientation can occur through an initial movement being strengthened by growth in commitment towards, and capability in, the new archetype.

Case Illustrations: Hill County and Garden County

Hill County is the one case of reorientation where a major oscillation occurred, that is, between 1975 and 1978 it moved *back* towards a professional bureaucracy. In all other cases of reorientation there were oscillations in particular structural elements, but in terms of the total change occurring the organizations continued towards the corporate archetype. So although Hill County illustrates the broad pattern identified above it has its own novel characteristics.

At the start of the research in 1972 Hill County, while being within the heteronomous professional bureaucracy archetype, was showing signs of corporateness. In terms of its task environment the pressures were for it to be a corporate bureaucracy. In fact, in the sample as a whole it had the highest score on environmental complexity and variability, facing problems of high unemployment, declining industries, relatively low levels of educational attainment in its population and significant numbers of social welfare recipients. But, in spite of these pressures, Hill County was, in organizational terms, arranged strongly along the lines of a heteronomous professional bureaucracy. It had a wide range of programme departments and committees (high differentiation), just one or two coordinating committees and managerial task forces (low integration), and the membership of committees and groups was on a 'need to know' basis rather than attempting to include a variety of viewpoints. Only in terms of its emergent and prescribed decision-making pattern was there any hint of a corporate possibility. Some attempts had been made to outline a system for policy and resource analysis and to begin to give the management team and the one major coordinating committee a more active role in decision making. However, these roles were sketchy and when articulated involved an advisory relationship to programme committees rather than a directive and controlling one.

When, in 1973, Hill County produced its report on what its structure would be from 1 April 1974 (the point of reorganization) there were statements favouring a corporate approach. The report did not contain a comprehensive and total commitment to all the elements discussed in the Bains Report or the local government literature, but there was a commitment to visualizing the local authority as governing the community and attempting to examine issues across the board rather than 'just' providing services. Following the report, various officers were recruited at the point of reorganization as a deliberate effort to build up the organization's corporate expertise. For the first time, the organization had managers responsible for corporate planning, research and intelligence, project coordination and personnel management. There was a 'high' measure of organizational capability.

The result was definite movement towards a corporate archetype by 1975, by building up the functions and responsibilities of the chief executive's office while leaving the programme departments untouched. The officers appointed for corporate planning, project coordination etc. reported directly to the chief executive. Each of these officers established and staffed a unit, varying in size from nine officers in project coordination to 50 officers in the corporate personnel office. These units, with the active encouragement of the chief executive, developed systems to facilitate cross-departmental analysis of policies, projects and budgets. As an additional development the research and intelligence unit put considerable activity into community reviews of consumer satisfaction with services. The central policy committee set up a structure of subcommittees to examine budget allocations, personnel and land issues and, in addition, introduced a performance review subcommittee. (This committee was one that was strongly recommended by the Bains Working Group but was actually one of the structural elements least often adopted by local authorities primarily because it was seen as too much of a threat by the professional departments (Greenwood et al., 1975).)

Clearly on this evidence Hill County was showing signs of developing towards a corporate bureaucracy. It had, by 1975, very markedly increased the level of prescribed integration, together with both prescribed and emergent decision-making criteria. However, at the same time it was beginning to oscillate. It became more not less professional on decision-making patterns. At the prescribed level, instead of moving to a more policy-oriented civil-service-style model of operation involving programme heads in corporate decision making, membership in such groups was severely curtailed. Also, the organization moved away from routing issues and reports through the management team and policy committee. In effect what had happened in Hill County by 1975 was a division of functions between programmes and the chief executive office and, along with that, a disjunction in reporting relationships. A corporate headquarters had been grafted onto a strengthened divisional structure.

How were these essentially structural and systemic developments connected to internal dynamic processes? There were clear competing value systems in the organization. The dominant elite, composed of the chief executive, chief financial officer, corporate unit heads and some (but not all) programme heads, was highly committed to continued corporate development. Other programme heads, together with their immediate subordinates, were opposed to any further extension of what they saw as 'the corporate octopus' and were in favour of dismantling the corporate structures and systems in place and returning to a 'clear and clean' professional bureaucracy. The distribution of power between those favouring further corporate advances and those preferring a retreat to earlier arrangements was balanced, or 'intermediate', between a highly centralized and concentrated one and a decentralized dispersed one. That is, the programme heads, such as the directors of education and highways, held a considerable amount of power and had direct access to key politicians. As a result their views were heard loud and clear.

Other factors intersected to produce a situation of contradiction, conflict and turmoil in Hill County. The organization was experiencing a very high level of expenditure growth. There was also a very high level of interest dissatisfaction which derived both from perceptions of an inequitable distribution of resources (the opponents of the corporate approach insisted that too many went to the chief executive's office) and from the feeling that the status of the service programmes had diminished relative to that of the corporate units. Together these produced feelings of dissatisfaction and a perception of falling effectiveness.

The retreat from the corporate approach was also affected by the absence of a strong transformational approach in this first period. The leadership exercised by the chief executive and through the corporate heads was deliberately (if possibly unwisely) low key and technical. There was a fairly strong view on the part of the corporate advocates that a corporate approach was self-evidently good and that the systems of programme and community review would demonstrate the usefulness of the approach. The low-key style of leadership could have backfired. However, the chief executive had considerable prestige which derived from his previous role within the *national* financial scene; thus, initial opposition locally was muted.

The result of these combined pressures over the 1975–8 period was to cause an oscillation. Having moved from a professional bureaucracy to a schizoid position by 1975, Hill County moved back to an embryonic professional bureaucracy. But this was not a simple step back. Hill County reduced its level of prescribed integration by eliminating the central performance review committee (a key element in a corporate approach) and the land and buildings committee (which had attempted to take a central hold over physical plant) and also disbanded two officer–member task forces. It continued to maintain a decision-making pattern that was programme department-centred. These arrangements were consistent with the professional bureaucracy approach. However, at the same time it reaffirmed and continued to develop the role of the corporate centre for scanning the local environment, for producing corporate issues and plans and for carrying out central reviews of expenditure. Groups were established or built up for these roles, centred around the chief executive's office. In effect, there was a significant corporate structural presence within a generally professional framework.

By 1978 there were both contextual and internal pressures for continued change. The previous high level of growth in expenditure had now turned into high overspending according to the definitions of central government. Grants had been reduced, but the reduction in expenditure had not kept pace. There was continued high dissatisfaction with the distribution of resources between the various departments. The effectiveness of the organization was now perceived as being low, a continuing decline. Along with this went a much increased propensity to change the organization, and to change it in the direction of a corporate bureaucracy. That is, there was a reformative commitment. The opposition of programme directors and their subordinates to the corporate approach had been replaced by a commitment to the approach advocated by the chief executive. The logic of his arguments, the usefulness of the materials produced by the corporate analysts and, significantly, the emerging recognition of the deterioration in the fiscal context pushed people to accept the need for a corporate approach.

The shift to a reformative commitment coupled with the demonstrable expertise in corporate planning made it possible for Hill County to redirect the organization and achieve orientation. And, by 1982, Hill County had moved from an emergent professional bureaucracy to a coherent corporate bureaucracy. A number of key events occurred in this period to harness the changes in interpretive schemes from a competitive to a reformative pattern. First, there were significant changes in personnel. Especially important was the retirement of the chief executive and the promotion of an immediate subordinate who was more transformational in style. Under the new chief executive the profile of the central units was reduced which led to some resignations and early retirements. The role of the chief financial officer was developed and the incumbent assumed a more active role in promoting the virtues of a corporate approach as a way of controlling expenditure and revenue problems. Overall, there was a reduced emphasis on the centre as the corporate part of the organization and a search for a wider involvement in problem solving.

The reconceptualization of the corporate approach was structurally exemplified by the major increase in both prescribed and emergent integration. The policy committee reintroduced a land and buildings committee and set up panels to deal with critical budgetary issues, key policy initiatives and economic development. There was a proliferation of task forces created to analyse the budgetary situation, to suggest ways of raising more revenue, to examine alternative budgetary processes and to allocate resources more effectively. But these groups and panels were not allowed to wander aimlessly about their business. Senior managers ensured that they reported systematically through the management team, whose composition was expanded to include all chief officers. The management team impressed itself upon the reports that it received rather than merely acting as a post box. Essentially, Hill County had achieved an organization which accepted the corporate approach because it broadened involvement, demonstrated the potential of corporate analysis and confronted a worsening fiscal situation.

Another instructive case is Garden County. When Garden County produced its report on what its structure would be at the point of reorganization, as with the other six organizations that reoriented it embraced a corporate approach. This is, perhaps, not surprising as one of the senior officers of the organization had been a member of the Bains Working Group. The officer retired before the formal reorganization took place in 1974 but he left behind him one of his former senior managers as the new chief executive together with a cadre of managers committed to change towards the new form. This again shows the importance of initial institutional values and their presence in particular organizations as the environment of Garden County was one which could produce either a professional or corporate bureaucracy.

What was not in place, however, at the beginning of the reorientation track was a history of actually operating corporate management systems. There was, however, considerable theoretical understanding within the organization of the practices of corporate planning and analysis. For several years Garden County had sent senior officers from its programme and central departments to various seminars and management training courses at which participants were exposed to the corporate practices and experiences of (for example) Wool City and Rootley. As a result, by 1974 when reorganization occurred, Garden County had a high commitment to corporate planning and a significant cadre of managers who had an understanding, if not experience, of the structures and systems of the corporate bureaucracy.

Not surprisingly, by 1975 Garden County had made a major movement towards the implementation of a corporate bureaucracy. It had moved to a schizoid position by becoming corporate on its prescribed and emergent structures for integration and had begun to alter its systems of decision making. The changes introduced were significant. Taken together, they meant that Garden County had in place a policy and resources committee with its resource subcommittees (as recommended by the Bains Report) and cross-departmental task forces with representatives from a wide range of departments. The management team and policy committees were trying to work in concert by processing all major issues through them. Thus a framework for corporate activity was in place. Furthermore, the first traces of a policy and resource system of analysis were in place. In other words, there was a high level of initial activity which seems to be necessary to an organizational transformation.

Garden County experienced very high expenditure growth in the three years just before and after reorganization. The increase in spending was the second highest in the sample, rising by nearly 70 per cent, and no doubt contributed to the widespread feelings of satisfaction with budgets and personnel establishments. Overall organizational performance was not rated as being particularly high but it was perceived as acceptable. In other words, the level of expenditure growth was not seen as problematic despite the first signs that central government was about to cut grants.

The management team of ten senior officers was acting in concert. There was a general commitment to the direction of the organization and a solidarity in expressing it. The chief executive carefully orchestrated this within the organization. Thus, the elite acted as a collective leadership and had some view of the major changes that Garden County was undergoing. There was nothing flamboyant or charismatic about this; it was a realization of the largeness of the undertaking and the need to sell it. In addition, a small chief executive's office was built up (five people) who were the architectural 'technicians' of the system. In terms of transformational leadership and expertise, in other words, Garden County experienced the advantage of high organizational capacity.

Garden County put in place a policy and resource allocation system that went across departmental boundaries. Budgetary analysis on a topic basis as well as a departmental basis was introduced and concepts of zero-based budgeting were seriously considered. A system of regular reviews of departmental programmes was set up with the explicit aim of performance assessment. These developments helped Garden County control its expenditure. It had reacted sharply to the cuts in central government expenditure, at least partly because the local political party was strongly in favour of the action that central government was taking to curb local government expenditure. The local reaction was helped by government calculations that Garden County, despite its recent high growth in spending, was not a significant overspender. The result of the downward pressure on spending was to create dissatisfaction amongst managers over their allocations (i.e. interests) but not acutely. There was also a decline in commitment to the corporate approach (from *competitive*, in which the elite wanted change, to *indifferent*, where there were no strong views either for or against the changes that had already taken place). The organization was in a position of some indifference about change; certainly the collective leadership was exercised in a more low-key way. In a sense equilibrium had been reached.

We argued in chapter 7 on inertia, however, that with a new organizational form, as in this case, transformational activity is required to maintain it. It might be suggested that Garden County had moved to what looked like a steady state too quickly and that its hold on the new archetype might be precarious. In fact, this organization moved into the full corporate archetype category by reducing its differentiation (in particular by reformulating its committee structure so that the politicians dealt with programme areas rather than single departments). But Garden County reduced the level of its corporateness on some of the other elements of organizational design, notably the extent of emergent integration and emergent decision-making pattern.

What this suggests is that by 1982 Garden County was poised either to consolidate its corporate position – which would require a reinvigorated transformational leadership – or to begin to retreat towards the heteronomous professional bureaucracy if its structures and systems frayed further. Garden County indicates the continuous process of change and realignment.

Case Illustration: Valeden

One further case is instructive of the reorientation track. There are three organizations which are, by the standards of British local authorities, quite small. They serve populations of between 77,000 and 102,000 and employ between 500 and 750 people. All three moved from being professional bureaucracies in 1972 to being embryonic corporate bureaucracies in 1975, the largest movement of any organizations in the sample. One of these three, Valeden, illustrates a different set of dynamics to those discussed so far.

Valeden was very much the creation of the reorganization of 1974. Much of that reorganization was aimed at eliminating small, supposedly inefficient local authorities. Indeed, the Royal Commission on Local Government (1969) recommended the total demise of a second, district tier of local government and the concentration of all sub-central government services at one level of local government. However, the Conservative government did not accept these recommendations but decided that a two-tier system would be retained but with the second tier being subject to a large number of amalgamations in order to increase their size. Valeden was an amalgamation of four previous local authorities, one of which, the traditional old-established borough, was the major component of the new organization.

In 1972, immediately prior to the announcement of amalgamation, this core borough was organized as a professional bureaucracy. However, in 1973 the four constituent organizations produced a plan for Valeden under the strong influence of the Bains Working Group's recommendations and within the text of the Valeden reorganization report was a very strong commitment to the idea of corporate planning. The language of commitment was as high and articulately expressed as could be found in organizations such as Wool City, Rootley and Steeltown. Yet, the senior managers who were to run Valeden had neither experience of managing a corporate bureaucracy (as they were essentially the same people who had managed the predecessor professional bureaucracy) nor had they any theoretical understanding of the new forms. There was, however, just one senior manager (the Director of Technical Services) who had detailed understanding of the concepts and techniques, a knowledge obtained from a ten week management development course.

In other words, Valeden began in 1974 in a schizoid position. Its 'history', in so far as the original core borough provided a history (the senior managers of Valeden came from that borough and carried with them the intellectual baggage of the heteronomous professional bureaucracy), was reflected in structures and systems that resembled the professional bureaucracy format. But there were structural features lifted from the Bains Report, thus reflecting the ideas of the corporate approach.

What we see with Valeden, as with the other two smaller organizations, Cheswich and Churchtown, is the impact of institutionally approved ideas. These organizations had increased their size dramatically overnight. But their task environment was not especially complex or uncertain. The range of tasks performed by these shire districts was small compared with other local authority organizations. Therefore, one would hypothesize that the impact of environmental and task complexity, together with increased scale, would be to heighten the degree of professional bureaucracy. But these organizations had been bombarded with messages, both general and organizationally specific, about the appropriateness of corporate management. These smaller organizations, moreover, lacked experience, expertise and confidence in themselves. As a result, the institutionally prescribed form was warmly embraced in order to demonstrate that they were innovative and efficient organizations (Meyer and Rowan, 1977).

A year later in 1975, largely through the drive and initiative of the corporately committed Director of Technical Services, Valeden had taken further steps towards a corporate bureaucracy archetype, arriving at an embryonic form. Both the prescribed and emergent decision-making systems were corporate in form. The management team, in concert with the policy and resources committee, had asserted itself to be a focal point for managing policy and resource issues. Also, programme and community reviews had been added to the machinery and processes of budgetary review. Valeden began to carry out a whole series of examinations of its policy objectives and spending patterns. While this involved the setting up of one task force of managers, and some attempt to systematize the policy-making system, Valeden still remained just within the professional bureaucratic archetype on these two dimensions of emergent integration and prescribed decision-making criteria.

The external and internal features of Valeden at this time were conducive to the organization taking the further final step towards a full corporate archetype. There had been low expenditure growth, the flow of funds from central government was generally adequate and as a result there were no taxation pressures. This was coupled with a perception on the part of both politicians and managers that Valeden was a highly effective organization in fulfilling its responsibilities. Indeed their financial performance was seen as very creditable and the chief executive and the management team argued that this was due to the corporate system of reviews and routing. There was some dissatisfaction with the internal allocation of resources, but this was essentially concentrated in one section of one department, amongst the land-use planners who objected to being part of the more general technical services department under the authority of an engineer. Such dissatisfaction was containable through the concentrated power structure organized around the chief executive and his four immediate subordinates.

While for the organization as a whole there was some indifference at the beginning of the period as to the organizational form, the collective leadership was committed to continuing on the corporate track. The leadership was not directly transformational in the sense of formally recognizing the need to garner commitment and attempt to change values. However, one important leadership initiative had occurred. The chief executive recognized soon after the formal reorganization in 1974 that there was a lack of expertise in corporate planning amongst the senior managers. As a result he, and two of his subordinates, went to a number of one day seminars on corporate management. Also, he appointed a young executive assistant who had spent three years working in the corporate planning unit of a large county. Thus the leadership built up their stock of knowledge, in the process reinforcing their own commitment to a corporate approach, and they began to develop a more transformational approach to leadership.

These developments helped Valeden continue its push towards the corporate archetype. More corporate groups were introduced to carry out policy and resource allocation tasks across professional boundaries. The policy and resource allocation systems were tied together to form a coherent process involving policy groups converging on the management team, resource subcommittees and, finally, policy and resource committees. By 1978 Valeden was a fully fledged corporate bureaucracy, despite the absence of task pressures for change in this direction.

The precipitating dynamic for the culmination of the movement to the corporate archetype was the growing commitment of the elite to change. From an initial indifference the elite had become strongly committed to the corporate system but were faced with an increasingly significant number of second and third level managers articulating the virtues of a professionalized system of management. That is, there was a competitive pattern of value commitments. The articulation of opposition was possible because of the relatively dispersed structure of power which provided arenas for the disaffected minority to express grievances and dissatisfaction. The first of these propositions is not supported by the data. Admittedly, four of the organizations that reoriented were set within task contexts that would support either archetype, but three were set within contexts that provided no pressures for change. The idea that organizations 'move' because of tensions with their task environment is not supported. The second proposition, however, receives significant support. All but one of the seven began with either a competitive or reformative value commitment and the one exception moved to a competitive position over the initial three years. In other words, there is support here for the influential role of strategic commitment to particular interpretive schemes as determinants of the push for transformation. The incompatibility that seems to matter most, and which acts to lever an organization out of its prevailing situation, is that between the organization's design and the pattern of commitment to alternative interpretive schemes. The pattern of commitment can be a potent precipitating dynamic for change. We would add, however, that this precipitating dynamic acted within an institutional context favourable to the direction taken by the organizations. Whether the role of value commitments is as influential in institutional contexts that are hostile or indifferent to those ideas and values is an unanswered issue.

The precipitating role of dissatisfaction with interests is not easily assessed from the data in this chapter. Certainly, high dissatisfaction with interests is not a necessary condition for change. Two of the seven organizations had low dissatisfaction in 1975 and in 1978 four organizations still had only 'medium' dissatisfaction. It is possible that interests is a reinforcing dynamic, in that it is unlikely to play a primary role as a precipitating dynamic, and works to strengthen the push for change associated with another precipitating dynamic. Dissatisfaction with interests could be harnessed by the proponents of change and channelled towards a dissatisfaction with the prevailing archetype. How far this is the case will be explored further in chapters 9 and 10.

Much more evident is the role of organizational capability. In chapter 7 the absence of capability was found to impede the ability of an organization to implement desired changes in structures and systems. We shall find the same point reinforced by the experiences documented in chapters 9 and 10. Here we observed that all but one of the seven reorientations had a combination of significant transformational leadership combined with a high measure of expertise. It is the combination of these factors which provides the necessary enabling dynamic for the displacement of an existing archetype.

We have to stress, however, that the impact of the precipitating and enabling dynamics should not be considered independently. What matters, as is evident from the material, is their interactive effect. These seven organizations show the greatest impact of the newly institutionalized values about the necessity for a corporate form of organization. But they do so because there was at some point a strong commitment by senior management to the corporate archetype and the use of external reports and authority figures as legitimating devices for moving in that direction. The issues for all of them become twofold, namely harnessing the changes in interpretive schemes to structures and systems and ensuring the presence of the necessary understanding and expertise on how to run the new management approach. In six of the seven cases this was successfully achieved.

There are other general observations that can be made about successful reorientations. In these seven organizations can be seen both incremental and quantum change. While all of them generated a high level of activity and change in the early period, the rate of movement was particularly quick in the three smaller organizations, Valeden, Cheswich and Churchtown, which moved in three years almost fully from a professional bureaucracy archetype to a corporate bureaucracy archetype. In other words, there was a degree of quantum change facilitated by a combination of (a) their relatively small size (and the consequent lack of complexity) and (b) the fact that they were the product of mergers and amalgamations which sharpened the subsequent search for a relevant organizational form to cope with the new situation. The search resulted in an answer derived from the strong legitimating organizational messages being sent from the local government community as a whole.

The four large organizations, each employing more than 10,000 employees, were much more incremental in their approach and showed more oscillation. As large internally complex organizations, there was a greater task of moving senior management forward towards acceptance of the new ideas and of devising appropriate structures and systems for dealing with a wide range of tasks. Clearly central in the process was the building of a collective leadership which not only embraced corporate values but which had a degree of expertise in designing appropriate processes and managing change, and so could contain the levels of dissatisfaction to a manageable level. This difficulty in managing transformation in large organizations almost inevitably meant that some oscillation would occur. The path to reorientation is not smooth and uninterrupted.

The result of these problems was not to cause Valeden to move away from a corporate bureaucracy but for it to alter the basic approach to corporate working. It placed less emphasis on corporate task forces and strengthened the role of the central units. The chief executive built up a small corporate unit reporting directly to him and responsible not only for managing the policy-making system but also for carrying out the priority reviews of policy and expenditure. Of the three people involved in this unit, one came from a local manufacturing organization and two were young ambitious members of the land-use planning section. Some of the teeth of the opposition were drawn. By 1982 Valeden had completed its reorientation and was on the inertia track.

9 Retaining an Archetype: Discontinued Excursions

Introduction

Organizations on a discontinued excursion track are those that experience a limited and temporary fraying of an initial design coherence. Parts of the structure or systems become detached from the ordering assumptions of the prevailing interpretive scheme and temporary movement towards an alternative archetype occurs. There were seven organizations in the sample that commenced within a coherent archetype, moved from that archetype at some point in the study period, but ultimately returned to their place of departure. Of these seven, four began and ended the research period within the heteronomous professional bureaucracy archetype and three began from and returned to the corporate bureaucracy archetype. Overall these seven organizations managed to retain a dominant archetype, although not without struggle and difficulty.

What might produce this track of discontinued excursions? Our theory states that the organizational starting point and history is important in understanding the subsequent dynamic processes of change. The seven organizations in the study that followed this track were divided at the start according to which of the two archetypes was dominant. That is, the discussion will begin with an analysis of the four organizations that were heteronomous professional bureaucracies and then will consider the three corporate bureaucracies.

Discontinued Excursions: Heteronomous Professional Bureaucracies

The position of the four organizations of concern here in the first phase of the research are given in table 9.1. The table summarizes the

Table 9.1 Discontinued excursions: heteronomous professional bureaucracies' compatibilities between context, choice, capabilities and design, 1975

| | Contextual pressures for change | | | Choice | | | Capabilities | |
Organization	Task/ environment	Fiscal	Institutional	Values	Interest dissatisfaction	Power	Expertise	Leadership
Shipton	Medium	Medium	High	Indifferent	Medium	Concentrated	Medium	Transactional
Seaport	Medium	Low	High	Indifferent	Low	Intermediate	Low	Transactional
Forestshire	Low	High	High	Competitive	High	Intermediate	Medium	In-between
Plainshire	Low	High	High	Status quo	High	Intermediate	Low	Transactional

extent of incompatibilities between the design archetype (heteronomous professional bureaucracy) and the contextual and strategic choice variables as measured in 1975.

One of the organizations – Plainshire – did not move until 1978, which means that there should have been few significant pressures for change in the first phase. The other three organizations, in contrast, began to lose their design coherence in 1975–8; therefore, the dynamics of those changes should be located in table 8.1. As in chapter 8 a convenient analytical starting point is the context, which is shown in terms of the institutional context and the task environment context. For these organizations, of course, there were strong institutional pressures to move towards the corporate approach but there was little if any pressure from the task environment. Therefore, any movement was a reflection of strategic choice to accommodate the institutional pressures and against the pressures of the task environment.

In Shipton and Seaport there was an indifference to the prevailing and the institutionally prescribed values. Put another way, neither organization had strong resistance to change, nor did they have any strong commitment to the alternative corporate approach. However, given the institutional pressures some change was likely given the absence of resistance. In Forestshire, on the other hand, there was a competitive pattern of commitment – some favoured change, some did not. Those in favour of change were the senior managers who held greater power. Therefore, change was likely. The push for change was reinforced in Forestshire and, to a lesser extent, in Shipton by the widespread dissatisfaction with the allocation of resources produced by the existing system: i.e. there was dissatisfaction with interests. And in Seaport organizational members saw the performance of the organization as a whole as poor. So, there were elements within these organizations' profile of values and interests that would support change even if, by themselves, they would not have caused change. It was the combination of these accommodating dynamics with the precipitating dynamic of institutional pressures that caused movement.

There are other significant features of these organizations that should be noted. First, the strength of value commitment to change was usually low or, at best, competitive. Second, there was at best only a modest capability and expertise in the corporate approach. In Shipton and Seaport there was virtually no experience or expertise in managing a corporate bureaucracy. Both had a history of operating with separate professionally organized programme departments, with a senior manager – not a chief executive – acting *primus inter pares* and providing administrative and legal functions across the organization. To compound the problem, both organizations lost some of their most experienced staff to other organizations in the early post-reorganization years and failed to recruit managers who were committed to and/or knowledgeable of a corporate mode of working. Third, there was no evident transformational leadership. Only Forestshire had a combination of some expertise and some transformational leadership. These 'deficiencies', following the discussion of chapter 8, would not presage confident and quantum movements to the corporate archetype. So what happened?

Shipton, Seaport and Forestshire began to experiment with new structures. These experiments were more pronounced in Forestshire, where the organization actually reached the schizoid position over a period of three years. Forestshire's degree of enthusiasm and commitment was high amongst the senior managers (it was much less so amongst middle managers – hence the competitive pattern of commitment noted in table 9.1) and there were notable efforts to develop corporate structures and decision systems. A small (four person) corporate planning unit was established to prepare methods and procedures of corporate analysis and planning. One of its first achievements was a statement of organization-wide objectives and priorities. The unit had the support of the chief executive who had been recruited, in 1973, supposedly because he had worked in an organization which practised corporate planning. However, the basic structural pattern of the organization, together with the budget system, remained strongly professionally based. By 1978, in Forestshire, there was a mixture of corporate and professionally based structures and systems.

The structural changes in Seaport and Shipton were less guided and more modest. Some lateral teams were established to encourage an awareness of links between professional departments and an attempt was made to process various policies and programmes through a management team headed by the chief executive. The planning of policies was under scrutiny. But the scale of experimentation was essentially constrained by the absence of any real expertise or capability in the designing of corporate planning and information systems (a feature echoing the problems of Midland City in chapter 8). The experiments occurred without resistance but there was no fundamental commitment generated (because of the absence of task pressures for change and/or transformational leadership) and there was a distinct feeling that experiments were running almost on automatic pilot.

In short, Shipton and Seaport may have been receptive to the institutional pressures for the corporate approach – despite their modest relevance – but had no real understanding of how to actually practise the corporate approach, nor had they any transformational leadership highly committed to the new approach. None of the senior managers in these organizations, including the chief executives, saw the institutional movement to a corporate form with any sense of mission or major change. No structures or systems were set up to spread the message, no attempt was made to treat the corporate approach as a gospel. There was a kind of mild interest in, and acceptance of, the idea of change without any underlying vision or emotion. As a result, no momentum for change was generated early in the process. The movement toward a corporate archetype was intellectualized as a logical, self-evident step. Some degree of change was simply accepted, but it was not driven.

Between 1975 and 1978, as the various design changes were occurring, important changes were happening in the fiscal context. And the internal context was changing as organizational members responded to the worsening fiscal situation and evaluated the design experiments. A snapshot of the position in 1978 is given in table 9.2.

The external task context of Shipton and Seaport had not changed. But the intensity of the institutional pressures for change had waned and the fiscal context had deteriorated, in the sense that the general pressure on spending had intensified even though these organizations were classified by central government as 'low' overspenders. What is interesting, however, is the way in which the pressure from the fiscal environment was interpreted by members of these organizations. For, despite the fact that in absolute terms the organization was within range of government spending targets, senior officers saw the problem as being of major concern and as a reason for retreating from structural experimentation.

The picture that came through the programme of interviews and the survey data of Shipton and Seaport is that the experiment with corporate structures lacked any strong push for change, either from the immediate situational environment or from internal motivation and commitment. The wider movement for change in the institutional environment was, more or less, 'accommodated' by trial-and-error experimentation of a limited form. Over time, however, the institutional push for the corporate approach receded and the heteronomous professional bureaucracy became, once more, a legitimate format.

Table 9.2 Discontinued excursions: heteronomous professional bureaucracies' compatibilities between context, choice, capabilities and design, 1978

| Organization | Contextual pressures for change | | | | Choice | | Capabilities | |
	Task/ environment	Fiscal	Institutional	Values	Interest dissatisfaction	Power	Expertise	Leadership
Shipton	Medium	Low	Medium	Status quo	Medium	Concentrated	Medium	Transactional
Seaport	Medium	Low	Medium	Indifferent	Low	Intermediate	Low	Transactional
Forestshire	Low	Medium	Medium	Indifferent	Medium	Intermediate	Low	In-between
Plainshire	Low	Medium	Medium	Status quo	Medium	Intermediate	Low	Transactional

Resurrection of the latter format essentially indicated to Shipton and Seaport – whose managers were largely indifferent to the corporate approach – that prevailing and traditional arrangements were acceptable: experimentation with new forms was not necessary. Moreover, the fiscal environment was changing in a manner that led managers to favour a return to known and tested organizational responses rather than continued experimentation with unclear and little understood ideas. These organizations did not, in fact, face significant overspending, but the strength of the message for restraint in the fiscal context persuaded senior managers not to risk losing control of expenditure. The attraction of tried and proven resource allocation mechanisms increased. The desire to return to understood arrangements was keenest in Shipton (hence the *status quo* commitment pattern – i.e. a commitment to the heteronomous professional bureaucracy – reported in table 9.2).

The same fiscal and institutional factors operated upon Forestshire in a rather more serious form. First, the level of overspending was greater and an issue of considerable concern. Second, the decline in the institutional support for the corporate approach had a serious impact upon the degree of support to the experiments taking place. We have already noted that the extent of experimentation was further advanced in Forestshire than the other authorities, because of the greater expertise. This expertise was located in a small corporate planning unit working to the chief executive. Three members of the unit were young highly educated 'whizz kids' recruited at the point of reorganization in 1974. To enhance their credibility in a professionally based organization (especially where there was *opposition* at middle management to the new system) a long-term administrator was appointed as head of the unit, a man with 20 years' service in the organization, an unparalleled network of contacts inside and outside the organization and considerable respect and trust from senior managers. Essentially, his role was to build commitment to the new approach, i.e. an initial institutional leadership structure was built. However, this structure clearly failed to build widespread commitment (hence the 'indifference' reported in table 9.2).

So, there would have been problems in maintaining the direction of change in Forestshire. In fact, the experiments collapsed and Forestshire became a coherent heteronomous professional bureaucracy. Partly, it may have been a consequence of pressures from the task environment – the corporate experiments were moving the organization *out* of a position of alignment. To us, however, of greater significance was the decline of expertise caused by the departure of key members of the corporate planning unit to other organizations (expertise fell to 'low' in 1978) and a decline in the commitment of senior managers (the pattern of commitments fell from competitive to indifferent). A crucial loss of support was the increasing disinterest of the chief executive.

It is intriguing to speculate on why the chief executive lost interest. One reason was that the level of his commitment to corporate planning was not particularly intense – he was in no sense an evangelist, emotionally and fervently believing in the corporate approach (in the way that Wool City's chief executive could be described). So in the face of opposition within the organization and reduced 'legitimation' from the institutional context, his position was increasingly uncomfortable. Nor could he strengthen his position by manipulating the kinds of change levers available to business sector counterparts. In the organizations dealt with here the chief executive does not have direct control over senior appointments. They are in an advisory role to politicians. Nor do chief executives have the power to dismiss senior management. Thus, the management of the degree of opposition or the distillation and dissemination of a new culture, through changes in personnel, is very difficult. Finally, the chief executive became involved in national activities which increasingly absorbed his energies and time. In effect, Forestshire suffered a decline in its capability to design corporate systems, a reduction in transformational leadership, a loss of commitment to the corporate approach and a decline in institutional support, all set within a task context that did not need corporate activities.

In summarizing the above discussion two general points can be made. First, the three organizations discussed thus far are similar to those that followed the inertial track in that they began the period with a congruence between design arrangements and the task and environmental context (levels of complexity). But these organizations, unlike those along the inertial track, lost that congruence, albeit temporarily. This confirms the point made at the end of chapter 8, that the pressures for congruence arising from task and environmental contexts can be overriden, at least temporarily, by a combination of institutional prescriptions for change and particular configurations of strategic choice. In chapter 7 we noted that Home County retained its heteronomous professional bureaucracy archetype despite the prescriptions of the institutional environment. The organizations discussed in this chapter, on the other hand, exhibited a fraying of the archetype. The difference between Home County and the three organizations that experienced some fraying of their archetype is in the degree of commitment within the organization to prevailing arrangements. In Home County there was a clear *status quo* commitment – hence, no change. In Seaport, Shipton and Forestshire there was either an indifferent commitment (thus enabling the institutional pressures to influence events) or a competitive commitment to change. This implies that strong institutional prescriptions plus a pattern of indifferent or powerful reformist value commitments will result in some change even where the changes create incompatibilities of design with the environmental context.

Second, the above conclusions refer to the precipitating dynamics that cause some organizations to lose their design coherence despite the initial compatibility between the prevailing design and the task context. An equally important question is why the changes introduced are abandoned. One set of answers is to do with the capability of the organization in terms of expertise and transformational leadership. The fact is that not one of the four organizations had a combination of high expertise and high transformational leadership. This suggests that maintenance of change requires the enabling dynamics of high expertise and high transformational leadership or (a possibility not illustrated in the above organizations) a continued pressure for change from the pattern of commitments.

We have said little of Plainshire. One reason for this is that this organization did not change at the same time as Shipton, Seaport and Forestshire. Whereas these three altered their structures in the years between 1972 and 1975 and had abandoned the experiments by 1978, Plainshire altered its structures in 1975–8 and reversed them between 1978 and 1982. That is, Plainshire experimented later than Seaport, Shipton and Forestshire. Furthermore, there was nothing in the profile of Plainshire's circumstances either in 1975 or 1978 that would suggest the likelihood of structural change. Its existing design was compatible with both the task context and the internal profile of values (a *status quo* pattern of value commitment). There was, it is true, some dissatisfaction with the way in which interests were being met but not with overall organizational performance. Here is a profile of an organization that we would predict would pursue an inertial track.

It would be misleading to suggest that a definitive answer can be given to the question as to why, for two to three years following 1975, a series of corporate developments took place in Plainshire. In particular, there was a strengthening of the routing of policy plans and budget proposals through a corporate team at the centre of the senior officer structure and the preparation of embryonic overall objectives and reviews of performance. Certainly the data in tables 8.1 and 8.2 provide no explanation. Some interesting suggestions can still be made. First of all, it has to be remembered that the degree of structural change was much less pronounced than in the other three organizations. Second, by the end of 1976 Plainshire was experiencing, for the first time, serious financial difficulties. It was in a position of high growth (its year-on-year increases since 1974 were very high relative to other organizations) and its levels of spending were noticeably higher than government targets. These trends were seen as a crisis by both politicians and managers. Plainshire was, and is, a traditional Conservative rural local authority where financial probity was regarded as an important value. High expenditure growth and a pattern of significant overspending was widely interpreted as meaning that (a) spending was out of control and (b) existing structural and budgetary arrangements must be inadequate. The labelling of the fiscal situation as a crisis inevitably led to a search for ways of better controlling expenditure.

The above story was borne out by the interviews conducted with managers in the organization. What we do not know is why they adopted structural solutions of a corporate form. Probably, they did so because they were 'there' in the institutional environment and had been proclaimed as the appropriate approach. Moreover, a common reaction to problems of perceived overspending is to tighten and centralize control. Thus, in Plainshire, the role of the management team was strengthened within the budget process: the chief executive appointed an assistant to conduct expenditure reviews, which led to some aspects of rational–analytic procedures being developed. All of this marked a departure from the professionally centred decentralized organization. Because of the value commitment to professional forms of organizing, however, plus the low capability to follow through the initial experimentation with new arrangements and the absence of transformational leadership, the experiment was short-lived. What we have is genuine experimentation. Plainshire illustrates, we believe, a third general point, which is that the process of change is influenced by the timing of critical events and the way that these are interpreted by organizational members.

Thus, the fiscal crisis was interpreted in three organizations as sufficient cause to *abandon* experiments, in favour of resumption of well-understood organizational practices – the heteronomous professional bureaucracy – which were not identified as the cause of the problem. The same fiscal crisis was interpreted in Plainshire as sufficient cause to *initiate* experiments with corporate arrangements because the prevailing professional bureaucracy format was associated with the fiscal problem.

In other words, very different responses (experimentation versus retreat) can follow the same events (in this case, fiscal pressure) depending upon the history of the organization and the associations between events and structures as perceived (interpreted) by strategic members.

Discontinued Excursions: Corporate Bureaucracies

There were three organizations that began in 1973 with a coherent set of structures and systems which constitute the corporate bureaucracy archetype, lost some of their internal coherence and subsequently returned to the archetype. Given the strong institutional pressures the puzzling feature is that there was movement *out* of the archetype. The relevant data are summarized in tables 9.3 and 9.4.

Each of these three organizations operated within environments that were ambivalent in terms of their relevance to the corporate and professional design archetypes. That is, the environment was moderately complex but by no means as complex as those of, for example, Wool City and Midland City. There were urban problems but of a more diminished scale and urgency: moreover, the areas served were more affluent and less densely populated. Task complexity, on the other hand, was high in Rootley and Milltown, although noticeably lower in Steeltown. These characteristics of the task and environmental context imply that the corporate and professional model were equally relevant and would be equally ill-fitting. That is, there would be some pressures or strains of accommodation between external context and design type.

The dominant feature within the organizations, in 1975, was the *status quo* pattern of value commitments. That is, there was a widespread commitment to the values of the corporate approach throughout senior and middle managers. There was compatibility

Table 9.3 Discontinued excursions: corporate bureaucracies' compatibilities between context, choice, capabilities and design, 1975

Organization	Contextual pressures for change			Choice			Capabilities	
	Task/ environment	*Fiscal*	*Institutional*	*Values*	*Interest dissatisfaction*	*Power*	*Expertise*	*Leadership*
Rootley	High/medium	High	Low	*Status quo*	Medium	Dispersed	High	Intermediate
Steeltown	Medium/low	Medium	Low	*Status quo*	High	Concentrated	High	Transformational
Milltown	Medium	Very high	Low	*Status quo*	Medium	Intermediate	High	Intermediate

Table 9.4 Discontinued excursions: corporate bureaucracies' compatibilities between context, choice, capabilities and design, 1978

Organization	Contextual pressures for change			Choice			Capabilities	
	Task/ environment	*Fiscal*	*Institutional*	*Values*	*Interest dissatisfaction*	*Power*	*Expertise*	*Leadership*
Rootley	High/medium	Low	Medium	*Status quo*	High	Intermediate	Medium	Intermediate
Steeltown	Medium/low	Very high	Medium	*Status quo*	Medium	Concentrated	High	Transformational
Milltown	Medium	Medium	Medium	Competitive	High	Intermediate	Medium	Intermediate

between this aspect of strategic choice and design arrangements. As a result, the configuration of the power structure was not important. The picture in 1978 was very similar, in that two of the organizations retained their *status quo* value commitment. Milltown, in contrast, had a competitive commitment but the elite wished to retain the *status quo* and had a concentrated power structure through which to do so. The clear prediction for these organizations, therefore, in terms of value commitments, was that they would remain as corporate bureaucracies throughout the period in much the same fashion as Wool City and Northern City.

In one sense the prediction was borne out in that the organizations remained around the corporate archetype for the full period and were within it for most of the period. In effect, these organizations reinforce the conclusion that patterns of value commitment are signally important as predictors of design choice irrespective of the high dissatisfaction with interests. There were differences, however, between these organizations and those corporately organized organizations that remained on the inertial track (i.e. Wool City and Northern City) and it is important to explore what these were, otherwise differences between the dynamics of the inertia and discontinued excursion tracks will be obscured.

Earlier it was suggested that modest change in structural coherence might occur for one or more of three reasons. There might be genuine experimentation with structural forms, especially in situations of recently established arrangements. There might be pressures from the inner or outer context to change. There might be 'drift' as an organization unwittingly loses coherence and then reasserts it as, and if, performance is affected. The first and third of these explanations appear relevant in Steeltown, Milltown and Rootley. All three experienced a measure of witting experimentation as they attempted to 'sort out' the benefits of the matrix and monocratic subvariants of the corporate archetype (Greenwood and Stewart, 1973). And all three made changes that were not evidently thought through in terms of the overall archetype. Some of these changes are illustrated below.

It is important, however, in outlining the events in these organizations to be able to explain why the degree of experimentation and drift in these organizations was greater than in Wool City and Northern City. In fact, the explanation rests with the combination of the other strategic variables although the particular interplay and interpretation is unique to each organization.

Rootley is an example where the strong and widespread commitment to the corporate approach 'allowed' only modest movement out of the archetype. Put simply, that movement was a function of (a) the external contextual pressures, which led managers to have a low perception of overall organizational performance and a feeling of the need 'to do something' in order to improve and (b) the need to work out the appropriate form of corporate working and to simplify the numerous experiments that had occurred in a short space of time.

Rootley, in 1975, had a high measure of organizational capability and transformational leadership. The chief executive, the directors of finance and administration and the senior corporate planning officer represented an institutional transformational leadership structure. They recognized the need to proclaim and sell their views continuously to other managers and politicians. Like Wool City they were interested in innovation and experimentation and became famous nationally for their schemes of area-based administration (which initiated in the directorate of administration) and their documents of corporate decision analysis (e.g. 'position statements', 'key issue analysis', 'community reviews'). Not only did these experiments attract national attention, they brought special programme funding into the organization from central government. Senior managers were quick to proclaim the virtues of the corporate approach and its responsibility for the special financial attention.

Rootley experimented much more than did Wool City or Northern City. In fact, Rootley introduced structural changes which were considered and rejected by Wool City. We believe that the problem of Rootley was that the transformational leadership was too broadly spread and the experiments occurring were not fully coordinated, i.e. there was a tension between those experiments consistent with the matrix version of corporate planning and those that were more consistent with the monocratic variant. Within this general receptivity to change and structural experimentation the service chief officers were seeking to improve service delivery on a professional basis. In effect, there was a lack of clarity in the direction and architecture of change. The underlying commitment to the corporate approach, however, prevented Rootley from spinning far from the corporate archetype.

By 1978 two things had happened to enable the organization to recover its coherence. First, the structure of the transformational leadership had changed. Various key figures had left the organization and the remaining leadership centred around the chief executive and the director of finance. There was, in short, a focusing of the elite. Second, there was the worsening of the fiscal context. It has become clear that this part of the environment was of considerable importance to the whole organizational population, although of particular import- ance was the way in which the issue was seen as a crisis, and how it was linked to existing policy-making arrangements. Warren (1984), in his study of Antioch College, points out the importance of a fiscal crisis as a lever for change in a public organization. In Rootley, the *rate* of spending growth was high, starting from a low base, and the level of overspending of government targets was low. However, the organization was controlled by the Conservative Party which identified itself with fiscal restraint and made it clear to managers that tighter controls over spending would be imposed. The chief executive and director of finance were not in a position to 'blame' the corporate approach for the high level of spending, given that Rootley had a national image of corporate progressiveness – an image which the senior managers enjoyed. It would have been difficult to jettison the corporate approach given the additional resources attracted from central government for the purpose of furthering understanding of that approach. (In fact, the chief executive did not wish to overthrow the corporate approach although, privately, he was lukewarm on the merits of the area-based system of policy making.) The natural course of events was a move towards a more internally consistent organizational design with stronger control at the centre. This is what happened. The organization moved from a dispersed power structure towards the concentrated form – it became more centralized and more concentrated. The elite, in effect, took more control. Again, therefore, we see elite values interpreting external events (the fiscal shift) and the importance of the temporal and evaluative context as influences upon the interpretation.

Steeltown, in all essentials, followed the same pattern and dynamics as Rootley. It was a situation in which a degree of experimentation around the corporate archetype occurred, until the fiscal crisis developed. The scale of the crisis was, in absolute terms, more serious in Steeltown than in most other organizations. Spending was way above government targets and the trend of expenditure growth was steeply upwards. In 1978 the chief executive reacted to the deterioration in the fiscal scene by stressing the importance of the corporate approach to the preparation of priorities and cutbacks. Again, he was hardly in a position to do otherwise. Steeltown, like Rootley and Wool City, had been selected as an organization worthy of additional funding and as a site of research, because of its corporately based approach to environmental problems. This national prominence effectively circumscribed the abilities of senior managers to abandon corporate structures. In fact, the chief executive was a highly successful salesman and architect of the corporate approach and restored the original coherence.

Milltown is different. We have suggested that Steeltown and Rootley drifted out of coherence through a process of resolving discrepancies of matrix and monocratic variations of the corporate theme, coupled with a measure of 'drift'. The impact of worsening fiscal conditions was instrumental in pulling the organizations into line with basic value commitments. In Milltown, in contrast, there was less evidence of drift and experimentation (or sorting out) and a greater suggestion that the level of commitment to the corporate approach was less stable.

Before 1974 Milltown was one of the most corporately inclined organizations in the whole organizational population. In drawing up its new organization in 1973 it produced a strong statement of intent committing it to corporate management. Along with Wool City and Rootley, Milltown was in the forefront of corporate development with both experience and expertise. Yet, during the period between 1973 and 1975, the managers and politicians responsible for the policy and direction of the organization saw it as performing badly. Much of that poor performance was seen as due to the time-consuming nature and perceived ineffectiveness of the corporate groups that made up the matrix organization. Decision making had become confused and directionless. Various integrative mechanisms (resource and policy committees, corporate task forces) were disbanded. Participation was desultory rather than energetic.

For the dominant coalition (trying to operate within an open matrix, underpinned by a somewhat decentralized power structure) the initial recasting of the structure was an attempt to deal with the issues of low perceived performance and some interest dissatisfaction. But one of the things that becomes important is how such changes are perceived by others in the organization and also what simultaneous changes are occurring elsewhere. Internally the changes were seen by some members of the organization as signs that the corporate form was no longer predominant. Externally, Milltown began to face financial pressure and, in the institutional context, alternatives to the corporate form of organization had become legitimate once again. Taken together these led to the emergence of a small 'opposition group' within this organization, committed to change in the direction of a professional bureaucracy. In other words, there was more (initially latent) opposition to the corporate approach than in the other organizations and the loss of coherence was less one of experimentation and drift than of struggle and disillusionment. Of course, by 1978 it had become institutionally legitimate to critically appraise and oppose the corporate form and in Milltown this occurred – hence the competitive pattern of value commitment. However, the return to coherence of design was enabled by the concentrated power structure. The senior elite impressed their interpretation of appropriate structural arrangements upon a growing number of managers who were highly dissatisfied with the pattern of interests and low in commitment to the values of a corporate bureaucracy. Such a position is much more fragile and less stable than the position of Steeltown or Rootley.

Conclusions

An evident conclusion from the analysis of Steeltown, Milltown and Rootley is that several of the themes already noted are confirmed. Perhaps the most important of these is the way in which the biography of an organization affects its interpretation of particular events. Thus, it was noticeable that in all three organizations – but especially in Steeltown and Rootley – the organizations had histories which effectively 'locked' them into a corporate way of working. By becoming prominent on the national scene, receiving additional government resources and by becoming sites of government research and advocates (at conferences and educational institutions) or 'their' way of doing things, managers become locked into ways of working even though the legitimacy of those ways of working may decline (but *not*, in these cases, disappear). These organizations had invested too much into the ideas of the corporate approach to overthrow them easily. As a result, changing financial circumstances caused a strengthening of resolve in favour of the corporate archetype.

A second point that we would make concerns the importance of transformational leadership and organizational capability. In all three organizations there was considerable understanding of the corporate notion and a degree of emotional commitment to it. But corporate systems were new and as such organizations entertained structural experimentation. This can lead to loss of coherence until and if the leadership initiates the drive for tighter coherence which in these cases occurred as a consequence of precipitating events in the fiscal context. Transformational leadership, we noted earlier, is necessary to sustain a new archetypal form even where that form has been formally adopted. There is no necessary momentum of the system that prevents drift and oscillation. Furthermore, the leadership has to be focused rather than diffuse. Rootley illustrates, in contrast to Wool City, how a cacophony of structural experiments can cause the loss of coherence even in the context of strong transformational leadership. Transformational leadership has to be focused.

A third point is more tentative. The three organizations with which we have been concerned were faced with ambivalent task contexts. Implicitly, much of organization theory, especially contingency theory, suggests that situational pressures will work in the same direction. If this is the case, the senior managers will receive a coherent signal for change or for inertia. However, with a mixed or ambivalent signal, as in these organizations, there is a greater probability that groups in an organization will interpret the meaning of those environmental signals. Depending on the particular mix of value commitments and power, this can lead either to relative inertia through the dominance of a particular structural form or to oscillation as alternative forms are put forward. But the organization will experience pressures from the environment which, in the absence of determined transformational leadership, can lead to modest experimentation and drift from coherence as parts of the organization seek to handle the ambivalent or inconsistent pressures.

Because of the importance of the relationship and total position, the long-run difficulties of a managerial choice based purely on a value position are illustrated. This is because such choices may create a contradiction with contextual pressures; also the operational structures and systems consequent on a particular value position may be poorly understood. The leaders, the senior managers, may not have the necessary knowledge and expertise at their disposal.

The situation is seen particularly in the organizations that started and ended as heteronomous professional bureaucracies. They were under strong institutional pressure (and some contextual pressure) to change. However, the senior managers lacked expertise, knowledge and leadership to guide the organization through the tensions that were created by the changes introduced. As might be expected from the nature of both archetypes the content of the organizational change away from the professional archetype was common; it was systems rather than structure oriented. All four of these organizations changed their systems of decision making, pattern and criteria, prescribed and emergent, into a corporate form. It is in the form and content of decision making that the crux of archetype meaning is found. Changing decision making presents the greatest challenge to a professional. The involvement of non-professionals, whether through task forces or by the intervention of chief executives, sharpens the value conflicts and has the potential to change resource allocation. Clearly this is a high impact system (Kanter, 1984).

Thus, the professional bureaucracies that went on a discontinued excursion were coping with a value propensity to change, contextual pressures to change, interest dissatisfaction, a less centralized power system, low capability in corporate management and transactional leadership. As a result of the tensions engendered they travelled a fair distance along the change track before returning.

Those organizations that started as corporate bureaucracies were in a different situation. Their major pressures were material, arising from a changing fiscal situation and consequential interest dissatisfaction. However, there were less likely to be competing values, the leadership structure and style was more transformational in nature and there was considerable expertise in managing corporate systems. Where this was less the case, in Milltown, the organization seemed poised for yet another excursion. In a sense all three of these organizations show 'low-level oscillation', movement around an archetype rather than between archetypes. However, in such movement there is the possibility that the changes create the possibility of further movement away from the archetype. Whether such movement and fragility will develop is liable to be dependent on two things.

First, there has to be some kind of articulated alternative organization form. Without an articulated archetype change will follow known and established patterns, i.e. there will be more of the same (Starbuck et al., 1978). Second, there has to be a leadership and power situation which allows those alternatives to be expressed in arenas that matter. Change can be blocked through a concentrated power structure (elite domination) and/or an active, transformational leadership that continuously reaffirms the importance, efficiency and effectiveness of the current archetype.

10 Unresolved Excursions

Introduction

Unresolved excursions occur where there is a failure to obtain design coherence over a period of time. These tracks are examples of failed or resisted attempts at reorientation. In this situation an organization remains in an intermediate category – i.e. between archetypes – over a long period of time. The track is potentially a very important one because of its neglect in the study of organization. There is a very real attraction to studying successful change, but the study of organizational change has to encompass both aborted and unresolved excursions. Miller and Friesen (1984), for example, cite five configurations, covering over one-third of their sample, that lacked coherence. Chapter 6 demonstrated that there were six organizations in our sample which followed this track.

The unresolved track has several patterns within it. That is, organizations classed as travelling along the track exhibit important differences in terms of the starting point, degree of oscillation and direction of movement. Table 10.1 shows these patterns. The first difference between the six organizations is whether they began from a position of coherence. Two organizations – Leafy County and Coastal County – began from the heteronomous professional bureaucracy (i.e. the institutionally *pro*scribed form) and moved partially towards the corporate archetype. In examining the dynamics of these two organizations we have to understand, first, why movement occurred but, second, remained incomplete. Four organizations were in an intermediate position between the two archetypes for the full ten year period. In many respects these organizations run counter to one of the basic hypotheses underlying the ideas of design archetypes and tracks, namely that organizations observed in an embryonic or schizoid state will move towards an archetypal position. The idea of 'momentum' or gravitational pull suggests that for organizations to spend up to ten years in an embryonic or schizoid state should be highly unlikely – although this begs the very important issue raised by our work, namely the periodicity of strategic change in organizations. Indeed, these four organizations are the ones that deny the idea that organizations gravitate towards a full and coherent archetype.

A second distinction may be drawn from table 10.1. Certain organizations – notably Southton, Seaside and Coalport – demonstrate circumstances of relatively stable unresolution. That is, they were never within, and usually not close to, organizational coherence, resisting all gravitational pulls, and they did not oscillate in any significant manner. Such stability contrasts with the greater degree of movement observed in Leafy County and Navalport. Coastal County is different again in that there was stability which was close to organizational coherence. The dynamics that produce stable unresolution are probably different to those that produce oscillation and it will be necessary to tease out these differences.

What, then, might produce these patterns of unresolved excursions? We would expect that Leafy County and Coastal County, the two organizations that began from a coherent archetype design, would

Table 10.1 Unresolved excursion tracks

Organization	1972	1975	1978	1982
Pattern 1				
Leafy County	PB[a]	EPB[b]	Schizoid	Schizoid
Coastal County	PB	EPB	EPB	EPB
Pattern 2				
Seaside	EC[c]	Schizoid	Schizoid	Schizoid
Southton	Schizoid	Schizoid	Schizoid	Schizoid
Coalport	Schizoid	Schizoid	EPB	Schizoid
Navalport	Schizoid	EPB	EPB	Schizoid

[a] Professional bureaucracy
[b] Embryonic professional bureaucracy
[c] Embryonic corporate bureaucracy

Table 10.2 Unresolved excursions: compatibilities between context, choice, capability and design, 1975

Organization	Contextual pressures for change			Choice			Capabilities	
	Task/ environment	Fiscal	Institutional	Values	Interest dissatisfaction	Power	Expertise	Leadership
Leafy County	Low	High	High	Reformative	Low	Intermediate	Medium	Intermediate
Coastal County	Low	Medium	High	Status quo	Low	Intermediate	Low	Transactional
Seaside	High	Medium/high	Low	Indifferent	High	Intermediate	High	Intermediate
Southton	High	Medium	High	Competing	High	Concentrated	Low	Transactional
Coalport	High	High	High	Status quo	Low	Intermediate	Low	Transactional
Navalport	Low	Low	High	Status quo	Low	Intermediate	Low	Transactional

Table 10.3 Unresolved excursions: compatibilities between context, choice, capability and design, 1978

Organization	Contextual pressures for change			Choice			Capabilities	
	Task/ environment	Fiscal	Institutional	Values	Interest dissatisfaction	Power	Expertise	Leadership
Leafy County	High	High	Medium	Competing	Medium	Intermediate	Low	Transactional
Coastal County	Low	High	Medium	Status quo	Low	Intermediate	Low	Transactional
Seaside	High	High	Medium	Indifferent	High	Dispersed	Medium	Intermediate
Southton	High	Medium	Medium	Indifferent	Medium	Intermediate	Low	Transactional
Coalport	Low	Very high	Medium	Status quo	Medium	Intermediate	Low	Transactional
Navalport	Low	Medium	Medium	Status quo	Low	Intermediate	Low	Transactional

exhibit similar circumstances to the three heteronomous professional bureaucracies that broke from their coherence and the seven organizations that reoriented. That is, there would be a pattern of value commitments that is not one favouring the *status quo*. We have already noted that a reformative or competitive commitment almost always leads to change. We have also found that an indifferent commitment, combined with strong institutional pressures for change, can lead to change. Unlike the reorienting organizations, however, there should be an absence of the enabling dynamic of transformational leadership and expertise. The failure to reorientate will be connected to inadequate capacity. Unlike the discontinued excursions, however, the changing fiscal context would not be interpreted as justifying retreat from the experiments. There will be something continuing to press for change without being able to secure resolution.

The four organizations that began in a position of unresolution – i.e. between archetypes – would certainly lack the enabling dynamics for change towards the corporate approach but would have some dynamics pressing consistently in that direction. There would be no waning of the pressure for change. The relevant data are given in tables 10.2 and 10.3.

The Dynamics of Unresolved Excursions

Pattern 1: Moving from an archetype

We have pulled out Coastal County and Leafy County as requiring separate discussion because there are two sets of explanation required. We need to know why they broke from the prevailing archetype and, second, why they did not complete a reorientation or return to their starting point. There may be similarities with the discontinued excursions and the reorientations in answering the first question, but there should be differences when answering the second.

In 1972 both Leafy County and Coastal County operated as coherent heteronomous professional bureaucracies and had done so for many years. By 1975 both organizations had moved towards the corporate archetype. The task context did not act to precipitate change. Throughout the period the degree of task complexity was 'low' to 'medium' and was much more in tune with a professional bureaucracy arrangement than the corporate alternative. So, once again, we see the organization changing *despite* its task context not because of it. Leafy County, however, had a reformative pattern of value commitment. There was a strong and universally shaped belief in the need for movement towards the corporate model – in effect, the managers had adopted the ideas disseminated from the institutional context even though they were not dissatisfied with organizational performance or critical of existing resource allocations and they had an organizational form appropriate for the task context. Furthermore, they had a significant amount of organizational capability. This combination of precipitating and enabling dynamics is exactly the combination which was found to produce organizational reorientations. Not surprisingly, therefore, by 1975 Leafy County had altered its structures and systems sufficiently to become an embryonic professional bureaucracy and would, over the next three years, move even further towards the corporate archetype.

This general movement away from the professional bureaucracy format was understandable both because of the institutional pressures and also because of Leafy County's stated intention in 1973 of becoming corporate. In a report produced then, detailing its future direction when the 'new' organization appeared on 1 April 1974, it stated the need to move towards a more corporate form while retaining the best of the professional bureaucracy. To do this an Assistant Chief Executive was appointed (one of very few such appointments in the country) whose responsibility was to oversee the development of the corporate process, assisted by a small central staff. The organization had reflected upon corporate approaches to organization and in the Assistant Chief Executive and a few others had staff with experience and expertise. So, by 1975, Leafy County was on the move away from its original archetype.

Change towards the corporate archetype occurred until 1978. However, by 1978 there were also changes taking place in the values and interests of managers, as well as the continuation of contextual pressures for change. The fiscal context was deteriorating sharply. Leafy County was classified as significantly overspending and was criticized by the central government. Cuts in expenditure growth were necessary and were introduced. One consequence was a marked rise in dissatisfaction with the pattern of resource allocations (i.e. with interests) and a decline in perceived organizational performance. As noted earlier, the onset of problems with resources can be interpreted by people in the organization as furthering the relevance of the new system or as triggering a desire to return to tried and trusted traditional arrangements. In Leafy County it was the latter that occurred. The heteronomous professional bureaucracy was seen as a surer, more tried organizational form for dealing with issues of resource allocation. The problems of overspending and the visible dissatisfaction with budget allocations were, in part, connected to the experimentation with a corporate archetype.

One aspect of Leafy County's evolving circumstances, which shows the interaction of the precipitating and enabling dynamics, was the loss in 1976–7 of three of the key corporate designers, including the Assistant Chief Executive, to other organizations. These were important losses to Leafy County because they were not replaced. For reasons of economy the small staff reporting to the Assistant Chief Executive was dispersed. As a consequence there was a decline in organizational capability at a time of fiscal challenge. The loss of capability and the symbolic act of cutting the central corporate unit contributed to the disillusionment of middle managers who were required to work the new corporate structures and yet failed to perceive their relevance to their task situation. In Clark's (1972) terms, corporate planning was a precarious value and these changes underlined its fragility. The chief executive and the immediate senior managers reporting to him, while favouring the corporate approach, lacked the necessary transformational skills, time, expertise and ability to continue the process towards reorientation. By 1978 Leafy County had a competitive pattern of value commitments and lacked organizational commitment. It could neither advance towards the corporate archetype (because it lacked the necessary organizational capability) nor retreat to the professional bureaucracy (because of the commitments of the senior managers).

Given the mixture of pressures and tensions acting upon Leafy County we would anticipate that it would not stay unresolved. The only dynamics for change towards reorientation were the value commitments of senior managers plus the waning institutional pressures. The mix of precipitating factors working in the other direction plus the strong enabling capability of managing the professional bureaucracy is likely to outweigh the push for change.

Coastal County is unlike Leafy County, except in that it moved from a coherent organizational design to the embryonic category. From 1975 until 1982 it remained in the embryonic position. Why did it move given that its profile of precipitating and enabling dynamics would not predict any movement? Coastal County should have remained as an heteronomous professional bureaucracy, i.e. on the inertia track. Our model cannot explain why this organization moved except with reference to the institutional pressures. Importantly, perhaps, the changes in Coastal County were only modest and concerned the use of prescribed integrative structures (i.e. use of interdepartmental teams and resource allocation committees of politicians). That is, there was a shift from the coherent archetype, running counter to the role of the precipitating and enabling dynamics discussed so far, but to a position close to the archetype.

One might have expected a fairly short discontinued excursion in this organization. However, interestingly, the discordant structures were retained in order to cope with the emerging pressure on resources caused by the organization's high expenditure growth and overspending. Coastal County continued to utilize both teams and task forces of managers to examine ways of controlling expenditure and build up central committees of politicians to look at across-the-board issues of resources allocation. The corporate structures at Coastal County were never used to look at substantive policy issues; their focus was expenditure control. Thus it never took on the full meaning of a corporate bureaucracy archetype.

This usage of a limited range of corporate structures for purposes of expenditure control was also found in Navalport (which is considered more properly under pattern 2 below).

In Navalport the organization seemed to be on track for a discontinued excursion by 1978, when it was rocked by problems of overspending. While the rate of overspending was only slightly above the average for the sample, the overspending followed several years of very low actual expenditure growth. As a result the amount of funds from central government became problematic and Navalport was faced with the possibility of politically unacceptably large tax increases. There was a strong perception of a fiscal crisis. The organizational outcome was the continued use of political committees to examine expenditure patterns, personnel downsizing and land disposition, together with marked changes in both the prescribed and emergent patterns of decision making. In particular, the management team of the organization began to be a resource allocation group, in marked contrast to its previous role as a minder of administrative housekeeping matters. So, as in Coastal County, a corporate oriented structure was brought into play to deal with problems of resource allocation; the focus was expenditure not policy.

Pattern 2: Initial and Sustained Unresolution

Three (Seaside, Coalport, Navalport) of the four organizations that began in 1972–3 with a mixture of corporate and non-corporate structures remained so, once again, despite a task context that was more appropriate for a heteronomous professional bureaucracy. This is not surprising because they were particularly susceptible[1] to the ideas prescribed by the Bains Report. These three organizations are small relative to the other organizations in the sample and in 1972 two of them had little understanding or expertise in the corporate approach. They had not taken advantage of the various management development courses that gave training in the corporate approach and the senior positions in the organizations were filled by existing personnel rather than through external recruiting.

Seaside was rather different in that certain senior positions were filled by officers with a deeper understanding of the corporate approach and of the need for transformational leadership. This organization had more organizational capability in corporate planning than any of the other five organizations on this track. However, much of this capability had left the organization by 1978.

In effect, at the beginning of the research period the three organizations 'looked like' the diagrams contained within the Bains Report. They had adopted the primarily structural prescriptions wholesale. The prescribed framework of these organizations conformed to the clearest available expression of the institutionally preferred design archetype. However, in all three organizations there were no worked-out systems or processes to ensure that planning was done and resource decisions were made on a corporate basis. In other words, they showed themselves to be doing the opposite of Kanter's (1984) emphasis on high-impact systems: they were tinkering with the prescribed framework and assuming that systems and emergent practices would follow.

Interestingly, the pattern of value commitments was either indifferent (Seaside) or favoured the *status quo*. Despite the inadequacy of the organizational form in that it was not fully corporate, as had been intended, there was no desire to change it. This satisfaction with, or indifference to, prevailing arrangements continued into 1978, despite the arrival of financial problems and, as a consequence, no changes were made to move back towards the professional bureaucracy. Lacking the enabling dynamic of an organizational capability in the corporate format (by 1978 Seaside had lost its capability), the full adoption of the corporate archetype was not possible. In effect there were no precipitating or enabling dynamics for change in either direction, other than the task context which, as we have learned from earlier chapters, was overridden by patterns of commitment.

Southton, however, was different. In many ways it resembled Wool City (which had become a coherent corporate bureaucracy before 1972 and remained as such through the full period of the research) in its high task complexity. Southton was a metropolitan district with a population of over 250,000 and having a wide range of functions. It faced high environmental complexity. For example, it had the fourth lowest proportion in the sample of professional employees living in the area, the second highest rate of unemployment (26 per cent) in the sample, the fifth highest population density and the largest amount of public housing (reflecting the relatively low socio-economic structure of the area). Southton's task context combined with the institutional context to prescribe the corporate approach as appropriate.

In 1975 the reasons for Southton's schizoid position were apparent. The precipitating dynamics of task and institutional context were supported by a competitive pattern of value commitment in which the elite wanted change towards the corporate model and, in this case, high dissatisfaction with interests. Here is the compatibility observed in Wool City between the situational context and the internal profile of value commitments plus the enabling dynamic of a concentrated power structure. But reorientation had not been achieved because of the lack of organizational capability. This is yet another example of an organization that interprets the external world using concepts and ideas derived from the institutional context but, in this case, without the capability to fully implement those ideas and concepts (figure 10.1). These observations reinforce those of chapter 9. In other words, we are building up a recurrent picture of organizational transformation requiring a combination of precipitating and enabling dynamics. A crucial enabling dynamic, and one that figures much more prominently than the power configuration, is the presence of significant organizational capability. Lacking such capability, Southton failed to complete its desired and (in task terms) appropriate reorientation.

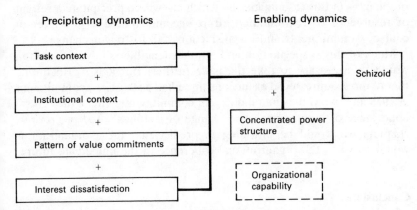

Figure 10.1 The dynamics of an unresolved excursion

What Southton also demonstrates, however, is that the precipitating push for change that can come from an elite commitment to change and the failure to fully change an organization can have interesting effects. Southton remained schizoid over the research period. But it reshuffled some of its structures between 1972 and 1975 whilst still remaining, overall, within the schizoid category. It was clear from the interviews with senior managers that the changes were *seen* as directionless and had, in themselves, caused perceptions of low organizational effectiveness and the dissatisfaction reported in table 10.2. Keeping the organization stable from 1975 to 1978, however, changed perceptions even though the organization was between archetypes. There was no apparent concern with performance or organizational problems. Even the fiscal pressure was seen as a manageable problem by both politicians and senior managers. The organization saw itself as being much more effective than in the previous period and, while there was still dissatisfaction over resource allocation, that dissatisfaction had declined.

Southton obviously illustrates that an organization can remain between archetypes if there are dynamics for reorientation but the capability to do so is absent. But there may also be signs that the schizoid position, rather than being one of interest tension and incompatibilities, is actually one that becomes 'accepted'. Thus, in Southton, the competitive pattern of commitments turned into indifference as the degree of structural shuffling ceased. Emerging problems – in this case financial – which elsewhere precipitate a retreat or resurgence of reorientation effort become treated as a matter of course. Commitments and dissatisfactions fail to trigger change.

Much of this is speculation and a rather lengthier study of Southton would be necessary to take the issue further. But it is worth noting that of the six unresolved excursions three had a *status quo* commitment in 1978 and two others had indifferent commitments. Given the central importance of a commitment to change or stability noted in previous chapters we would be unwilling to predict that these organizations would move to full organizational coherence in the immediate future.

Conclusions

The unresolved excursion track is important because it shows that organizations will not necessarily move towards an archetypal position. This suggests two things. First, the periodicity of strategic change in organizations may be much longer than most organizational theorists have acknowledged. We do not normally study organizations, in this detail, over long periods of time. The work of Child and Smith (1987) and Pettigrew (1985; 1988) shows that when one does, the results are not always as mainstream organizational theory might predict. Perhaps periods of 15 or 20 years are needed to study changes of a major strategic nature. This suggests that there is no natural break in the study of change; change is not a special topic, it is ubiquitous.

The second point is that an unresolved excursion may be sustained because particular elements of a new archetype may be useful in solving certain, specific problems. In the cases of Coastal County and Navalport aspects of corporate decision making were recognized as relevant to solving problems of resource shortage and fiscal crisis. Those elements were maintained in the face of a set of pressures to return to a different archetype.

In one sense the discussion of unresolved excursions has not fully supported the general thrust of the hypotheses set out at the beginning of the chapter. Only one of the two organizations that started from and left a coherent position had any clear precipitating dynamic for doing so. Further, of the six organizations, only one, Leafy County, had any interpretive dynamics pressing for change towards the corporate archetype. However, we have suggested that behind these results may be interesting patterns. The first is that by 1978 five of the six organizations were either indifferent to change or wanted to stay in the intermediate position (i.e. a commitment to the *status quo* as one of unresolution). The logic of the archetype thesis, as we have already mentioned, is that organizations are pulled towards coherence. What may be happening is that these organizations were content with the incoherent pattern because they believed their arrangements were corporate (i.e. consistent with institutional prescriptions). They had no organizational expertise to tell them otherwise. And, unless organizational members perceived performance as poor – which they did not – there was little perceived pressure to change. In effect we are returning to the point that without further longitudinal study it is very difficult to know whether positions between archetypes can become stable.

There is also a further point about unresolved excursions which derives from the general dynamic of our theory. We suggest that it is incompatibilities between the various precipitating and enabling dynamics that causes movement. Given the number of such dynamics (situational context, values, interests, power and capacity) there are many potential incompatibilities and, as a result, many potential different patterns that can produce an unresolved excursion. In other words, one might expect this track to have the least coherent patterns.

Notes

1 These three organizations responded similarly to the three small organizations on the reorientation track – Cheswich, Valeden and Churchtown – in being susceptible to the institutionally prescribed message.

11 Conclusions

Introduction

The aim of this final chapter is not to try and summarize the book. There have been attempts to summarize as the book has progressed, at the end of each chapter. A summary, in the sense of a precis of what has gone before, would not be appropriate. Rather we wish to raise what seem to us to be the key questions that come out of our approach and the empirical study that has been used to explore it. The major aim has been to establish a theoretical analysis of organizational change and stability which is holistic in nature, which is concerned with examining fundamental shifts in organizational design and basic orientation, i.e. strategic change, and which examines organizations over a relatively substantial period of time. Hopefully, we have also illustrated its usefulness as a theoretical and empirical tool. There is, of course, no sense in which a study of 24 organizations in a particular institutional setting at a particular point in time can be definitive. But the theory developed is strongly linked at many points with previous theorizing and empirical research on organizational change.

We are suggesting that this holistic and long-term approach to the analysis of change and stability is necessary if we are to advance understanding of these crucial and critical phenomena as interlinked and subject to the same causal forces. It is necessary in order to stop examining organizational change as though it were a special and, to a certain extent, unique area. It is the study of stability at one point in time that should be seen as unusual and unique.

This chapter will first attempt to reiterate the key ideas that make up the basics of the theoretical analysis, emphasizing those that are particularly new and different. Second, it will abstract the key elements in the findings from the analysis of the four tracks to see what kind of overall understanding of the dynamics of change and stability has been established. The third section of the chapter will examine what new and continuing research directions are suggested by these ideas and findings. The final section deals with the particular issue of time and history in organizational analysis.

The Key Ideas

What, then, do we see as the key ideas that drive the theoretical analysis, especially those that are somewhat new and different? There are two that are directly part of the analytical framework and four others that are important in the unfolding of the analysis. The two central ideas are (a) *archetype* and (b) *track*; the four that are important to the subsequent analysis are (c) change and stability as two sides of the same coin, (d) institutional setting, (e) the particular historical point and (f) contradictions, incompatibilities and tensions as essential dynamics.

It is crucial to the way of understanding strategic change and major transformations developed in this book that there are organizational design archetypes. Because an archetype is a 'combination of structural coherence and underpinning interpretive schemes' (Greenwood and Hinings, 1988) large-scale change is difficult. The idea of a design archetype emphasizes both the legitimate long-term concern of organizational analysis with typologies as coherent sets of structural and systemic properties that are efficiently related to particular contexts, and the more recent concern with organizations as cultural phenomena with value systems that underpin structures. While the approach of cultural theorists such as Schein (1986), Allaire and Firsirotu (1984) and Smirchich (1983) covers more than structure and systems, the essential point for us is that there is a coherent and systematic linkage between interpretive schemes and structures.

Studies of change have a long history of examining the interaction of the technical with the social and seeing the unanticipated consequences of the former for the latter as a problem (Bennis et al., 1984). Culture theorists and recent writers on major organizational change have been concerned with examining the way in which such change implies, and is hampered by, organizational, group and individual values (Kimberley and Quinn, 1984). Again, the concept of organizational design archetype brings these together in a coherent and systematic way, linking particular values about domain, modes of organizing and criteria of effectiveness to particular structural and systemic forms.

We are suggesting that the understanding of organizations requires this kind of holistic approach to conceptualizing organization design in order to move away from the notion of structure and systems as essentially neutral elements. It is central to the dynamics of our theory that strategic change involves movement away from one design archetype to another and therefore, explicitly or implicitly, defines change as holistic and as dealing with *interpretive schemes* as well as structures and systems.

Our second crucial idea is that of *tracks*. While the idea of archetype is used (rather differently) by Miller and Friesen (1984) and is also linked to the notion of ideal types, we feel that the concept of tracks is relatively unique. It is central to our approach that all organizations are in motion, i.e. on tracks, regardless of whether they are involved in strategic design change or not. The most important fact of organizational life is change, either within or between archetypes. So, all organizations are on tracks as they move through time, yet there has been very little attempt in organizational analysis to conceptualize and describe this movement. Perhaps the two main attempts are the idea of an organizational life cycle (Kimberly et al., 1980) and the concern of population ecologists with death and survival (Hannan and Freeman, 1977). The concept of an organizational track is meant to provide a language for talking about organizations as longitudinal phenomena, drawing on the life-cycle notions of transitions but recognizing that 'not all organizations pass through transitions or the same set of stages, nor do they depart from similar positions or have common destinations' (Greenwood and Hinings, 1988).

Tracks, then, emphasize the necessity of studying organizations over time and allow for the possibility not only of radical transformation but also of abortive shifts between design archetypes and of the absence of strategic or transformational change (inertia). Because organizations are conceptualized as archetypes, tracks are configurations of interpretive decoupling and recoupling arising from the loss or retention of structural coherence and the displacement or stability of underpinning interpretive schemes. For us, a major task of organizational analysis is to explore the nature of the tracks that organizations follow.

Our aim is to explain different tracks; tracks are the dependent variable. The concepts of archetypes, incompatibilities, precipitating and enabling dynamics are there to provide the explanation for an array of questions that are derived from the idea of tracks. Why organizations follow particular tracks is a question about relative stability as well as relative change. Why do some organizations complete a transformation while others do not?

This leads on to the four general ideas which underlie the subsequent analysis. Clearly the concepts of both tracks and archetypes emphasize both strategic design change and strategic design stability. There is an inertia track as well as a reorientation track. Organizations retain archetype coherence as well as lose it and move to a different archetype coherence. The attempt to explain why organizations follow different tracks is not just a theory about coping with change; it is about why organizations are structured as they are and whether this involves change or stability. As we note later in this chapter, the issue of whether an organization is changing or stable is largely a matter of the time span of examination. It is our position that all organizations are changing but at different rates.

Miller and Friesen (1984), Tushman and Romanelli (1985), Pettigrew (1985; 1988) and Child and Smith (1987) have all begun to develop theories about the sequences of evolution and revolution, the punctuated nature of change. Clearly in an evolutionary phase it may well look as though an organization is not changing; it is certainly in a relatively stable state. In a period of revolution change can easily be seen with the naked eye. Yet, in these two developing theories stability and change are inextricably linked as an organization moves through time. It is vitally necessary for the study of organizations to bring a time focus back in. Our conceptualizations need a time focus as a centrepiece of theorizing, not as a special topic of study. One of the major attempts of the theory of tracks is to give the study of organizations just such a focus.

Again, it is just such a focus that leads to the other general analytical ideas of institutional setting, the partciular historical point and contradictions. If one is to understand the tracks that organizations follow through time then a more thorough understanding of the institutional setting has to be achieved than is often the case in contemporary organization theory. The search for universals, using an initially universal set of concepts and theoretical principles has not been a particularly successful endeavour. A major result has been the generation of alternative, competing paradigms (Burrell and Morgan, 1979). We are arguing that one has to be careful about, for example, taking a set of brokerage houses and a set of hospitals and treating them as self-evidently comparable. Child and Smith (1988) outline an 'analysis of firms within sectors' approach to the study of organizational transformation.

In a sense this is somewhat similar to the search of the taxonomists for populations (McKelvey, 1982). The underlying thesis is that there are key aspects of sectors, populations or institutional settings that have to be understood because of the way they bind a set of factors together to produce particular outcomes. Child and Smith (1987) outline three aspects of a sector which are important for understanding how organizations in that sector will react. These are objective conditions, cognitive arenas and networks. Similarly, Hinings and Greenwood (1988) suggest that some institutional sets have tight networks which serve to disseminate ideas about objective conditions and organizational ideas. In other words, the relationships of precipitating conditions, enabling dynamics and organizational tracks takes place within an *ordered* institutional setting which plays an important role in determining the nature of those relationships.

Not only can organizations not be disembodied from their institutional setting, neither can they be isolated from the particular historical moment. Once again, the idea of tracks, with its emphasis on organizations always being on the way from somewhere to somewhere (even if they are the same place!), means that whenever analysts study them they are intervening at a particular historical point. Organizations have histories which are intimately tied to their current position and their potential future actions. Kimberly (1987) and Kimberly and Rottman (1988) have developed the idea of an organizational biography and emphasized its importance as a determinant of an organization's current and future outcomes. Many of the current approaches in organization theory make the assumption, usually implicitly, either that nothing has happened to an organization prior to the point at which it is subject to investigation or that whatever has happened has no relevance to understanding its current situation. Yet students are always told that one of the skills they should develop is 'reading' any organization that employs them, which includes understanding at least its recent history.

The final general idea that we would emphasize is that of incompatibilities (or contradictions or tensions). The concept of equilibrium or balance is a generally important one in science and social science. In organization theory the idea of fit has been important

(Donaldson, 1985; Drazin and Van de Ven, 1985; Van de Ven and Drazin, 1985). The flip side of the concept of fit is that of incompatibility. We are arguing that an essential dynamic in producing either stability or change, and the degree of that change, is the extent to which the various design elements of an organization fit within an archetype and with the precipitating pressures of situational context, values and interests, and the enabling dynamics of power and capacity. The actors within organizations may well strive for fit but the essential dynamic for that striving is lack of fit or incompatibility.

As a result, in order to adequately understand organizational stability or change, it is necessary to start from incompatibilities, not fits. An incompatibility between design and dynamic elements produces degrees of tension in an organization between the various actors. Of course it is always the case that a particular organization can tolerate high degrees of tension, or that it can set up insulating devices which mean that the tensions arising out of the incompatibilties do not surface in arenas that matter (Lukes, 1974; Walsh et al., 1981). But incompatibilities are a central dynamic because of two conditions. One condition is that there are always unanticipated consequences of action (Giddens, 1979). Thus, the setting in train of courses of action will produce incompatibilities. A second condition is that external contexts do not stand still; markets change, technologies change, government regulation changes and so on. Changing contexts produce precipitating pressures when they produce incompatibilities. Therefore, a central feature of organizational life is the striving that takes place to deal with the tensions engendered by incompatibilities.

These, then, are what we regard as the major general ideas that underlie this work, and which, in their particular emphasis and combination give a different thrust to the analysis. The question that now has to be addressed is 'So what?' What value have we added to the analysis of strategic design change and stability?

The Key Findings

To reiterate, it is not the intention of this section to provide a precis or summary of the full empirical results contained in chapters 6–10. Rather it is to establish the overall patterning of the dynamics of change and stability, and the extent to which they operate similarly or differently over the four tracks.

Given some of the points that we have just made in the previous section it is necessary to reiterate the nature of the institutional setting that was being studied. The systematic empirical part of the book (as against the rather less systematic use of cases such as Chrysler, Cadbury's, People Express, National Steel, !CI and The Bay) dealt with the reorganization of local government in England and Wales during particularly turbulent times. It is part of the nature of local government as an institutional system that it is dependent on another level of government, central government. It is central government which passes the laws which define the powers and responsibilities of the next level of government. It was central government that decided what the particular form of local government reorganization would be on 1 April 1974. As Hinings and Greenwood (1988) pointed out there is an active network of institutional associations in local government which link closely with central government in the dissemination of 'best' practice.

What all of this means is that, institutionally, individual local government organizations have little choice over their activities, and no choice at all over the 'markets' that they serve. Their strategic choices have to be over relative priorities and, more importantly, over ways of delivering services. These conditions mean that a great deal of attention can be focused on issues of strategic organizational design. As a result one has very clearly articulated competing design archetypes, namely the heteronomous professional bureaucracy and the corporate bureaucracy.

A further important aspect which we have emphasized is the particular historical point of the study. The years from 1970 onwards have been continuously turbulent for local government organizations in Britain. By 1970 it had become apparent that the system was to be reorganized; the only question was the nature of that reorganization. From 1972 when the Local Government Act was finally passed until 1 April 1974 when the new system came into existence new structures and systems were being designed and managers were applying for jobs in their own and other local authorities. There was considerable personnel movement both from a large number of early retirements that took place and from movements between organizations. A notion developed that if one came out of reorganization without a promotion then it was a personal failure.

As we have previously mentioned, within a year of reorganization central government embarked on a programme of cutting its grants to local government. The fiscal crisis had begun and continues. Indeed, so difficult was the fiscal situation, at least from a central government viewpoint, that additional general legislation was introduced in 1978 and 1982 that gave the centre greater control over the activities of local government. This activity culminated with a further Act of Parliament in 1984 which abolished the Greater London Council and the six metropolitan counties. Every year between 1975 and 1985 local government had to face new circumstances of service delivery.

In terms of our approach this presented a situation where one would expect considerable numbers of incompatibilities to arise in the individual organizations. The situational fiscal context was continuously changing producing a precipitating pressure. The institutional ideas about appropriate organizational design and service delivery were similarly changing throughout the period producing further precipitating pressure. Taken together these could produce value and interest incompatibilities. Thus, we were examining and developing our analysis in a situation where attempts at strategic change should be the norm. In a sense, such a historical setting means that the potentially interesting organizations are those that do not change.

This point is important as it plays up the interaction of the particular institutional setting with the particular time period and the necessity of taking it into account in developing a research approach. So much organizational analysis, we have suggested, implicitly takes stability as the normal condition that change becomes the separate special approach. Yet here we have a setting where stability should be far from a normal condition. The norm is change, and that is what we find. As chapter 6 points out, only two organizations managed to remain stable against the tide, during the ten year period; that is, they remained heteronomous professional bureaucracies. Even taking account of those that were corporately stable, 20 out of 24 organizations were subject to change. If our approach had been to take these 24 organizations as a non-institutionally specific, non-historically located set, the idea of change as the expected condition would not have come up.

What, then, can we say about any general patterns? Given that the inertia track was both not predicted as major within this institutional sample and that it was, indeed, the least frequent, it can be used as a template against which the other tracks can be examined.

The inertia track bears out the general thrust of the theory very well. It is here that we find fit and a lack of incompatibility. There is a strong relation between task environment and design archetype and a commitment to the *status quo*. These features would seem to override any dissatisfaction with interests. The congruence between environment, values and design meant that the power structure becomes unimportant in terms of explaining strategic design stability; given the value commitments the nature of power is irrelevant. However, power and organizational capacity were important in the one situation where there was continued incompatibility between the task environment and the design archetype. But by the end of the period there were signs that this organization was beginning to go on an excursion.

One other feature of the inertia track is of particular importance because it highlights something which has a general significance across all tracks. There has to be an organizational capacity to operate whatever design archetype an organization is within. This may sound somewhat banal in the sense that it says you have to know what you are doing. But there is a tendency in organization theory either to take expertise for granted or to ignore the necessity of technical knowledge in favour of cultural and behavioural expertise. For an organization to remain in a situation of stability there has to be knowledge present about how to run such an organization.

In addition, a somewhat counter-intuitive finding: some inertial organizations require active, transformation leadership. This point underscores the importance of history and biography. An organization on an inertial track can be within an archetype of either long-term or recent attainment. The more recent it is, the more the stabilizing phase requires activity on the part of the institutional leadership; this will be particularly the case where the design archetype being stabilized is new not just to the organization but to the institutional sector.

Those organizations that were on a reorientation track underscore these observations from the inertial track. As chapter 8 puts it, 'The issues for all of [these organizations] become twofold, namely harnessing the changes in interpretive schemes to structures and systems and ensuring the presence of the necessary understanding and expertise on how to run the new management approach' (p. 157). This, together with a necessary level of collective transformational leadership, was the enabling dynamic that allowed these organizations to complete a transformation successfully. However, it is the enabling system that is particularly important in ensuring that a reorientation rather than a discontinued or unresolved excursion takes place. The precipitating dynamic was primarily the power of the institutional ideas about a corporate approach which showed themselves in reformative or competitive commitments within senior management.

While there is a sense in which we see 'pure' strategic choice in action here with a strong value commitment to a particular way of organizing overriding contextual pressures, this is not entirely the case. We see the impact of the scale of these organizations. A reorientation was achieved much more quickly and painlessly in the smaller organizations. Managing such a change in the very large organizations with tens of thousands of employees and hundreds of thousands of clients took much longer. In order to achieve such a reorientation it became critical to develop the necessary organizational capacity, in terms of both an informed leadership and a relatively high level of expertise in the technical operation of a corporate system. Again, while it might seem somewhat self-evident, the point about expertise requires further stressing. It is too easy to take it for granted that expertise is present. These organizations climbed over the hump of change problems through the combination of value commitment, transformational leadership and expertise. There would be people in the organization who could go beyond visions to concrete implementation that produced the desired and satisfactory outcomes.

A number of other points need to be made about reorientations. We see power come into play as a way of ensuring that movement continues along the desired track both actively and passively. With a concentrated power structure the dominant elite can enforce their value preferences and continue to manage the momentum. The same form of power structure, in a situation of competitive commitment, enables senior management to ensure that the concerns of others are not heard; it becomes a way of insulating and thus neutralizing a potential incompatibility.

Further, these organizations, through their combination of commit-ments, leadership, capacity and power, are able to generate a high degree of activity at the beginning of the change period. Not only is there a higher degree of activity than for organizations on other tracks, but it tends to be emergent and systems oriented rather than prescribed and structural. However, we do see the emergent and prescribed aspects of archetype change reinforcing each other as the change develops. The early changes have a high symbolic and real impact as they concentrate on those modes of decision making central to both archetypes. What reorienting organizations do is develop a sustainable momentum.

Finally, as far as reorientations are concerned they give support to the notions of punctuated evolution in two senses that require disentangling. First, there was a high pace of change in the first period, a much lower one in the second period and another high pace in the third period. This is punctuation in the sense of the revolution–evolution sequence. But change is punctuated in a second sense, namely that oscillations, either minor or major, occur. Moving from one design archetype to another is not a linear progression. Design elements can change both forward and backwards in response to inabilities to contain competitive value commitments completely, as ways of attempting to deal with incompatibilities that arise from contextual pressures and as a response to design innovations that have unanticipated consequences, in the sense of not working in the expected way.

Discontinued and unresolved excursions are subthemes of inertial and reorientation tracks. Those discontinued excursions that started from the position of an heteronomous professional bureaucracy show an initial disregard for, and overriding of, the task environment in favour of the stronger precipitating pressure of the ideas emanating from the institutional environment. These combine with the strategic choice of senior managers to begin the process of transformation. The picture is the same as for reorientations. However, the enabling dynamics are different which means that the transformation cannot be completed. There is neither the organizational capacity nor the power structure to see the change through. Sufficient momentum is never mounted or sustained. There is too much concern with prescribed structure rather than emergent systems. As a result, the historical experience of the organizations reasserts itself; the organizational biography defines reality.

The same is true for those organizations that went on discontinued excursions from a corporate bureaucracy archetype. All three organizations had recent histories which locked them into corporate ways of working. They all operated in task environments which were ambiguous as to a choice between the two archetypes, so once again choices could be made without necessarily having severe performance effects. But maintaining a new archetype is difficult; drift from the archetype can and does occur. There is a need for a clear focus of design activity and for limits to be put on experimentation. In these organizations experimentation with a new form was one of the elements that caused movement.

However, all the organizations on a discontinued excursion track suggest that there may be long-run difficulties in maintaining a choice based purely on managerial preferences. These organizations, throughout the research period, were constantly facing incompatibilities from task environment, design archetype, value commitments or capacity difficulties. An issue that became important was the extent to which the fiscal pressures were interpreted as crisis. The organizations changed both forward and backward as they attempted to resolve these incompatibilities.

While inertial tracks are at least likely in the particular historical and institutional setting dealt with here, unresolved excursions are the ones that are least compatible with the theoretical ideas of design archetypes. The organizations that followed this track demonstrate a number of things. One is that the time frames for studying strategic design change may be much longer than most of us have acknowledged. Certainly they demonstrate that there is really no natural break in the study of change. A second point derives from the nature of the theoretical dynamic, i.e. the existence of incompatibilities. With the interrelation of situational context, interpretive schemes, interest, power, capacity and design archetypes there can be many different forms of incompatibility. As a result an unresolved excursion can potentially arise from a myriad of different circumstances and to a certain extent our findings show this as there is a less clear pattern here than with the other tracks.

However, these organizations do suggest that particular elements of a new design archetype may be adopted to solve specific problems and the conseqences of incompatibility ignored, essentially through the buffering of power. Also, senior managers in these organizations may believe that their arrangements are corporate, particularly because of the emphasis on prescribed structures and the lack of an organizational capacity which suggests otherwise. This is illustrated by the finding that these organizations actually had the lowest rates of change. There was certainly no value drive in these organizations; rather there were singular responses to situational pressures with no underlying design logic.

Where, then, does this leave us? We would suggest the importance of two conditions, a high value propensity to change and a low resistance to change. Indeed we would say that in themselves they are sufficient conditions to produce structural change regardless of context, interests and power. On the other hand, sufficient conditions for no change are a high resistance to change by a dominant coalition with a concentrated power structure, regardless of the values held by the non-elite. Also, there will be no change where there is a low propensity to change, with either low or high resistance to change, irrespective of interests and power. This is contingent on momentum deriving from the logic of task accomplishment which can change with the task context.

Two observations follow from this. One is that there is a recurrent picture of an organizational transformation requiring a combination of precipitating and enabling dynamics. Value pressures are important on the precipitating side of the equation. But contextual changes produce pressures and the more such changes produce an interpretation of crisis, the greater the need for a response. However, the interpretation of a changing context is made in relation to an existing archetype, its support by the dominant elite and its perceived effectiveness. The second observation is that on the enabling side of the equation capacity (expertise and leadership) appears to be more important than power. This fits with much general research in the sense that while we can often explain power (Hinings et al., 1974), we are much less certain about the effects of a particular power structure. Power is a crucial enabling dynamic in certain circumstances but, unlike capacity, does not seem to have a general role. In understanding strategic change it is important not to underestimate the crucial role of understanding and expertise.

One further point is worthy of emphasis. Throughout the chapters dealing with the dynamics of change it has become increasingly apparent that the same pressures can produce different consequences, and that different pressures can produce the same consequences. This is because the effects are dependent on three factors.

1 It is the joint and interactive effect of external and internal pressures and the ways in which these produce incompatibilities that matter.
2 These joint and interactive effects will differ according to the particular position of an organization at a particular point in time (history and institutional location).
3 Not only is the position of an organization important, but in understanding consequential change it is necessary to know in which direction it is currently moving.

These observations reinforce the general point that change is ubiquitous and that a theoretical position based on the concept of tracks means that starting and ending points of study always have a strong element of arbitrariness in them. Consistently we were led to speculate about an organization being in a position where consequential change would occur. Once again we are led to the point about the periodicity of change.

Research Directions

The more systematic research reported here is a small set of organizations in a particular institutional sector at a particular point of time. As such it can be no more than indicative of possible substantive findings and much further research is clearly necessary. However, rather than calling for more research on everything, i.e. an extension and replication, there seem to be five issues of particular interest because they are at the heart of the more generic study of change. They are the role of prescribed and emergent structures in change, the presence of oscillations, the persistence of unresolved excursions, the development of new archetypes and the periodicity of change.

Strategic design change has both a prescribed and emergent aspect. While we have worked with this distinction in discussing the various tracks, it requires more thought and attention in the future. Much discussion of change, both theoretical and practical, suggests some form of conflict between prescribed and emergent organizational arrangements with many attempts at reorganization concerned with handling the resistance from emergent practices that follow alterations of prescribed structures (Bennis et al., 1984). The concept of a design archetype sees prescribed and emergent elements as interlinked and requiring at least equal attention.

Kanter's work on change (1983; 1984), as well as that of Pettigrew (1985), suggests that certain kinds of emergent systems are crucial in signalling change, that is, they are high impact systems. We have argued that in the corporate bureaucracy the high impact systems were concerned with decision-making patterns and criteria generally and with their emergent aspects in particular. The successful transformation of an organization in the present sample required attention to these high impact, emergent elements. Future research needs to delineate the equivalent high impact elements and systems in other specific organizational settings and, critically, to see how far the various tracks can be separated in terms of the extent to which change originates in the high impact elements. Not all elements of organizational structures and systems should be seen as equal. Because design archetypes are structures and systems underpinned by provinces of meaning, it is the relationships with such meaning that are important in understanding change. Not all elements have the same meaning or the same dramatic relationship to meaning. It may be relatively easy to amalgamate certain departments, thereby reducing differentiation, in some organizations because that does not have a strong impact on the underlying values, but other elements, such as removing a level in the hierarchy or changing the routing of involvement, may produce a much stronger impact precisely because of its crucial relationship to those values. Thus there is an important research issue which distinguishes more clearly between the meaning of the various commonly used elements of structure and systems in particular design archetypes and their subsequent role in the change process.

The second research issue concerns the presence of oscillations. Strategic design change is not usually a smooth linear evolution or an instantaneous revolution. Organizations move forward on some elements, stand still on others and move backwards on others. Changes are experimented with and abandoned. A track such as a discontinued excursion is a major oscillation. But there are both minor and major oscillations within both the reorientation track and that of an unresolved excursion. This observation is very much in line with the theorizing and research findings of Tushman and Romanelli (1985), Pettigrew (1985) and Child and Smith (1987) with ideas such as punctuated evolution.

These ideas need taking further both theoretically and empirically. Essentially it is a matter of capturing the real processual and dynamic of change in organizations with its hesitations, it struggles, its disappointments, its retreats, its renewed attacks and its tactical withdrawals. Such an approach requires tracking organizations in detail in real time within a framework as proposed here which starts from the assumption that change is ubiquitous and that changes will not proceed smoothly in most circumstances.

The third point that requires further consideration as a research direction is the persistence of unresolved excursions. The body of literature embracing contingency theory, ideas of design archetypes and tracks, and even most of the work on strategic choice, has an implicit or explicit assumption that some form of organizational fit takes place. The differences rest on the causes and dynamics of that process rather than its ultimate existence. Explanation of less than perfect correlations in such studies has been based on the fact that at any one time (cross-sectional) some organizations will be temporarily out of fit. But in our sample there are six organizations that remain in an unresolved design archetype for periods of up to ten years. This hardly seems to illustrate moving in, out and back into fit. Rather, it suggests that lack of fit can be a long-term situation for some organizations.

Of course, it could be argued that if these organizations had been private sector and profit-making organizations then they would have either gone bankrupt or been taken over because of the effect of being embryonic or schizoid on performance. Thus, it may be an institutional effect. Given the emphasis in so much theorizing on the relationship between lack of fit and performance (Donaldson, 1985) the existence of long-term incompatibility is potentially important. We would suggest that the existence, tracking and further examination of unresolved excursions is important. It would involve greater understanding of the dynamics of such a track and, more particularly, the relationship of the position to performance.

Much organization theory is centred around the ideas of particular types being adapted to specific situations in order to enhance performance (Mintzberg, 1979; Miller and Friesen, 1984). Our research suggests (as does that of Miller and Friesen (1984) as well as that of Burns and Stalker (1961)) that organizations are often between types. But the extant theorizing does not start from the likelihood and commonness of this phenomenon; rather, it suggests that lack of fit is unusual and, therefore, does not require attention. The whole question of being between types persistently requires much more attention.

Both the issue of oscillations and that of unresolved excursions lead to a fourth research point that we have raised earlier, that of the periodicity of change. Periodicity has two aspects to it, one being the actual time periods over which strategic design change takes place, and the other being the time period that should be adopted to study such change adequately. Neither has been the subject of much theoretical speculation or empirical observation. We will leave the second of these for the final section of the chapter.

Again, the first of these issues, the nature of actual periodicity in change has not been central to theorizing. In dealing with oscillations we mentioned ideas of punctuated equilibrium that have been suggested. These concepts concern the pace and direction of change in particular periods. They are ideas that require extending to take account of the time periods over which evolutionary and revolutionary change takes place. What can occur in a six month period as against a five year period? How long does a strategic reorientation take? Child and Smith (1987) and Pettigrew (1985; 1988) take a view of decades rather than years. Clearly a historical dimension is crucial to the study of change, and within that the mapping of the time periods over which particular sorts of changes occur. Organization theory can gain a great deal from such mapping.

Our final point is somewhat different from the previous ones as it goes beyond the theoretical bounds laid out. It concerns the development of new archetypes. In this book we have outlined two design archetypes and given some explanation of their origin. Along with Tolbert and Zucker (1983) our explanation is that there are initial task pressures which are the precipitating dynamics that produce the search for alternative modes of organizing, and that these are followed by institutional value precipitators which produce widespread take-up of these ideas. Hinings and Greenwood (1988) give more details of the institutional network dynamics of the process of diffusion. An underlying issue raised by our approach is whether various design archetypes are specific to different institutional sectors. We also need to learn about how archetypes arise. Child and Smith (1987) outline the development of the Mars model of strategy and organization in the confectionery industry and its gradual adoption by Cadbury's. What are the design archetypes in the cement industry or the chemical industry? How do they arise? How are they diffused? The dense institutionally specific mechanisms of professional associations, local authority associations and acknowledged leaders together with the authoritative hierarchical position of central government which are so clear in British local government are unlikely to be present in many sectors. The work of Meyer and Rowan (1977) requires extending to answer the question of the interorganizational trading of organizational ideas. Organization theory should begin to ask the question of where ideas about organizing come from, not in the sense of metaphors of understanding (Morgan, 1986) but in the world of organizational dynamics. Questions of this kind pose the issue of the relative importance of tasks, values and politics; not which is the only one that matters, but how they interact with each other in the production of organizational design archetypes.

A Note on Time and History

Before concluding this final chapter a short diversion on time perspectives is necessary. Truly dynamic theories and longitudinal studies of organizations raise the issue of a 'proper' time period for study, pointing out such questions as what lags in effect occur and what variables are determinant at different levels of analysis. These issues are raised by the approach outlined here and there is a sense in which the previous chapters have moved through successively more immediate levels of analysis.

Generally speaking, the longer the time period adopted, the more likely it is that determinant causes will be seen in terms of large-scale movements of socio-cultural and economic phenomena. While this is pre-eminently the role of the historian, in organization theory we can see such an approach in the work of the population ecologists (cf. Hannan and Freeman, 1977). Here organizational form and change is conceptualized as being the effect of forces beyond the control (and even the comprehension) of managers. To test such theories long runs of longitudinal data are required (cf. Delacroix and Carroll, 1983). Contingency theory and resource dependency have a similar flavour to them but a somewhat more medium-term requirement.

Theories and studies which focus on the actor tend to have either an immediate cross-sectional approach or are very short term, i.e. a three year period would be a long one. The shorter the time frame adopted the more likely it is that the important causal variables are immediate situation and actor connected.

Perrow (1972) put these points well when he said that, if one takes a long-term view of what causes organizations to be as they are, the major factors seem to be cultural; in the medium term they are technological and, in the short term, economic. A somewhat similar view in examining strategic change is that of Tichy (1983) with his distinctions between cultural, political and technical processes. He conceptualizes these as cycles with different periodicities, with cultural processes having the greatest periodicity and technical processes the shortest.

In the theory presented here we are attempting to deal with three levels of analysis which are likely to have different cycles. Design archetypes according to the theory presented here have a considerable degree of stability. As a result, studying them, either in an inertial or reorienting phase, requires a medium-term focus (ten years?). However, the notions of dynamics of stability and change can be done on a rather shorter time period (three to five years?) as one can study context, values and interests at work and how they either support or challenge design archetypes on a year-on-year basis. Finally, the concept of capacity, i.e. the structure and exercise of leadership and the existence of expertise, can be studied on almost a day-to-day basis. Certainly, when new senior managers enter an organization it is instructive to study them at least from month to month. Because capacity can be studied more easily over the short run and, as Meindl and Ehrlich (1987) point out, because it gives an intensely human component to analysis, leadership may well seem dominantly determinant.

Our interest is in the interplay of these levels of analysis and their different periodicities. Each is determinant over its own appropriate time span. It may well be that, in the longest of runs, organizational capacity does not matter, only socio-economic shifts. But in attempting to understand how the University of Alberta copes with a 3 per cent cutback for the 1987–8 academic year, the structure and exercise of leadership and the availability of skills and expertise to elaborate new structures, systems and processes may be vital. Hopefully, as we move into further research which elaborates the theory of tracks and design archetypes and the associated dynamics of change and stability, the empirical support for various levels of determination will become apparent. Certainly, in order to do this the critical need in the study of organizations is real-time longitudinal studies to which researchers commit substantial periods of their lives.

Bibliography

Alexander, A. (1982) *Local Government in Britain since Reorganization*. London: George Allen and Unwin.

Alford, R. (1975) *Health Care Politics*. Chicago: University of Chicago Press.

Allaire, Y. and Firsirotu, M. (1984) Theories of organizational culture. *Organization Studies*, 5: 193–226.

Bains Working Group (1972) *The New Local Authorities: Management and Structure*. London: HMSO.

Barnard, C. I. (1938) *The Functions of the Executive*. Cambridge, MA: Harvard University Press.

Barnes, Z. (1987) Change in the Bell system. *Academy of Management Executive*, 1: 43–6.

Barrett, A. L. and Cammann, C. (1984) Transitioning to change: lessons from NSC. In J. R. Kimberley and R. E. Quinn (eds) *Managing Organizational Transitions*. Homewood, IL: Richard D. Irwin.

Bennis, W., Benne, K. D. and Chin, R. (eds) (1984) *The Planning of Change*. New York: Holt Rinehart and Winston.

Benson, K. (1977) Organizations: a dialectical view. *Administrative Science Quarterly*, 22: 1–21.

Blau, J. R. (1984) *Architects and Firms*. Cambridge, MA: MIT Press.

Brown, R. H. (1978) Bureaucracy as praxis: toward a political phenomenology of formal organizations. *Administrative Science Quarterly*, 27: 365–82.

Burns, J. M. (1978) *Leadership*. New York: Harper and Row.

Burns, T. (1977) *The BBC*. London: Macmillan.

Burns, T. and Stalker, G. M. (1961) *The Management of Innovation*. London: Tavistock Press.

Burrell, G. and Morgan, G. (1979) *Sociological Paradigms and Organizational Analysis*. London: Heinemann.

Chandler, A. (1962) *Strategy and Structure*. Cambridge, MA: MIT Press.

Chapman, R. A. (1984) Administrative culture and personnel management: the British civil service in the 1980s. *Teaching Public Administration*, 4: 1–14.

Chester, D. N. (1968) Local democracy and the internal organization of local authorities. *Public Administration*, Autumn.

Child, J. (1972) Organization structure, environment and performance: the role of strategic choice. *Sociology*, 6: 1–22.

Child, J. (1974) Managerial and organizational factors associated with company performance, part 1. *Journal of Management Studies*, 11: 175–89.

Child, J. (1975) Managerial and organizational factors associated with company performance, part 2: a contingency analysis. *Journal of Management Studies*, 12: 12–27.

Child, J. and Smith, C. (1987) The context and process of organizational transformation: Cadbury Ltd in its sector. *Journal of Management Studies*, 24: 565–94.

Clark, B. (1972) The organizational saga in higher education. *Administrative Science Quarterly*, 17: 178–84.

Clegg, S. and Dunkerley, D. (1982) *Organization, Class and Control*. London: Routledge and Kegan Paul.

Cole, R. E. (1982) Diffusion of participatory work structures in Japan, Sweden and the United States. In P. S. Goodman and Associates (eds) *Change in Organizations*. San Francisco: Jossey-Bass.

Committee on Management of Local Government (1967) Report, Volumes 1–5. London: HMSO.

Cyert, R. and March, J. (1963) *The Behavioral Theory of the Firm*. Englewood Cliffs, NJ: Prentice-Hall.

Daft, R. and Macintosh, N. (1984) The nature and use of formal control systems for management control and strategy implementation. *Journal of Management*, 10: 43–66.

Dalton, M. (1964) *Men Who Manage*. New York: John Wiley.

David, S. M. and Kantor, P. (1980) Political theory of transformations in urban budgetary areas: the case of New York City. In D. R. Marshall (ed.) *Urban Policy Making*. London: Sage.

Dearlove, J. (1979) *The Reorganization of British Local Government*. Cambridge: Cambridge University Press.

Delacroix, J. and Carroll, G. R. (1983) Organizational foundings: an ecological study of the newspaper industries of Argentina and Ireland. *Administrative Science Quarterly*, 28: 274–91.

Department of the Environment (1973) *The Sunderland Study*. London: HMSO.

Donaldson, L. (1985) *In Defence of Organization Theory*. Cambridge: Cambridge University Press.

Drazin, R. and Van de Ven, A. H. (1985) Alternative forms of fit in contingency theory. *Administrative Science Quarterly*, 30: 514–39.

Dror, Y. (1968) *Public Policy Making Re-examined*. New York: Chandler.

Fiedler, F. E., Chemers, M. M. and Mahar, L. (1977) *Improving Leadership Effectiveness: the Leader Match Concept*. New York: Wiley.

Foster, C. D., Jackman, R. and Perlman, M. (1980) *Local Government Finance in a Unitary State*. London: George Allen and Unwin.

Galbraith, J. (1975) *Organizational Design*. Reading, MA: Addison-Wesley.

Giddens, A. (1979) *Central Problems in Social Theory*. London: Macmillan.

Gouldner, A. (1955) *Patterns of Industrial Bureaucracy*. London: Routledge and Kegan Paul.

Greenwood, R. (1984) Incremental budgeting: antecedents of change. *Journal of Public Policy*, 4: 277–306.

Greenwood, R. and Hinings, C. R. (1988) Organizational design types, tracks and the dynamics of strategic change. *Organization Studies*, forthcoming.

Greenwood, R. and Stewart, J. D. (1971) *Corporate Planning in English Local Government*. London: Charles Knight.

Greenwood, R. and Stewart, J. D. (1973) Towards a typology of English local authorities. *Political Studies*, 21.

Greenwood, R., Norton, A. L. and Stewart, J. D. (1969) Recent changes in the internal organization of county boroughs, part III. *Public Administration*, Autumn, 289–306.

Greenwood, R., Hinings, C. R. and Ranson, S. (1975) Contingency theory and the organization of local authorities, part 1: differentiation and integration. *Public Administration*, 53: 1–23.

Greenwood, R., Hinings, C. R. and Ranson, S. (1977) The politics of the budgetary process. *Political Studies*, 25: 25–47.

Greenwood, R., Walsh, K., Hinings, C. R. and Ranson, S. (1980a) *Patterns of Management in Local Government*. Oxford: Martin Robertson.

Greenwood, R., Hinings, C. R., Ranson, S., and Walsh, K. (1980b) Incremental budgeting and the assumption of growth: the experience of local government. In M. Wright (ed.) *Public Spending Decisions: Growth and Restraint in the 1970s*. London: George Allen and Unwin.

Greiner, L. (1972) Evolution and revolution as organizations grow. *Harvard Business Review*, 50: 37–46.

Hackman, R. H. (1984) The transition that hasn't happened. In J. R. Kimberley and R. E. Quinn (eds) *Managing Organizational Transitions*. Homewood, IL: Richard D. Irwin.

Hall, R. H. (1977) *Organizations, Structure and Process*. Englewood Cliffs, NJ: Prentice-Hall.

Hall, R. H., Haas, J. E. and Johnson, N. J. (1963) An examination of the Blau–Scott and Etzioni typologies. *Administrative Science Quarterly*, 12: 118–39.

Hambrick, D. C. (1983) Taxonomic approaches to studying strategy: some conceptual and methodological issues. *Journal of Management*, 10: 27–42.

Hannan, M. T. and Freeman, J. H. (1977) The population ecology of organizations. *American Journal of Sociology*, 82: 929–64.

Heclo, H. and Wildavsky, A. (1974) *The Private Government of Public Money*. London: Macmillan.

Hedberg, B. L. T. (1981) How organizations learn and unlearn. In P. C. Nystrom and W. H. Starbuck (eds) *Handbook of Organizational Design*. New York: Oxford University Press.

Hedberg, B. L. T., Nystrom, P. and Starbuck, W. (1976) Camping on seesaws: prescriptions for a self-designing organization. *Administrative Science Quarterly*, 21: 41–65.

Hickson, D. J., Hinings, C. R., Schneck, R., Lee, C. A. and Pennings, J. (1971) A strategic contingencies theory of power. *Administrative Science Quarterly*, 16: 216–29.

Hickson, D. J., Butler, R. J., Cray, D., Mallory, G. R. and Wilson, D. C. (1986) *Top Decisions*. Oxford: Blackwell.

Hinings, C. R. and Foster, B. D. (1972) The organization structure of churches. *Sociology*, 7: 93–106.

Hinings, C. R. and Greenwood, R. (1988) The normative prescription of organizations. In L. Zucker (ed.) *Institutional Patterns and Organizations*. Chicago: Ballinger.

Hinings, C. R. and Slack, T. (1987) The dynamics of quadrennial plan implementation in national sport organizations. In T. Slack and C. R. Hinings (eds) *The Organization and Administration of Sport*. London, Ontario: Sports Dynamics.

Hinings, C. R., Hickson, D. J., Pennings, J. M. and Schneck, R. E. (1974) Structural conditions of intra-organizational power. *Administrative Science Quarterly*, 19: 22–44.

Hinings, C. R., Greenwood, R. and Ranson, S. (1975) Contingency theory and the organization of local authorities, Part 2: contingencies and structure. *Public Administration*, 53: 169–220.

Hinings, C. R., Greenwood, R., Ranson, S. and Walsh, K. (1980) The organizational consequences of financial restraint in local government. In M. Wright (ed.) *Public Spending Decisions: Growth and Restraint in the 1970s*. London: George Allen and Unwin.

Hinings, C. R., Brown, J. L. and Greenwood, R. (1987) *Content and Authority in Change: The Case of a Public Accounting Office*. Edmonton: Human Resources Management Research Centre.

Hood, C. and Dunsire, A. (1982) *Bureaumetrics*. Farnborough: Gower.

Iacocca, L. (1984) *Iacocca, An Autobiography*. New York: Bantam Books.

Jackman, R. and Sellars, M. (1978) The distribution of RSG; hows and whys of the new need formula. *CES Review*, July.

Jones, G. and Stewart, J. D. (1983) *The Case for Local Government*. London: George Allen and Unwin.

Kanter, R. (1983) *The Change Masters*. New York: Simon and Shuster.

Kanter, R. (1984) Managing transitions in organizational culture: the case of participative management at Honeywell. In J. R. Kimberley and R. E. Quinn (eds) *Managing Organizational Transitions*. Homewood, IL: Richard D. Irwin.

Kimberly, J. R. (1987) The study of organization: toward a biographical perspective. In J. W. Lorsch (ed.) *Handbook of Organizational Behaviour*. Englewood Cliffs, NJ: Prentice-Hall.

Kimberly, J. R. and Quinn, R. E. (eds) (1984) *Managing Organizational Transitions*. Homewood, IL: Richard D. Irwin.

Kimberly, J. R. and Rottman, D. (1988) Environment, organization and effectiveness: a biographical approach. *Journal of Management Studies*.

Kimberly, J. R., Miles, R. H. and associates (eds) (1980) *The Organizational Life-Cycle*. San Francisco: Jossey-Bass.

Langhorn, K. and Hinings, C. R. (1988) Integrated planning and organizational conflict. *Canadian Public Administration*, forthcoming.

Laumann, E. O. and Pappi, F. U. (1976) *Networks of Collective Action*. New York: Academic Press.

Lawrence, P. and Lorsch, J. G. (1967) *Organizational and Environment*. Cambridge, MA: Harvard University Press.

Livesay, H. C. (1977) Entrepreneurial persistence through the Bureaucratic Age. *Business History Review*, 51: 415–43.

Lukes, S. (1974) *Power: A Radical View*. London: Macmillan.

Lundberg, C. (1984) Strategies for organizational transitioning. In J. R. Kimberley and R. E. Quinn (eds) *Managing Organizational Transitions*. Homewood, IL: Richard D. Irwin.

McCall, M. W. and Lombardo, M. M. (1978) *Leadership: Where else can we go?* Durham, NC: Duke University Press.

McKelvey, W. (1982) *Organizational Systematics*. Berkeley: University of California Press.

Meindl, J. R. and Ehrlich, S. B. (1987) The romance of leadership and the evaluation of organizational performance. *Academy of Management Journal*, 30: 91–109.

Meindl, J. R., Ehrlich, S. B. and Dukerich, J. M. (1985) The romance of leadership. *Administrative Science Quarterly*, 30: 78–102.

Merton, R. K. (1968) *Social Theory and Social Structure*. Glencoe, IL: Free Press.

Meyer, A. D. (1982) How ideologies supplant formal structures and shape responses to environments. *Journal of Management Studies*, 29: 45–61.

Meyer, J. and Rowan, B. (1977) Institutional organizations: formal structure as myth and ceremony. *American Journal of Sociology*, 83: 340–63.

Meyer, J. and Scott, W. R. (eds) (1983) *Organizational Environments*. Beverley Hills: Sage.

Meyerson, D. and Martin, J. (1988) Cultural change: an integration of three different views. *Journal of Management Studies*, forthcoming.

Miles, R. H. and Randolph, W. A. (1980) Influence of organizational learning styles on early development. In J. R. Kimberly, R. H. Miles and Associates (eds) *The Organizational Life Cycle*. San Francisco: Jossey-Bass.

Miles, R. and Snow, C. (1978) *Organizational Strategy, Structure and Process*.

New York: McGraw-Hill.

Miller, D. (1981) Towards a new contingency approach: the search for organizational gestalts. *Journal of Management Studies*, 18: 1–26.

Miller, D. and Friesen, P. (1980) Archetypes of organizational transition. *Administrative Science Quarterly*, 25: 269–99.

Miller, D. and Friesen, P. (1984) *Organizations: A Quantum View*. New York: Prentice-Hall.

Miner, J. B. (1975) The uncertain future of the leadership concept: an overview. In J. G. Hunt and L. L. Larson (eds) *Leadership Frontiers*. Kent, OH: Kent State University Press.

Mintzberg, H. (1979) *The Structuring of Organizations*. Englewood Cliffs, NJ: Prentice-Hall.

Mitroff, I. and Emshoff, J. R. (1979) On strategic assumption-making: a dialectical approach to policy and planning. *Academy of Management Review*, 4: 1–12.

Morgan, G. (1986) *Images of Organization*. Beverley Hills: Sage.

Newman, P. (1985) *Company of Adventurers*. Markham: Penguin Books.

Nystrom, P. C. (1986) Comparing beliefs of line and technostructure managers. *Academy of Management Journal*, 29: 812–19.

Ouchi, W. (1981) *Theory Z*. Reading, MA: Addison-Wesley.

Perrow, C. (1967) A framework for the comparative analysis of organizations. *American Sociological Review*, 32: 194–208.

Perrow, C. (1972) *Complex Organizations: A Critical Analysis*. Glenview, IL: Scott, Foresman.

Peters, T. and Waterman, R. (1982) *In Search of Excellence*. New York: Harper and Row.

Pettigrew, A. (1973) *The Politics of Organizational Decision-Making*. London: Tavistock.

Pettigrew, A. (1985) *The Awakening Giant*. Oxford: Blackwell.

Pettigrew, A. (1988) Context and action in the transformation of the firm. *Journal of Management Studies*.

Pfeffer, J. (1981) *Power in Organizations*. Boston: Pitman.

Pfeffer, J. (1982) *Organizations and Organization Theory*. Boston: Pitman.

Pfeffer, J. and Salancik, G. (1974) Organizational decision-making as a political process: the case of a university budget. *Administrative Science Quarterly*, 19: 135–51.

Pfeffer, J. and Salancik, G. (1978) *The External Control of Organizations: A Resource-Dependence Framework*. New York: Harper and Row.

Pugh, D. S. and Hickson, D. J. (eds) (1976) *Organization Structure in its Context: The Aston Programme 1*. Farnborough: Lexington Books.

Pugh, D. S. and Hinings, C. R. (eds) (1976) *Organization Structure: Extensions and Replications*. Farnborough: Lexington Books.

Pugh, D. S. and Payne, R. (eds) (1977) *Organizational Behaviour in its Context: The Aston Programme III*. Farnborough: Lexington Books.

Pugh, D. S., Hickson, D. J., Hinings, C. R. and Turner, C. (1969) An empirical taxonomy of work organizations. *Administrative Science Quarterly*, 14: 91–113.

Quinn, J. B. (1982) *Strategies for Change: Logical Incrementalism*. New York: Richard D. Irwin.

Raine, J. (ed.) (1981) *In Defence of Local Government*. Birmingham: INLOGOV, University of Birmingham.

Ranson, S., Hinings, C. R. and Greenwood, R. (1980) The structuring of organization structures. *Administrative Science Quarterly*, 25: 1–17.

Romanelli, E. and Tushman, M. (1983) Executive leadership and organizational outcomes: an evolutionary perspective. *Research Working Paper No. 35*. Graduate School of Business, Columbia University.

Royal Commission on Local Government in England, 1966–69 (1969) Report, Volume 1. London: HMSO.

Schein, E. H. (1986) *Organizational Culture and Leadership*. San Francisco: Jossey-Bass.

Schick, A. (1980) Budgetary adaptations to resource scarcity. In C. H. Levine and T. Rubin (eds) *Fiscal Stress and Public Policy*. London: Sage.

Schoonhoven, C. B. (1980) Problems with contingency theory: testing assumptions hidden within the language of contingency theory. *Administrative Science Quarterly*, 25.

Scott, W. R. (1965) Reactions to supervision in a heteronomous professional organization. *Administrative Science Quarterly*, 10: 65–81.

Selznick, P. (1949) *T.V.A. and the Grass Roots*. Berkeley: University of California Press.

Selznick, P. (1957) *Leadership in Administration*. Evvanston, IL: Row Peterson.

Skelcher, C. K. (1980) From programme budgeting to policy analysis. *Public Administration*, 58: 155–72.

Slack, T. and Hinings, C. R. (1987) Planning and organizational change: a conceptual framework for the analysis of amateur sport organizations. *Canadian Journal of Sport Sciences*, 12: 185–93.

Smirchich, L. (1983) Concepts of culture and organizational analysis. *Administrative Science Quarterly*, 28: 339–59.

Smith, C., Child, J. and Rowlinson, M. (1988) *Innovations in Work Organization: Cadbury Limited 1900–1985*. Cambridge: Cambridge University Press.

Starbuck, W. H. (1976) Organizations and their environment. In M. D. Dunnette (ed.) *Handbook of Industrial and Organizational Psychology*. Chicago: Rand McNally.

Starbuck, W. H. (1983) Organizations as action generators. *American Sociological Review*, 48: 91–102.

Starbuck, W. H., Greve, A. and Hedberg, B. L. T. (1978) Responding to crises. *Journal of Business Administration*, 9: 111–37.

Staw, B. and Szwajkowski, E. (1975) The scarcity–munificence component of organizational environments and the commission of illegal acts. *Administrative Science Quarterly*, 20: 345–54.

Stewart, J. D. (1971) *Management in Local Government*. London: Knight.
Stewart, J. D. (1980) From growth to standstill. In M. Wright (ed.) *Public Spending Decisions: Growth and Restraint in the 1970s*. London: George Allen and Unwin.
Stoizman, J. D. (1975) Objective and subjective concepts of interest in sociological analysis. *Sociological Analysis and Theory*, 5: 107–15.
Tannenbaum, A. S. (1968) *Control in Organizations*. New York: McGraw-Hill.
Tichy, N. (1983) *Managing Strategic Change: Technical, Political and Cultural Dynamics*. New York: Wiley-Interscience.
Tichy, N. and Ulrich, D. (1984) Revitalizing organizations: the leadership role. In J. R. Kimberley and R. E. Quinn (eds) *Managing Organizational Transitions*. Homewood, IL: Richard D. Irwin.
Tolbert, P. and Zucker, L. (1983) Institutional sources of change in the formal structure of organization: the diffusion of civil service reform, 1880–1935. *Administrative Science Quarterly*, 28: 22–39.
Tung, R. (1979) Dimensions of organizational environment: an exploratory study of their impact on organization structure. *Academy of Management Journal*, 22: 672–93.
Tushman, M. and Romanelli, E. (1985) Organizational evolution: a metamorphosis model of convergence and reorientation. In L. Cummings and B. Staw (eds) *Research in Organizational Behavior*. Greenwich, CT: JAI Press.
Van de Ven, A. and Drazin, R. (1985) The concept of fit in contingency theory. In B. M. Staw and L. L. Cummings (eds) *Research in Organizational Behavior*, 7: 333–65.
Walsh, K., Hinings, C. R., Ranson, S. and Greenwood, R. (1981) Power and advantage in organizations. *Organization Studies*, 2: 131–52.
Warren, D. (1984) Managing in crisis: nine principles for successful transition. In J. R. Kimberley and R. E. Quinn (eds) *Managing Organizational Transitions*. Homewood, IL: Richard D. Irwin.
Weick, K. E. (1979) *The Social Psychology of Organizing*. Reading, MA: Addison-Wesley.
Wheatley Report (1973) *The New Scottish Local Authorities – Organization and Management Structures*. London: HMSO.
Wildavsky, A. (1975) *Budgeting*. Boston: Little Brown.
Worthy, J. C. (1985) *Shaping an American Institution: Robert E. Wood and Sears Roebuck*. Burbana, IL: University of Illinois Press.
Zaltman, G., Duncan, R. B. and Holbek, J. (1973) *Innovation and Organizations*. New York: Wiley.
Zucker, L. G. (1984) Organizations as Institutions. In S. B. Bacharach (ed.) *Perspectives in Organizational Sociology: Theory and Research*. Greenwich, CT: JAI Press.
Zucker, L. G. (1988) Normal change or risky business: institutional effects of the 'hazard' of change in hospital organizations, 1959–1979. *Journal of Management Studies*.

Index